Issues in Historiography

The Debate on the English Revolution

Issues in Historiography

General editor
R. C. RICHARDSON
King Alfred's University College

Forthcoming titles

The Debate on the Norman Conquest
Marjorie Chibnall

The Debate on the Wars of the Roses
DeLloyd J. Guth

The Debate on the American Revolution
Gwenda Morgan

The Debate on the Economy and the Industrial Revolution
Philip Ollerenshaw and Katrina Honeyman

The Debate on the Industrial Revolution and Society
John Rule

The Debate on the French Revolution
Gwynne Lewis

The Debate on the American Civil War
H. A. Tulloch

The Debate on the Russian Revolution
David Saunders

The Debate on the Holocaust
Steve Paulsson

Issues in Historiography

The Debate
on the English Revolution

THIRD EDITION

R. C. RICHARDSON

MANCHESTER
UNIVERSITY PRESS
MANCHESTER AND NEW YORK

distributed exclusively in the USA by St. Martin's Press

First edition published 1977 by Methuen
Second edition published 1988 by Routledge

This edition published 1998 by Manchester University Press
Oxford Road, Manchester M13 9NR, UK
and Room 400, 175 Fifth Avenue, New York, NY 10010, USA

Distributed exclusively in the USA by
St. Martin's Press, Inc., 175 Fifth Avenue, New York, NY 10010, USA

Distributed exclusively in Canada by
UBC Press, University of British Columbia, 6344 Memorial Road,
Vancouver, BC, Canada V6T 1Z2

British Library Cataloguing-in-Publication Data
A catalogue record for this book is available from the British Library

Library of Congress Cataloging-in-Publication Data applied for

ISBN 0 7190 4740 4 *paperback*

Third edition first published 1998

05 04 03 02 01 00 99 98   10 9 8 7 6 5 4 3 2 1

Typeset by Best-set Typesetter Ltd., Hong Kong
Printed in Great Britain
by Bell & Bain Ltd, Glasgow

CONTENTS

For Joan Thirsk
in friendship and gratitude

PREFACE

History, E. H. Carr reminded his readers, is 'an unending dialogue between the present and the past'. 'When you read a work of history', he went on, 'always listen out for the buzzing. If you can detect none, either you are deaf or your historian is a dull dog'.[1] The attention regularly given to historiography in first-degree courses in higher education presumably rests on agreement with the views which Carr offered. It rests also, of course, on the belief that history's own past needs to be explored, and that the very latest books and articles on a given subject are not the only ones worth reading. 'Exciting new techniques', it has been observed, 'can imprison the mind as surely as old prejudices. Reading old history can help one escape the tyranny of new, and be a useful cerebral hygiene.'[2]

One of the most realistic and fruitful approaches to historiography is by way of case studies. Twenty years ago, when the first, and very different, edition of this book appeared, hardly any were available; Pieter Geyl's *Napoleon For and Against* (London, 1949) stood in relatively lonely eminence. Now there are a great many. Rosemary O'Day explored *The Debate on the English Reformation* (London, 1985) in a study which placed the current concerns of today's historians in a longer genealogy and located older writers such as Heylyn, Burnet, Milner, Cobbett and Froude in the different contexts which shaped their attitude and approach to the subject. Pat Hudson has surveyed historians' writings on *The Industrial Revolution* (London, 1992). French history also has its examples – J. A. W. Hefferman's *Representing the French Revolution* (Hanover, NH, 1992) and S. L. Campbell's *The Second Empire Revisited* (New Brunswick, NJ, 1978), to cite but two. On recent German historiography there is R. J. Evans's *In Hitler's Shadow: West German Historians and the Attempt to Escape from the Nazi Past* (London, 1989). P. J. B. Bosworth wrote on *Explaining Auschwitz and Hiroshima: Historical Writing and the Second World War* (London, 1993). A large crop of case studies in American historiography has appeared, some of them (not surprisingly) to do with the Presidency. B. Schwartz wrote on *George Washington: The Making of an American Symbol* (New York, 1987). M. D. Peterson surveyed *Lincoln in American Memory* (New York, 1994). Case studies of a thoroughly different (though still quintessentially American) kind have come into print as D. D. Walker's *Clio's Cowboys: Studies in the Historiography of the Cattle Trade* (Lincoln, Nebraska, 1981) clearly demonstrates.

The present book has had a long shelf life. It originally appeared in

1977 and was the product of an undergraduate course which I had been teaching. It made no claim to completeness; it presupposed some basic knowledge of the original events themselves. It was an *introduction* to the historiography of the English Revolution and was planned to be an aid to further reading which would help students go on to look at more of the texts on which it was based and at other works on the development of history. A second, considerably enlarged, edition appeared in 1988. Ten years on a third edition is now called for, appropriately to launch Issues in Historiography, a new series of case studies. It has been very extensively revised. Chapters 8, 11 and 12 are new. All the others have been amended and recast to take account of recent publications.

The dynamics of the debate on the English Revolution are as strong and lively as ever and the flow of publications in the field continues to be of tidal proportions. New textbooks, monographs, volumes of essays, journal articles all bear witness to the continuing fascination exerted by this subject. Its historiography is exhilaratingly plural and competitive. The redefinition of political history continues in the hands of the 'Revisionists' with political culture now firmly on the agenda. The need to connect the English Revolution with its British context has been signalled by Conrad Russell and others. Interdisciplinary studies of the Revolutionary period drawing on literature, drama, and art are registering their impact. The social complexities of the age are better understood though over-arching social interpretations of the Revolution have fewer followers. The inter-dependence of local and national affairs continues to come under enlightening scrutiny. 'History from below' is clearly here to stay and, refreshingly, supplements and challenges the view from the top. Numerous new biographies have appeared, some of them implementations of psychohistory. We are getting closer to a women's history of the English Revolution.

And the cast list has changed. The new names who came in with the second edition of 1988 – Jonathan Clark, Ann Hughes, Ronald Hutton, Mark Kishlansky, Kevin Sharpe – are all now well-established, senior academics in this country and in the United States. Newcomers to this version of the book include John Adamson, Julian Davies, Jacqueline Eales, Sean Kelsey, Timothy Lang, Alastair MacLachlan, and Mark Stoyle. There have been losses. Since the second edition leading figures in the field – J. H. Hexter, Roger Howell, J. P. Kenyon, and C. V. Wedgwood – have all died. The evolution of this book over its own lifetime is itself a significant historiographical phenomenon. (Technologically, however, this author confesses how he has lagged behind the times. The first edition was produced on a manual typewriter, the second on an electric (not electronic), and the third on a word processor which my more progressive colleagues regard as a museum piece.)

The spelling and punctuation in quotations from seventeenth- and eighteenth-century works have occasionally been modernized where this seemed necessary in the interests of clarity.

The dedication records a long-standing and highly valued link which goes back to my days as an undergraduate.

Notes

1 E. H. Carr, *What is History?* (Harmondsworth, 1964), p. 23.
2 David Hume, *History of Great Britain: The Reigns of James I and Charles I*, ed. D. Forbes (Harmondsworth, 1970), p. 18.

ABBREVIATIONS

Agric. H. R.	*Agricultural History Review*
AHR	*American Historical Review*
BIHR	*Bulletin of the Institute of Historical Research*
Ec. H. R.	*Economic History Review*
EHR	*English Historical Review*
Hist.	*History*
Hist. and Theory	*History and Theory*
Hist. Workshop J.	*History Workshop Journal*
HJ	*Historical Journal*
JBS	*Journal of British Studies*
J. Hist. Ideas	*Journal of the History of Ideas*
JMH	*Journal of Modern History*
PP	*Past and Present*
Proc. Brit. Acad.	*Proceedings of the British Academy*
R. Soc. Econ.	*Royal Society of Economics*
Soc. Hist.	*Social History*
THES	*Times Higher Education Supplement*
TLS	*Times Literary Supplement*
TRHS	*Transactions of the Royal Historical Society*

1

Introduction: the characteristics of the debate

Fashions in historical interpretation change. Each generation has to write its own history for itself. At new points on the road new land-scapes are seen. Different answers are given because different ques-tions are asked. (R. H. Tawney, undated lecture at the LSE, quoted in R. Terrill, *R. H. Tawney and his Times: Socialism as Fellowship* (London, 1974), p. 9)

The final, dispassionate, authoritative history of the Civil Wars cannot be written until the problems have ceased to matter; by that time it will not be worth writing. (C. V. Wedgwood, *The King's Peace 1637–1641* (London, 1955), p. 14)

The Civil War . . . has raged on paper ever since the blood stopped flowing. (R. Hutton, *EHR*, CII (1987), p. 214)

We are all at heart either Royalists or Roundheads. (Kevin Sharpe, *Sunday Times, Books* (3 November 1996))

Different labels have been attached by historians to England's mid-seventeenth-century crisis. One of them – now largely superannu-ated because of its narrowness – is 'Great Rebellion'. Another, more capacious and therefore more useful, is 'English Revolution'. This is the label adopted here and by it is understood that complex period which involved the downfall of Charles I's government, civil wars, social upheaval, and the creation of a republic. It has long attracted the attention of historians, and the available literature on the subject is now formidably large and indigestible. This book does not set out to provide another 'straight' history of the origi-nal events, either in the form of a general survey or of a mono-graph on a particular aspect. Its concern is, in fact, not primarily with the mid-seventeenth century itself but with the posthumous history of that period, with the ways in which it has been interpreted and analysed by successive generations of historians. Following a chronological sequence, chapters 2–5 look at writings on the English Revolution in the seventeenth, eighteenth, and nineteenth centuries respectively. Chapters 6–12 deal with various aspects of the twentieth-century historiography of the subject. The book as a whole is designed as a sustained attempt to answer two distinct but closely related questions:

(1) Why has the English Revolution remained such a provocatively controversial subject for historians?

(2) How have historians approached and explained its causes, course, and consequences?

The explanation of the continuing importance attached to the English Revolution rests partly, of course, on the undoubted impact of the original events themselves. Civil wars and revolutions are by their nature divisive. They divide between those who support, oppose, or hold aloof from the struggle. They divide between those who win and those who lose, between those who benefit from, and those who simply suffer as a result of, political upheaval or social and economic change. The English Revolution produced just this range of contemporary responses and results. It was traumatic in its nature and inherently controversial. Its events were momentous and far-reaching in their significance and effects. 'If in time, as in place', wrote Thomas Hobbes (see p. 28), 'there were degrees of high and low, I verily believe that the highest of time would be that which passed between the years of 1640 and 1660.' Civil wars in themselves were not new in England; there were several medieval precedents and the last of them (the Wars of the Roses) was relatively recent. But in the seventeenth century for the first time a defeated king was denounced as a traitor, put on trial in the name of his people, found guilty and publicly executed. The traditional hierarchies of the monarchical state and the Anglican Church were systematically dismantled. The institutions of government were restructured, the House of Lords was abolished, feudal tenures were ended, bishops were dispossessed, the Church was remodelled, a standing army came into existence. For the first, and only, time in English history the country became a republic. Though the monarchy and the Church were restored in 1660 there could be no question of putting back the clock to where it had stood before the Civil Wars.

The events themselves, then, were inherently dislodging, divisive, and controversial; there could be no general agreement among contemporary historians about the causes and significance of what had taken place. How far back in time did they need to go to discover the origins? Were the real causes to be found in the immediate past (Clarendon)? Was rebellion the perverse product of a period of peace and prosperity?

> The first and general cause was the Sins of the People, who (taking a surfeit of ease, plenty and pleasure) and growing wanton thereby, gazed after novelty (that magnetical attraction of the plebeian rout) and, discontented with their present condition, sought felicity in things they wanted, and were still unsatisfied even in the accomplishment thereof: whence is occasioned the hatred of tranquillity, the desire of motion, the loathing of present things, and seeking after future.[1]

So wrote the anonymous author of *Britania Triumphalis; a brief history of the Warres* in 1654. Clement Walker agreed (see p. 16). Or did the Civil War represent the avenging hand of God at work in defence of injured puritans and Parliamentarians (Thomas May)? And where in fact should historians look for an explanation? Did responsibility rest squarely with the King's dark designs and political ineptitude (Thomas May, Joshua Sprigge, John Vicars)? Or was it Parliament's ambition that was to blame (Thomas Hobbes, John Nalson, William Dugdale)? Was the rebellion the work of a subversive conspiracy (Hobbes, Nalson)? Could the upheavals be explained in purely political terms or was it necessary to take into account changes in society and the distribution of wealth (James Harrington)? What part did religion play? Could one agree with Peter Heylyn (see p. 12) when he discussed the Scottish rebellion 'that though Liturgy and Episcopacy were made the occasions, yet they were not the causes of this war, religion being but the vizard to disguise that business, which covetousness, sacrilege, and rapine had the greatest hand in'?[2] What was the role of individual actors in the drama such as Charles I, Strafford, Laud, Pym, and Cromwell?

The kind of explanations which were put forward by the earliest historians of the Revolution reflected, of course, the differences in the range of sources which they had at their disposal. As their own personal experiences – the controlling factor – contrasted sharply, these differences were in fact greater than at any later point in the historiography of this subject. In other words, seventeenth-century historians of the Civil Wars could not make use of a common body of evidence. The different explanations they put forward also reflected changes in the prevailing political situation. Could a Royalist speak freely before 1660, and conversely could a Parliamentarian historian really speak his mind in the uncongenial period 1660–88?

But the explanations which they offered were also bound up with the state of history at that time and the kinds of expectation that were entertained about its political and moral utility. In the sixteenth and seventeenth centuries, the study of history was undergoing a number of important changes; one writer, indeed, has spoken of a 'revolution' in historical writing and thought taking place in this period.[3] It is true that the older moral purposes of history were not abandoned, and the growth of puritanism lent added weight to historical explanations based on notions of divine intervention. But in general, the study of history in post-Reformation England became noticeably more secularized. Its writers and its audience were no longer – as in the Middle Ages – drawn largely from the clergy. Historians now catered increasingly for the varied interests of a lay audience, and as a subject history began to play an important part in the political and social education of the gentry and middle classes.[4] History, it was increasingly believed, taught patriotism, political wisdom, and true religion. Francis Bacon granted history an important place in his schemes for the advancement of learning. Harrington's political philosophy was historically based. The antiquarian researches of lawyers and others in the public records placed history at the service of politics.[5] The Civil Wars, in fact, re-emphasized the importance of history; both sides in the war ransacked the past for historical precedents with which to buttress themselves. In the Civil Wars, then, there emerged not simply opposing parties and opposing armies, but opposing theories of history.[6] (See pp. 15, 22.)

The impact of the English Revolution and its effects on historical study long outlived their original context. The political and religious dimensions of the seventeenth-century crisis remained intensely relevant and controversial far beyond 1660. They became, in fact, part of the very substance of eighteenth-century political life and religious disagreements and historians ignore them at their peril.[7] The 'Glorious Revolution' of 1688 added new perspectives. So did the English experience of the French Revolution.[8] In the eighteenth century the history of the English Revolution became inseparably bound up with the party political rivalries of Whigs and Tories and with the mutual animosities of Anglicans and Dissenters. Historical objectivity, even if it was aimed at, was unlikely to be respected. It was the readers, the users of history, as much as the writers who created Whig and Tory versions of the past in the eighteenth century. (The 'philosophical' history which emerged in the eighteenth century should be seen partly as the historian's bid for political independence.) Histories of the seventeenth-century crisis were far too valuable as political ammunition to be left in the hands of scholars. The eighteenth-century historiography of the English Revolution, then, was a series of contests. The works of Clarendon and Echard, which appeared in the first two decades of the century, were denounced as Tory propaganda by a succession of Whig writers (Oldmixon, Rapin). In the second half of the century Hume's anti-Whig *History* was proclaimed as a moderate Toryism and as such held the field until it was itself displaced from popularity in the nineteenth-century Whig revival (Brodie, Hallam, Macaulay).

The English Revolution continued to be politically relevant in the nineteenth century; one has only to study political attitudes to Oliver Cromwell to appreciate that.[9] Radicals like Godwin extolled the neglected virtues of England's seventeenth-century republic and extracted predictable lessons from the past for their own contemporaries. Mainstream Whigs, and Macaulay above all, with a new nationalism around them and the Romantic Movement behind them, re-emphasized the glorious achievements of the parliamentary struggle against Charles I for the political and religious liberty of the English people. Macaulay's *History of England* rapidly became one of the great Victorian classics. Published at a time when upper- and middle-class Englishmen were congratulating themselves that their country had escaped the 1848 revolutions in Europe, its agreeable political message was communicated in unforgettable prose style. This was history at the peak of its popularity, and the subject matter of Macaulay's seventeenth-century narrative became as familiar to his readers as the plot of a novel by Dickens or Thackeray.

The same could not be said of the work of those so-called 'scientific' historians in the second half of the nineteenth century who set out, by the application of a rigorous methodology, to achieve a truer, and more objective view of the English past. Macaulay's *History* was a bestseller; the first instalment of S. R. Gardiner's great work of meticulous scholarship proved quite unsaleable and was ignominiously pulped. But scientific history did not destroy the Whig interpretation of history; it merely diluted it.[10] The *Cambridge Modern History*, planned by Lord Acton as a great monument to objective history and published in the early years of the twentieth century, was recognizable as the swan-song of Victorian liberalism. Gardiner's mammoth history of seventeenth-century England, despite all its scholarly moderation and its unyielding adherence to chronology, was still Whig history of a kind, inferentially displaying the author's own political sympathies and present-mindedness.

The main novelty in historical scholarship in the later nineteenth century lay not in any total break with the complacent, present-based Whig interpretation of the English past, but in the emergence of the historian's profession and the refinements in methodology. The major historians of the later nineteenth century were not, as earlier, gentlemen amateurs or political party hacks. They were professionals, men with university appointments, proud of their academic status and of their research methods, and always at pains to stress the great difficulties of the work they undertook. Under their influence history left the open political arena, and historians themselves – now in sole charge of their subject – busily made new rules for the game. That the new historical product still bore some resemblance to the one which it aimed at replacing, we now see as being fundamentally inevitable. A historian, even one who claimed to be a detached academic, is always a part of his own society, and consciously or unconsciously will use the present in his approach to the past. The main difference between Macaulay and Gardiner was that the first historian openly and proudly approached the seventeenth-century crisis from a nineteenth-century Whig standpoint, while the second did something similar despite himself.

The historical study of the English Revolution has been closely bound up with political and social change. In a real sense, as Croce's famous dictum has it, 'all history is contemporary history'. The real break with the nineteenth-century Whig interpretation came not in the late nineteenth century, but in the harsher, less bracing climate prevailing after the two World Wars. It is true, of course, that the Marxist alternative to the liberal version of determinism dates back to the nineteenth century. But before the inter-war period the historical work of Marx and Engels on economic inevitability, on the place of class struggle in the general pattern of social and economic change, and on the role of the proletariat, had made a negligible impact in England. Christopher Hill's earliest articles and the book on the English Revolution which he edited in 1940 were deliberately designed to publicize what was still for most English historians of the seventeenth century, reared on Gardiner, Firth, and Trevelyan, a new and alarmingly radical way of looking at the past (see pp. 125–6).

Partly under the influence of Marxist ideas – both directly and indirectly (in attempts to counter and disprove the dangerous heresy) – and partly due to the influential work of R. H. Tawney (see pp. 113–19), historians of the English Revolution began to unfix their gaze on seventeenth-century constitutional struggles and to look instead at the relatively uncharted territory of the society and the economy out of which the crisis had emerged. The gentry controversy (see pp. 118–21) was one rather spectacular and noisy example of this new-found interest in social and economic history. But it demonstrated the ease with which alluringly plausible hypotheses could outrun the research needed to support them, and hinted at the potential dangers of constructing a separate social and economic interpretation which did not take full account of political divisions, regional differences, and the conservatism of many Parliamentarians. Hence one of the most recent stages in the historiography of the English Revolution has been a revival of interest in political events, processes, participation, and machinery – a revisiting of the region explored by Gardiner but with the aid of new maps, new travelling aids provided by the twentieth-century economic, social, and regional historians. Political historians of the English Revolution are now mindful that they must place English affairs within a British context and position their accounts of the aspirations, protestations and actions of the elite alongside the strivings of the 'people'. The 'Revolution from Below' has been charted by Christopher Hill and others. Belatedly, the experience of women in this troubled period has begun to be examined. Increasingly, too, historians of the English Revolution are realizing the necessity of looking at the seventeenth century as a whole. They have developed a new interest in the concept and typology of revolution and have busied themselves with comparisons between England's seventeenth-century upheavals and those experienced by other European countries at the same time.[11] The links between England and New England in this period have been explored.[12] More ambitiously still, comparative studies of the English, American, French, and Russian Revolutions have been attempted.[13] The help of other disciplines – literary criticism, sociology, and anthropology, for example – has been invoked in the historian's search for a deeper understanding of the divisions in, and culture of, early seventeenth-century society.[14]

But historians continue to disagree about the causes and consequences of the English Revolution; on this subject there is no generally accepted historical orthodoxy. New research sometimes takes on a dual function, on the one hand of undermining old myths and on the other of reinforcing old prejudices.[15]

Although specifically concerned with the historiography of the English Revolution, this book is also a case study of the development of historical research and writing in the last three centuries. It reveals historians variously at work in their capacities as explorers, builders, advocates, prosecutors, judges, and demolition experts. History as a subject is a means of questioning the past, but as society itself changes, and history with it, no two generations are likely to agree about the kind of questions that need asking nor are they necessarily satisfied with each other's answers. History, said the nineteenth-century Swiss historian Jacob Burckhardt, 'is on every occasion the record of what one age finds worthy of note in another'.[16] This book examines changes in the historical perception of the English Revolution in the light of Burckhardt's judgement.

Notes

1 Quoted in R. MacGillivray, *Restoration Historians and the English Civil War* (The Hague, 1974), p. 19.
2 Quoted *ibid.*, p. 41.
3 F. S. Fussner, *The Historical Revolution: English Historical Writing and Thought 1580–1640* (London, 1962). See also J. M. Levine, *Humanism and History: Origins of Modern English Historiography* (Ithaca, NY, 1987), D. R. Woolf, *The Idea of History in Early Stuart England: Erudition, Ideology and 'The Light of Truth' from the Accession of James I to the Civil War* (Toronto, 1990), and D. R. Kelley and D. H. Sacks (eds), *The Historical Imagination in Early Modern Britain: Historical Rhetoric and Fiction 1500–1800* (Cambridge, 1997).
4 Fussner, *The Historical Revolution*, esp. pp. 44–59; P. Burke, *The Renaissance Sense of the Past* (London, 1969), *passim*; L. B. Wright, *Middle-Class Culture in Elizabethan England* (1935, reissued London, 1964), esp. pp. 297–338.
5 Fussner, *The Historical Revolution*, pp. 253–74; M. McKisack, *Medieval History in the Tudor Age* (Oxford, 1971); P. Styles, 'Politics and historical research in the early seventeenth century', in L. Fox (ed.), *English Historical Scholarship in the Sixteenth and Seventeenth Centuries* (London, 1956); C. C. G. Tite, *Impeachment and Parliamentary Judicature in Early Stuart England* (London, 1974), pp. 24–53; A. B. Ferguson, *Clio Unbound: Perception of the Cultural and Social Past in Renaissance England* (Durham, NC, 1979); K. Sharpe, *Sir Robert Cotton 1586–1631: History and Politics in Early Modern England* (Oxford, 1979).
6 J. G. A. Pocock, *The Ancient Constitution and the Feudal Law: A Study of Historical Thought in the Seventeenth Century* (Cambridge, 1957, 2nd edn, 1987).
7 The consequences of the great divide between seventeenth- and eighteenth-century specialists are provocatively examined in J. C. D. Clark, *Revolution and Rebellion: State and Society in England in the Seventeenth and Eighteenth Centuries* (Cambridge, 1986).
8 See H. T. Dickinson, *Liberty and Property: Political Ideology in Eighteenth-Century Britain* (London, 1977); H. T. Dickinson, 'The eighteenth-century debate on the Glorious Revolution', *Hist.*, LXI (1976), pp. 28–44; J. P. Kenyon, 'The Revolution of 1688: resistance and contract', in N. McKendrick (ed.), *Historical Perspectives* (London, 1974), pp. 43–69; G. M. Straka, '1688 as the Year 1: eighteenth-century attitudes to the Glorious Revolution', in L. T. Milic (ed.), *Studies in Eighteenth-Century Culture* (Cleveland, Ohio, 1971), I, pp. 143–67; A. Cobban, *The Debate on the French Revolution 1789–1800* (2nd edn, London, 1960); A. Goodwin, *The Friends of Liberty: The English Democratic Movement in the Age of the French Revolution* (London, 1979); Marilyn Butler, *Burke, Paine, Godwin and the Revolution Controversy* (Cambridge, 1984).

9 See R. C. Richardson (ed.), *Images of Oliver Cromwell: Essays for and by Roger Howell Jr* (Manchester, 1993), esp. chs 5 and 6.

10 See H. Butterfield, *The Whig Interpretation of History* (London, 1931).

11 See, for example, T. Aston (ed.), *Crisis in Europe 1560–1660* (London, 1965); G. Parker and L. M. Smith (eds), *The General Crisis of the Seventeenth Century* (London, 1978); P. Zagorin, *Rebels and Rulers 1500–1660: Society, States and Early Modern Revolution* (2 vols, Cambridge, 1982).

12 See T. H. Breen, *Puritans and Adventurers: Change and Resistance in Early America* (New York, 1980); P. M. Gura, *A Glimpse of Sion's Glory: Puritan Radicalism in New England 1620–1660* (Middletown, Conn., 1984); A. Zakai, *Exile and Kingdom: Reformation, Separation and the Millenial Quest in the Formation of Massachusetts and its Relationship with England* (Ann Arbor, 1984); Margaret and J. Jacob (eds), *The Origins of Anglo-American Radicalism* (London, 1984).

13 See, for example, C. Brinton, *The Anatomy of Revolution* (New York, 1938, rev. edn 1965).

14 See, for example, C. Hill, 'Literature and the English Revolution', *The Seventeenth Century*, I (1986), pp. 15–30; J. Dollimore, *Radical Tragedy: Religion, Ideology and Power in the Drama of Shakespeare and his Contemporaries* (Brighton, 1984); G. Parry, *The Golden Age Restor'd: The Culture of the Stuart Court 1603–1642* (Manchester, 1981); M. Butler, *Theatre and Crisis 1632–1642* (Cambridge, 1984); R. C. Richardson and G. M. Ridden (eds), *Freedom and the English Revolution: Essays in History and Literature* (Manchester, 1986); A. Macfarlane, *Witchcraft in Tudor and Stuart England: A Regional and Comparative Study* (London, 1970); D. Underdown, *Revel, Riot and Rebellion: Popular Politics and Culture in England 1603–1660* (Oxford, 1986); R. Bauman, *Let Your Words be Few: Symbolism of Speaking and Silence Among Seventeenth-Century Quakers* (Cambridge, 1983).

15 Compare the utterly different reviews of Brian Manning's *The English People and the English Revolution* (London, 1976) by John Miller (*THES*, 28 May 1976, p. 16), and Christopher Hill (*Spectator*, 3 July 1976, pp. 21–2).

16 J. Burckhardt, *Judgements on History and Historians*, ed. H. R. Trevor-Roper (London, 1959), p. 158.

2

The seventeenth century: the debate begins

> Happy those English historians who wrote some sixty years since before our civil distempers were born or conceived, seeing then there was a general right understanding betwixt the nation. But alas! such as wrote in or since our civil wars are seldom apprehended truly and candidly save of such of their own persuasion. (Thomas Fuller, *An Appeal of Injured Innocence* (London, 1659), p. 1)

The historical debate on the English Revolution began, of course, in the seventeenth century and itself formed part of the contemporary struggles. The first historians of the Revolution – Clarendon, May, Hobbes, Harrington, and the others discussed in this chapter – were participants in or observers of the events they described, and what they wrote was in the full sense of the term *contemporary* history. History of this sort has obvious dangers and pitfalls as well as a particular value, a fact which the church historian Thomas Fuller (1608–61) entirely appreciated. Fuller firmly believed that 'the most informative histories to posterity and such as are most highly prized by the judicious are such as were written by the eye-witnesses thereof, as Thucydides the reporter of the Peloponnesian War'. But equally – like Ralegh before him – he recognized that, in writing contemporary history,

> I must tread tenderly because I go not, as before, on men's graves, but am ready to touch the quick of some yet alive. I know how dangerous it is to follow truth too near to the heels; yet better it is that the teeth of a historian be struck out of his head for writing the truth than that they remain still and rot in his jaws by feeding too much on the sweetmeats of flattery.[1]

Fuller's apprehensions about writing on recent events proved well founded, and his *Church History of Britain* published in 1655, despite its moderate tone and ostensibly non-political subject, did not save its author from savage attacks. Chief of his opponents was the Laudian Peter Heylyn (1600–62), whose *Life of Archbishop Laud* was published posthumously in 1668. But before this date Heylyn had already set out his objections to the bias of Fuller's *Church History*. Far from being neutral, Fuller's work, said Heylyn, offered unmistakable evidence of the author's puritan sympathies.

> All things pass on smoothly for the Presbyterians, whom he chiefly acts for. . . . No professed Puritan, no cunning Nonconformist or open Separatist comes upon the stage whom he follows not with plaudits and some fair commends . . . [Whereas] the Fathers of the Church and conformable children of it are sent off commonly in silence and sometimes with censure.[2]

The question of puritanism, like that of the strictly political issues at stake in the English Revolution, was exceedingly controversial, and by discussing this subject Fuller had put his hand into a wasps' nest.[3]

But in the seventeenth century the historical controversy over the English Revolution was primarily political and constitutional. With the Civil Wars still fresh in their minds, contemporaries on both sides of the political fence vigorously debated the issues which had been defended and fought over in the 1630s and 1640s. Royalists and Parliamentarians both found their historians, who based their rival accounts on the abundant pamphlet literature of the period, on party manifestoes and reports of parliamentary speeches, on newspaper evidence, and last but by no means least on their own personal experience and prejudice.[4]

One of the first contemporary writers to give an account of the politics of the English Revolution was Thomas May (1595–1650), who in 1647 produced the officially commissioned *History of the Parliament of England*, following it three years later with *A Breviary of the History of the Parliament of England*. Although he recognized that the subject of the Civil War was extremely contentious, May pleaded with his readers in the preface to the first of his two books that what he was offering to them was the truth, a plain, naked narrative and explanation of events. May's position, however, as one of the Long Parliament's secretaries made such an objective history impossible, and in practice he wrote from the biased standpoint of the King's opponents; the 1647 book was designed as an apology for Parliament itself, while its companion, which was published after the second Civil War and the execution of the King, was written to praise the army and the Independents. Clarendon, who had formerly been May's confederate, bluntly dismissed him once

> he fell from his duty and all his former friends and prostituted himself to the vile office of celebrating the infamous acts of those who were in rebellion against the King; which he did so meanly that he seemed to all men to have lost his wits when he left his honesty; and so shortly afterwards died, miserable and neglected and deserved to be forgotten.[5]

Clarendon was perhaps too severe. May at least made some effort to be fair to the Royalists and took no delight in the hostilities between King and Parliament ('this unnatural war', 'the unhappy distractions of these kingdoms'). But ultimately it was Parliament's case which Thomas May put forward, believing that,

> the Parliament of England . . . was more misunderstood in England than at Rome; and that there was a greater need to remind our own countrymen than to inform strangers of what was past, so much . . . have they seemed to forget both the things themselves and their own former notions concerning them.

And it was Parliament's case from both his own situation and political preferences that May was best qualified to present.

> My residence hath been during these wars in the quarters and under the protection of the Parliament; and whatsoever is briefly related of the soldiery . . . is according to the light which I discerned there – If in this discourse more particulars are set down concerning the actions of those men who defended the Parliament than of those who warred against it, it was because my conversation gave me more light on that side.[6]

May's Parliamentarian history of the English Revolution, not surprisingly, stressed the untrustworthiness of James I and Charles I, their disregard of Parliament's rights and liberties, their illegal and inept actions, and their apparent abandonment of the

Protestant cause. James I, May lamented, although he had some good qualities, showed too much favour towards the papists. Moreover, his relations with his Parliaments deteriorated, 'projects against the laws were found out to supply the King's expenses, which were not small', and government increasingly devolved into the grasping, unscrupulous hands of the Duke of Buckingham. All this, as May pointedly reminded his readers, stood in marked contrast to the actions of Queen Elizabeth 'of glorious memory' who had made 'the right use of her subjects' hearts, hands and purses in a parliamentary way' and during whose reign 'the prosperity of England seemed at the height'.[7]

Under Charles I, grievances multiplied as the situation went rapidly from bad to worse.

> Forty years old was King Charles, and fifteen years had he reigned when this Parliament was called [i.e. in 1640]; so long had the laws been violated . . . the liberties of the people invaded and the authority of Parliament, by which laws and liberties are supported, trodden under foot: which had by degrees much discontented the English nation.[8]

The King's acceptance of the Petition of Right was quickly forgotten, peace was made with Spain without Parliament's consent, titles and offices were sold freely to the highest bidder, 'multitudes of monopolies were granted by the King', the judiciary was interfered with, and from 1629 Parliament was dispensed with altogether. The ambitions and crimes of Strafford and Laud ('an English Pope') were rehearsed, and May lost no opportunity of emphasizing the Queen's popish preferences and her influence over the court. 'The countenancing of looseness and irreligion was no doubt a good preparative to the introducing of another religion, and the power of godliness being beaten down, popery might more easily by degrees enter.' No wonder, then, that Civil War finally erupted in England; all such causes worked relentlessly in this direction.

> It cannot but be thought, by all wise and honest men, that the sins of England were at a great height, that the injustice of governors and vices of private men were very great, which have since called down from Almighty God so sharp a judgement, and drawn on by degrees so calamitous and consuming a war.[9]

14

Thomas May's two publications, issued in 1647 and 1650, occupy a prominent place in what was in fact a growing Parliamentarian historical literature on the Civil War. The Parliamentarian cause indeed, more so than that of the King, was based on historical foundations. It had to be! Not to proclaim themselves as defenders of tradition would have been for Parliamentarians to admit that they were rebels. To deny the importance of Parliament in the past was implicitly to minimize its significance in the present. And what the Parliamentarians were defending, as they saw it, was the ancient constitution, the common law which had existed (so Coke said) since time immemorial, and the rights and liberties of all free-born Englishmen which Levellers and other radicals believed had been subverted by the Norman Conquest.[10]

Joshua Sprigge (1618–84) in his *Anglia Rediva* (1647), for example, presented the contemporary struggles as a necessary defence of Parliament, laws, and liberties, and dedicated his work to all true Englishmen 'that have with bleeding hearts and distilling eyes been spectators of the common sufferers under the insulting paces of arbitrary power and unlimited prerogative'.[11] Also in the 1640s John Vicars (1580?–1652) was busily engaged in bringing out the three parts of his fiercely puritan *England's Parliamentarie Chronicle* (1644–6). The work was dedicated to the members of the Long Parliament, 'the most renowned reformers, breach repairers, and revivers of a despised, distressed, and almost destroyed Church and State'. The MPs' virtues appeared all the more obvious in Vicars's eyes when contrasted with the Royalists: 'the most boisterous and rebellious rout of atheistical and papistical philistines and viperous malignants who would have maliciously immured, damned, yea dried up and destroyed the precious wells of our Bethlem. . . .' Vicars went on in the course of his enthusiastic text to applaud Parliament's action in taking away 'that state staggering Star Chamber Court [and continuing in the same spirit] dissolved and dissipated into smoke the crushing courts of the President and Council of the North, and limited and confined the unlimited bounds of business at the Council table'. The King's advisers in general Vicars contemptuously dismissed as 'living grievances', 'stinking channels of wrong and oppression'. But his bitterest spleen was reserved for Strafford and Laud.

That insulting arch-traitor the Earl of Strafford who as he had well nigh stabbed the state to the heart by his deep and most dangerous plots both abroad and at home, so the stroke of justice retaliated with blood [for] his most bold and bloody designs. . . .

That lamb-skinned wolf the Archprelate of Canterbury who had so long and so craftily and cruelly worried Christ's innocent lambs.

To the same 1640s vintage belongs the hostile *History of Independency* (1648) by Clement Walker (d. 1651), a stubborn and quarrelsome MP excluded by Pride's Purge and imprisoned on account of his historical work. It was Walker who provided an extremely explicit statement of the seventeenth-century view that rebellion in England was the unlooked-for product of a corrupting period of peace and prosperity. His cyclical view of history was that:

> A long Peace begat Plenty, Plenty begat Pride, and her sister Riot, Pride begat Ambition, Ambition begat Faction, Faction begat Civil War: and if our evils be not incurable . . . our War will beget Poverty, Poverty Humility, Humility Peace again. . . . The declining spoke of the wheel will rise again. But we are not yet sufficiently humbled.[12]

In the 1650s came two works of a very different kind, the one a work of political theory, and the other a valuable and extensive collection of contemporary source material. The first, published in 1656, was *The Commonwealth of Oceana* by James Harrington (1611–77). Properly speaking, Harrington was not a historian at all, and his later influence, too, in France and America to a greater extent than in England, was mainly in the sphere of political ideas. But his place in the historiography of the English Revolution is assured on two counts. First, Harrington believed in the importance of history and offered a general theory of historical development.

> No man can be a politician except he be first a historian or a traveller, for except he can see what must be or what may be he is no politician. Nor if he has no knowledge in history he cannot tell what is; but he that neither knows what has been nor what is can never tell what must be nor what may be.[13]

Second, Harrington's analysis has come to occupy an important position in twentieth-century debates on the origins of the Civil Wars. On the first count Professor Zagorin goes so far as to claim that Harrington 'rose to a degree of sophistication in his historical thinking that makes even the greatest historical work of his time seem primitive by comparison'.[14] For the insights he offers into the nature and causes of the English Revolution Harrington is rated by Zagorin more highly than Clarendon. Certainly, Harrington's work has found itself at the centre of modern historical controversies such as that over the rise of the gentry. (See pp. 118–21.) Both sides in the debate, of course, have used Harrington, who arguably was more concerned with the decline of the aristocracy than with the rise of the gentry, in different ways. Other historians – surprisingly, since Harrington did not think in terms of a class struggle – have seen in *Oceana* a prototype of the Marxist critique. Another writer has found in Harrington's book the blueprint of an 'opportunity state' while, such is the diversity of opinion on the subject, Professor Pocock, who has done most to enhance Harrington's modern reputation as a political theorist, has argued that he 'was primarily a historian of feudalism and only in a most rudimentary sense an observer of contemporary social processes'.[15]

Despite the expedient use of fictitious names – Oceana (England), Marpesia (Scotland), Emporium (London), Parthenia (Elizabeth I), Morpheus (James I), Olphaus Megaletor (Oliver Cromwell), Leviathan (Thomas Hobbes), and so on – Harrington's republican tract was firmly grounded in the harsh, but promising, reality of mid-seventeenth-century England. The political system outlined in *Oceana* was not an impracticable Utopia. Given the situation in England at the time, and the redistribution of power which had already occurred, Oceana, as Harrington conceived it, was the logical, indeed necessary, outcome. *Oceana* was intended to place the English Revolution in historical perspective, to show that there had been an irreversible drift towards republicanism, and that in the circumstances Harrington's settlement was the only one possible.[16] But an act of will to create an equal commonwealth was still needed in the 1650s, as J. C. Davis has argued; Harrington knew that it was not enough merely to submit to the inevitable.[17]

Harrington was convinced that the main key to events in the seventeenth century was the economic one. (R. H. Tawney's famous essay on 'Harrington's interpretation of his age' was an elaboration of this point.)[18] Civil War took place in England because the political structure had ceased to correspond with economic reality.

The dissolution of the late monarchy was as natural as the death of a man. . . . Oceana, or any other nation of no greater extent must have a competent nobility, or is altogether incapable of monarchy: for where there is equality of estates, there must be equality of power; and where there is equality of power there can be no monarchy. . . .

Nor was there anything now wanting unto the destruction of the throne but that the people not apt to see their own strength should be put to feel it; when a prince, as stiff in disputes as the nerve of monarchy was grown slack, received that unhappy encouragement from his clergy which became his utter ruin, while trusting more unto their logick than the rough philosophy of his Parliament, it came unto an irreparable breach; for the house of Peers which alone had stood in this gap, now sinking down between the King and the Commons, showed that Crassus was dead and Isthmus broken. But a monarchy divested of her nobility hath no refuge under heaven but an army. Wherefore the dissolution of this Government caused the War, not the War the dissolution of this government.[19]

Harrington's prescription for England's troubles was the 'popularly based but aristocratically led society' outlined in *Oceana*, with the Agrarian Law designed to provide a stable economic base for the government and to prevent excessive concentrations of wealth.[20]

The other major work in this field to appear in the 1650s was the first volume of the *Historical Collections* of John Rushworth (1612?–90). Published in 1659 and dedicated to Richard Cromwell, Rushworth's work was as provocative in the short term as it has proved valuable in the long term to subsequent historians.[21] The preface which Rushworth supplied to Volume One declared his objectives and expounded his conception of historical method; it is worth quoting at length on both counts.

Yet certainly of some use it may be to us, and of concernment also to those that may come after us . . . to consider indifferently how we came to fall out among our selves and so to learn the true causes, the rises and growths of our late miseries, the strange alterations and revolutions with the characters of divers eminent persons, the mutability of councils, the remarkableness of actions, the subtilty of pretensions, and the drifts of several interests. From such premises the best deduction which can be made is to look up to and acknowledge God who only is unchangeable and to admire His wisdom and providence even in human miscarriages. For empires, and kingdoms and common-wealths everywhere in the world have their periods, but the histories thereof remain and live for the instruction of men and glory of God. . . .

I began early to take in characters, speeches, and passages at conferences in Parliament and from the King's own mouth when he spake to both the Houses, and have been upon stage continually and an eye and ear witness of the greatest transactions; employed as an agent in and entrusted with affairs of weightiest concernment; privy also both to the debates in Parliament and to the most secret results of councils of war in times of action: which I mention without ostentation only to qualify me to report to posterity what will rather be their wonder at first than their belief. It is a pity they should altogether be deprived of the advantages which they may reap from our misfortunes. Hereafter they will hear that every man almost in this generation durst fight for what either was or pretended to be Truth. They should also know that some durst write the Truth, whilst other men's fancies were more busie than their hands forging relations, building and battering castles in the air, publishing speeches as spoken in Parliament which were never spoken there, printing declarations which were never passed, relating battles that were never fought, and victories which were never obtained, dispersing letters which were never writ by the authors, together with many such contrivances to abet a party or interest. . . . Such practices and the experience I had thereof and the impossibility for any man in after ages to ground a true history by relying on the printed pamphlets in our days which passed the Press whilst it was without control, obliged to all the pains and charge I have been at for many years together to make a great collection; and whilst things were fresh in memory to separate truth from falsehood, things real from things fictitious or imaginary. Whereof I shall not at all repent if I may but prove an ordinary instrument to undeceive those that come after us. . . .

I allow and accept it as a good memento which I meet with in a late Author: that most writers nowadays appear in public, not crook-backed (as it is reported of the Jews) but crook-sided, warped and bowed to the right or to the left. For I have heartily studied to declare myself unbiassed and to give an instance, that it is possible for an ingenuous man to be of party and yet not partial.

I pretend only in this work to a bare narrative of matter of fact digested in order of time, not interposing my own opinion or interpretation of actions. I infuse neither vinegar nor gall into my ink. . . . If I speak of any transactions which I myself did not see or hear

I do so with all the caution imaginable, having first consulted records, conferred with persons of unquestionable esteem interested in the very actions or perused their known handwritings of those times. And where I make mention of any letters or passages scattered in print I first well weighed the same and out of whose closets they came and found many of them concredited before I inserted them. . . .

As I never did approve so neither could I persuade myself to tread in their steps, who intermingle their passion with their stories and are not content to write of unless they write also for a party or to serve an interest, and so declare themselves far better Advocates than Historians. I profess that in singleness of heart I aim at Truth which to me has always seemed hugely amiable, even without the attires and advantages of wit and eloquence.

Rushworth's theory of historical method, unfortunately, was more difficult to translate into practice than he imagined. Despite his professed impartiality, his career in the republic's civil service, in which for a time he was Cromwell's secretary, and his dedication of the book to the Protector's son, identified him with the King's opponents and so exposed him to attacks from the right in the Royalist-dominated period of historiography between the Restoration and 1688.[22]

The most polemical of these was John Nalson's *Impartial Collection of the Great Affairs of State from the Beginning of the Scotch Rebellion in the Year 1639 to the Murder of King Charles I* (2 vols, 1682–3). The contradictions in the title chosen by Nalson (1638?–86) announced where his own allegiances lay. Moreover the work enjoyed royal patronage, and the official records were made available to this preferment-seeking author who obsequiously dedicated the finished publication to Charles II. Nalson, none the less, described himself as a 'votary of truth' while indulging in the 'liberty of an historian to tie up the loose and scattered papers with the circumstances, causes and consequences of them'. It was Nalson's express aim:

To manifest the innocence of the government and vindicate it from those notorious detractions and calumnies which some factious and turbulent spirits who have had all along a design to subvert the establishment both of Church and State persuading the nation of strange designs to introduce arbitrary government and re-establish popery, whereas the truth is and I doubt not to make it appear, that these popular bugbears were only the contrivance of the anti-monarchical and schismatical faction to draw in a party, thereby to enable them to carry on their own wicked designs of at least reducing the monarchy to an impotent Venetian seigniory, and utterly to extirpate the most apostolical government of episcopy and set up the anarchy of Toleration and Liberty of Conscience in the church.

[I vigorously condemn those who] under the smooth surface of pretences to maintain Liberty, Property, Protestant religion, and Privileges of Parliament, betrayed us into the most deplorable shipwreck that ever England saw, even to the entire loss of all these valuable things which were pretended to be preserved.

Rushworth's *Historical Collections* came in for special attack, its editor being roundly denounced for his sympathies with the Parliamentarian rebels, for his distortions and suppression of the evidence.

The truth is if Mr Rushworth leans apparently to one side I would attribute it to his having grown so long, even from his very first taking root in the world, under the influences of that whirlwind of Rebellion. . . . Mr Rushworth hath concealed Truth, endeavoured to vindicate the prevailing detractions of the late times as well as their barbarous actions and with a kind of re-bound libelled the government at secondhand. . . . His *Collections* are the malicious part of the transactions of public affairs, picked out of the whole mass and represented with all the disadvantages that can be found out to justify the actions of the late rebels. . . . [Rushworth seems] so wholly transported with partiality to a party that he has recorded little but what relates to the justification of those he favours and their proceedings. . . .

I would render this preface a volume to trace this gentleman in all his omissions, mutilations, abridgements, and, I may justly fear, additions. . . . The truth is those speeches which were loyal he has generally omitted but those who have fallen upon the popular theme of grievances he has carefully indeed collected and displayed to insinuate into the credulous and unwary that the heavy complaints of grievances were vox populi and the universal and just cry of the nation, and by consequence that the King, his ministers and government were wholly unjust, oppressive, cruel and tyrannical. . . .

Having mercilessly exposed Rushworth's bias, Nalson then proceeded to set the record straight and, in what he deluded himself was a calm and objective manner, began to narrate 'those affairs which brought ruin upon this excellent government' of Charles I. Nalson continued,

> To palliate the horrid sin of Rebellion they [the Parliamentarians] endeavoured to render his Majesty the aggressor and themselves engaged in a defensive war for the liberty of the subject, the laws of the land, and the true Protestant religion. . . . They razed the very foundations of the government both civil and ecclesiastical and erected upon the ruins of this glorious and imperial monarchy the title of the Commonwealth of England.
>
> These were the men who pretended religion and a thorough Reformation and these were some of the arts by which they betrayed the easy people into rebellion, and the nation into ruin. These were the fatal consequences and effects of these popular fears and groundless jealousies of popery and arbitrary government, and this the dismal period of that horrid Rebellion.

As Nalson saw it, there was only one conclusion to be drawn from the wicked revolt against Charles I: 'that true loyalty to their prince is both their interest and their duty, as they are men, christians and Englishmen. And that without it the fairest pretences to religion and Reformation are the most pernicious vizards and covers of the most dangerous of all kinds of rebellion.'[23]

Nalson's account was the most polemical of the anti-Parliamentarian histories to appear after the Restoration, but it was not an isolated one. The Royalist version of English history in general as well as of the Civil Wars in particular, stressing the sovereign and paternal aspects of monarchy and utilizing Brady's and Spelman's ideas on feudalism, was rapidly developing in the more congenial climate of the later seventeenth century.[24] James Heath (1629–64), for instance, earlier a staunch supporter of the cause of the exiled Charles II, in 1661 published his *Chronicle of the late Intestine War in the Three Kingdoms*, and dedicated it to General Monck. And in 1681, the anti-puritan, anti-Parliamentarian William Dugdale (1605–86) brought out his *Short View of the Late Troubles in England*. Dugdale could find little good to say about 'that viperous brood which not long since hath so miserably infested these kingdoms' and who had contrived the 'nefarious murder of King Charles I'. To Dugdale, the real origin of the Civil War lay in the hypocritical and subversive religion of the Parliamentarian leaders.

THE DEBATE BEGINS

That all rebellions did ever begin with the fairest pretences for reforming of somewhat amiss in the government, is a truth so clear that there needs thereof no manifestation from examples. Nor were they ever observed to have greater success than when the colours for religion did openly appear in the van of their armed forces; most men being desirous to have it really thought (how bad and vile soever their practices are) that zeal to God's glory is no small part of their aim. Which gilded bait hath been usually held forth to allure the vulgar, by those whose ends and designs were nothing else than to get into power, and so to possess themselves of the estates and fortunes of their more opulent neighbours.[25]

What had taken place in mid-seventeenth-century England could only be described as a rebellion against justly constituted authority. Contrasts were drawn between Charles I 'a most pious and gracious prince', 'the happy Restoration of Charles II', and 'that grand impostor Cromwell', and analogies made between the Civil War and the Baronial Wars of Henry III and the French Wars of Religion. Dugdale had been active on the King's side in the Civil War, and the first part of his history (covering the years up to 1646) was written in the Royalist stronghold of Oxford. At the root of the Civil War troubles were religious extremists whose 'fair and smooth pretences set forth in several declarations and remonstrances by which the too credulous people were miserably deluded and drawn from their due allegiance'. In Parliament they constantly and unreasonably obstructed the King, and in the country they curried favour 'by planting schismatical lectures in most corporate towns and populous places throughout the realm so to poison the people with anti-monarchical principles'.

If the reflections on what is past are sometimes severe let it be imputed to the just indignation conceived against those men who under specious pretences masked the most black designs, and [to] an abhorrence of those proceedings which embroiled the nation in a civil war, perfidious in its rise, bloody in its prosecution, fatal in its end and which to this day proves mischievous in its consequences. . . .

That the meeting of these members of Parliament from all parts of the realm (being many of them men of turbulent spirits, and principles totally anti-monarchical), gave opportunity for those contrivances which afterwards were put in action, there is nothing more sure. For in the first place, they took care to infuse fears and jealousies into the people everywhere that the government was designed to be arbitrary,

23

and popery like to be introduced, to promote which scandals many seditious preachers took no small pains in their pulpits especially in and about London.

Dugdale's conclusion echoed the persistent message of his text: that the Parliamentarian leaders had wilfully misled the people, and, for no good reason, contrived the downfall of the monarchy.

And the people of England may now see how by bracing them too far in the forbidden paths of a conceived liberty they not long since fell into the known slavery of the French peasant. A misery which some of them felt but a little, when for fear of it they first petitioned to be put into a posture of defence, but justly brought upon themselves by those undue courses which they took to prevent it, God in his wisdom thinking it fit to punish this nation by a real slavery unto some of their own fellow subjects for fancying to themselves an imaginary [one], under their lawful sovereign as a ground to justify their rebellion when there was no cause for it.

The book ends by quoting Sir Edward Coke's *Institutes* on treason, thus turning Parliamentarian legal theory against the rebels.[26]

Dugdale's emphasis on the subversive role of religious extremists is similar in this respect to *Behemoth or the Long Parliament* by Thomas Hobbes (1586–1679), written in the 1660s and eventually published in 1682. But Hobbes's work had at least something in common, too, with Harrington's *Oceana*, since again this was not a historical study in the conventional sense. For as the student remarks to the doctor in the first dialogue of *Behemoth*,

I suppose your purpose was to aquaint me with the history, not so much of those actions that passed in the time of the late troubles, as of their causes, and of the councils and artifice by which they were brought to pass. There be divers men that have written the history, out of which I might have learned what they did, and somewhat also of the contrivance; but I find little in them of what I would ask.[27]

Like Harrington, Hobbes was first and foremost a philosopher, and he turned to history largely to find a tool with which to test his own science of politics which he had already systematically expounded in *The Elements of Law* (1640), *De Cive* (1642), and in *Leviathan* (1651). As Professor Goldsmith says,

Behemoth is more than a brief history of the Civil War. It is not only an attack on what Hobbes regarded as false and dangerous prevailing opinions, but also an attempt to show how Hobbes's science explains the historical phenomena of the Great Rebellion. Even more it is Hobbes's triumphant vindication of the doctrines he had expounded since 1640 and of his proposal that Hobbism should be established by authority.[28]

Hobbes, therefore, had a less exalted view than Harrington of the nature and value of history, and unlike Harrington his interpretation of the English Revolution was not primarily a materialist one. There were elements of such an interpretation, however, in Hobbes's analysis, and Professor Macpherson has highlighted them in his book on *The Political Theory of Possessive Individualism*.[29] According to Macpherson, Hobbes attributed the outbreak of the Civil War to the new strength of market morality and to market-made wealth. Hobbes, his argument goes on, saw the Civil War as an attempt to replace the old constitution with one which was more economically favourable to the middle classes. Hobbes believed that each man was 'so much master of whatsoever he possessed that it could not be taken from him upon any pretence of common safety without his own consent'. Presbyterianism took root because it was a comfortable religion which did not 'inveigh against the lucrative vices of men of trade or handicraft . . . which was a great ease to the generality of citizens and the inhabitants of market towns'. 'The city of London and other great towns of trade, having in admiration the great prosperity of the Low Countries after they had revolted from their monarch, the King of Spain, were inclined to think that the like change of government here would to them produce the like prosperity.' The Parliamentary army was maintained by 'the great purse of the city of London and contributions of almost all the towns corporate in England'. The main grievance at the time was taxation 'to which citizens, that is merchants, whose profession is their private gain are naturally mortal enemies, their only glory being to grow excessively rich by the wisdom of buying and selling'.[30]

Such passages, however, should not be given an exaggerated importance. Unlike Harrington, Hobbes offered a mainly ideological rather than a materialist interpretation of the seventeenth-century crisis. To Hobbes, the Civil War was basically a struggle for sovereignty and, as in his works on political philosophy, he argued in *Behemoth* in favour of undivided rule. 'There can be no government', he repeated endlessly, 'where there is more than one sovereign.' The Parliamentarians, on the other hand, said Hobbes, at the beginning of the Civil War 'dreamt of a mixed power of the King and of the two Houses. That it was a divided power in which there could be no peace was above their understanding.' The Earl of Essex, the Parliamentarian commander, 'was carried away with the stream [in a manner] of the whole nation to think that England was not an absolute but a mixed monarchy: not considering that the supreme power must always be absolute whether it be in the King or the Parliament'.[31] As this quotation makes clear, therefore, Hobbes's theory of undivided sovereignty was inherently ambiguous, as he himself admitted in an apology to Charles II in 1662. Hobbes begged the King not 'to think the worse of me, if snatching up all the weapons to fight against your enemies I lighted upon one that had a double edge'.[32]

So the Civil War, in Hobbes's view, was basically a struggle for sovereignty, first between King and Parliament and later between Cromwell and the army on the one hand and Parliament on the other. And how did these struggles originate? To a large extent, argued Hobbes, they were the outcome of a subversive conspiracy stemming from the universities, 'the core of rebellion', breeding grounds for advanced, extravagant, and seditious ideas. 'The universities', Hobbes declared in a striking phrase, 'have been to this nation as the wooden horse was to the Trojans.' The corrupting influences nurtured in the universities were of two kinds: lawyers and, above all, clergymen – war-mongering Presbyterian divines.

> Had it not been much better that those seditious ministers, which were not perhaps 1000, had all been killed before they had preached? It had been (I confess) a great massacre; but the killing of 100,000 [in the Civil War] is a greater. . . . They that preached us into the rebellion . . . will say they did it in obedience to God, inasmuch as they did believe it was according to the Scripture; out of which they will bring examples, perhaps of David and his adherents that resisted King Saul. . . . Besides you cannot doubt but that they, who in the pulpit did animate the people to take arms in the defence of the then Parliament, alleged Scripture, that is, the word of God, for it. If it be lawful then for subjects to resist the King, when he commands anything that is

against the Scripture, that is, contrary to the command of God, and to be judge of the meaning of the Scripture, it is impossible that the life of any King, or the peace of any Christian kingdom can be long secure. It is this doctrine that divides a kingdom within itself, whatsoever the men be, loyal or rebels, that preach it publicly.[33]

Although it was the Presbyterian clergy who came in for particular denunciation (because of the power and influence they wielded), Hobbes had no great love for clergymen of any persuasion, or indeed for any religious group, and by many he was accounted an atheist. (Aubrey's *Brief Lives* has it that after the Restoration some of the bishops tried to get 'the good old gentleman burnt for a Heretique'.)[34] Papists as well as puritans were exposed and criticized in *Behemoth*. What Hobbes favoured was the establishment of a single Erastian church in which ecclesiastical doctrine and practice would be a matter of civil law.[35] Given the situation which had finally erupted into civil war, to Hobbes the message was obvious: restoration of stability to the commonwealth would mean that the independent powers of universities, lawyers, and clergy would all have to be drastically curtailed by a totalitarian state.

> The core of rebellion, as you have seen by this, and read of other rebellions, are the universities; which nevertheless are not to be cast away, but to be better disciplined; that is to say, that the politics there taught be made to be (as true politics should be) such as are fit to make men know, that it is their duty to obey all laws whatsoever that shall by the authority of the King be enacted till by the same authority they shall be repealed; such as are fit to make men understand that the civil laws are God's laws, as they that make them are by God appointed to make them; and to make men know, that the people and the Church are one thing and have but one head, the King; and that no man has title to govern under him that has it not from him; that the King owes his crown to God only, and to no man, ecclesiastic or other; and that the religion they teach there be a quiet waiting for the coming again of our blessed Saviour, and in the meantime a resolution to obey the King's laws (which also are God's laws); to injure no man, to be in charity with all men, to cherish the poor and sick, and to live soberly and free from scandal; without mingling our religion with points of natural philosophy, as freedom of will, incorporeal substance, everlasting nows, ubiquities, hypostases, which the people understand not, nor will ever care for. When the universities shall be

thus disciplined, there will come out of them, from time to time, well-principled preachers, and they that are now ill-principled, from time to time fall away.[36]

Hobbes emphasized the supreme importance of what had taken place in the middle of the century.

> If in time, as in place, there were degrees of high and low, I verily believe that the highest of time would be that which passed between the years of 1640 and 1660. For he that thence, as from the Devil's Mountain, should have looked upon the world and observed the actions of men, especially in England, might have had a prospect of all kinds of injustice, and of all kinds of folly, that the world could afford, and how they were produced by their dams' hypocrisy and self-conceit, whereof the one is double iniquity, and the other double folly.[37]

Hobbes's political philosophy, his views on undivided sovereignty, aroused many opponents in the seventeenth century, but of all these for our purposes the most noteworthy was Edward Hyde, Earl of Clarendon (1609–74), constitutional Royalist and empirical theorist of mixed monarchy. To Clarendon Hobbes was a trimmer, who wrote about high politics from the distant standpoint of an outsider, a novice, an impractical scholar, and irreligious mathematician.[38] He himself was quite different. With Clarendon we move unmistakably to historical writing on the grand scale. His *History of the Rebellion and Civil Wars in England* was the first full-length, systematic treatment of events in the early seventeenth century, and has been described as 'epoch-making in the development of English historical writing'.[39] First published in 1702–4, and reissued in at least twelve subsequent editions in the next 150 years, Clarendon's work is indeed a historical classic.

Clarendon, of course, was a prominent participant in the events he described. In the early 1640s he emerged as the leading constitutional Royalist and was one of the chief architects responsible for the creation of the King's party. In eclipse during the period of fighting when his message of moderation lost its relevance, Clarendon re-emerged in the 1650s and honours were heaped upon him after the Restoration which, in a diplomatic sense, he more than anyone had helped to make possible. Yet by 1667 Clarendon was in disgrace and made a scapegoat for his country's humiliating defeat in the war against the Dutch (which in fact he had opposed). The Lord Chancellor was deprived of office and banished from England by his royal master. His *History of the Rebellion* reflects the extreme vicissitudes of his career. A conflation of an earlier work written in the 1640s for the private instruction of the King and his counsellors, and of a self-justifying autobiography begun in exile in France twenty years later, Clarendon's *History* gives the most famous Royalist account of the English Revolution.[40] Clarendon, in fact, ranks much more highly as a historian than as a politician.

> Whatever his defects as a politician [Christopher Hill has observed] Clarendon was a great historian. His profound social insight, tempered by acute penetration in analyzing individual character; his lack of illusions, his scepticism, tempered by recognition of the fact of human progress even if he disliked the means which brought it about; all this fitted him to understand the conflicts of his age better than any contemporary and most later historians.

Clarendon's *History*, concludes Ronald Hutton (in no sense an admirer of Charles II's Lord Chancellor whom he finds 'greedy and unforgiving'), 'remains his most enduring monument and has ensured him a fame and a sympathy which his political acts alone would never have done'.[41] Christopher Hill uses Clarendon's work to support his own social interpretation of the English Revolution. Whether Clarendon's *History* – which is principally a political narrative – contains such an astute and extended analysis of the social causes and social nature of the Civil War struggles as Dr Hill would have us believe, is another matter. Clarendon, however, was certainly well placed and well qualified to write his *History of the Rebellion*.

> And as I may not be thought altogether an incompetent person for this communication, having been present as a member of parliament in those councils before and till the breaking out of the rebellion, and having since had the honour to be near two great kings in some trust, so I shall perform the same with all faithfulness and ingenuity; with an equal observation of the faults and infirmities of both sides, with their defects and oversights in pursuing their own ends. . . . I know myself to be very free from any of those passions which naturally transport men with prejudice towards the persons whom they are obliged to mention, and whose actions they are at liberty to censure.

There is not a man who acted the worst part in this ensuing year with whom I had ever the least difference or personal unkindness, or towards whom I had not much inclination of kindness, or from whom I did not receive all invitations of further endearments.[42]

To explain the outbreak of the mid-seventeenth-century troubles it was not necessary to go very far back in time. (Here, as in other respects, Clarendon was at odds with his former friend Thomas May.)

That posterity may not be deceived, by the prosperous wickedness of these times, into an opinion, that less than a general combination, and universal apostasy in the whole nation from their religion and allegiance, could, in so short a time, have produced such a total and prodigious alteration and confusion over the whole kingdom; and so the memory of those few, who, out of duty and conscience, have opposed and resisted that torrent, which hath overwhelmed them, may lose the recompense due to their virtue; and, having undergone the injuries and reproaches of this, may not find a vindication in a better age; it will not be unuseful, at least to the curiosity if not the conscience of men, to present to the world a full and clear narration of the grounds, circumstances, and artifices of this rebellion: not only from the time since the flame hath been visible in a civil war, but, looking further back, from those former passages, accidents, and actions, by which the seed-plots were made and framed, from whence these mischiefs have successively grown to the height they are now at.

I shall not lead any man farther back in this journey, for the discovery of the entrance into these dark ways than the beginning of this king's reign. For I am not so sharp-sighted as those, who have discerned this rebellion contriving from (if not before) the death of Queen Elizabeth, and fomented by several princes and great ministers of state in Christendom, to the time that it brake out. Neither do I look so far back as believing the design to be so long since formed; (they who have observed the several accidents, not capable of being contrived to the several successes, and do know the persons who have been the grand instruments towards this change, of whom there have not been any four of familiarity and trust with each other, will easily absolve them from so much industry and foresight in their mischief;) but that by viewing the temper, disposition, and habit of that time, of the court and of the country, we may discern the minds of men prepared, of some to do, and of others to suffer, all that hath since happened; the pride of this man, and the popularity of that; the levity of one, and the morosity of another; the excess of the court in the greatest want, and the parsimony and retention of the country in the greatest plenty; the spirit of craft and subtlety in some, and the rude and unpolished integrity of others, too much despising craft or art; like so many atoms contributing jointly to this mass of confusion now before us.[43]

So Clarendon set out to produce a magisterially balanced and impartial account of English events in the first half of the seventeenth century, aiming 'to do justice to every man who hath fallen into the quarrel in which side soever'. The extent to which Clarendon actually achieved this aim can be gauged first by examining his treatment of individuals on the opposing sides, and then by looking at his more general comments on a force like puritanism and on a whole nation such as the Scots.

Clarendon's *History* is justly famous for the character studies strategically interspersed in the narrative of events. When he dealt with the King's side in the war Clarendon, who before 1640 had been a reformer and moderate critic of Charles I, was faithful to his constitutional royalism. He was not blind even to the failings of the King himself. In his estimate of Charles I Clarendon emphasized,

> how difficult it was for a prince, so unworthily reduced to those straits his majesty was in, to find ministers and instruments equal to the great work that was to be done; and how impossible it was for him to have better success under their conduct, whom it was then very proper for him to trust with it; and then, without my being over-solicitous to absolve him from those mistakes and weaknesses to which he was in truth sometimes liable, he will be found not only a prince of admirable virtue and piety, but of great parts of knowledge, wisdom and judgment; and that the most signal parts of his misfortunes proceeded chiefly from the modesty of his nature, which kept him from trusting himself enough, and made him believe, that others discerned better, who were much inferior to him in those faculties; and so to depart often from his own reason, to follow the opinions of more unskilful men, whose affections he believed to be unquestionable to his service. . . .
>
> His kingly virtues had some mixture and allay, that hindered them from shining in full lustre, and from producing those fruits they should

have been attended with. He was not in his nature very bountiful . . . and he paused too long in giving, which made those to whom he gave, less sensible of the benefit. . . . He was fearless in his person, but not very enterprising.[44]

If his assessment of Charles I contained an element of 'whitewashing', this is no doubt as much due to the sources of information available to him as to his personal proximity to the King. Clarendon was more outspoken in his comments on the Queen, Henrietta Maria, and on her meddling in politics.[45] On Thomas Wentworth, Earl of Strafford, the King's chief servant, Clarendon had this to say:

> He was no doubt of great observation, and a piercing judgment, both into things and persons; but his too good skill in persons made him judge the worse of things . . . discerning many defects in most men, he too much neglected what they said or did. Of all his passions, his pride was most predominant: which a moderate exercise of ill fortune might have corrected and reformed; and which was by the hand of Heaven strangely punished, by bringing his destruction upon him by two things he most despised, the people and Sir Harry Vane. In a word, the epitaph, which Plutarch records that Sylla wrote for himself, may not be unfitly applied to him; 'that no man did ever pass him, either in doing good to his friends, or in doing mischief to his enemies'; for his acts of both kinds were most exemplary and notorious.[46]

Archbishop Laud, in Clarendon's account, emerged as one more sinned against than sinning.

> He was always maligned and persecuted by those who were of the Calvinist faction, which was then very powerful, and who, according to the useful maxim and practice, call every man they do not love, papist; and under this senseless appellation they created him many troubles and vexations. . . . No man was a greater or abler enemy to popery; no man a more resolute and devout son of the church of England. . . . Much hath been said of the person of this great prelate before, of his great endowments, and natural infirmities; to which shall be added no more in this place, (his memory deserving a particular celebration), than that his learning, piety, and virtue have been attained by very few, and the greatest of his infirmities are common to all, even to the best men.[47]

Strafford and Laud received from Clarendon's pen a charitable rather than an enthusiastic appraisal. But for Lucius Cary, Viscount Falkland, the King's secretary of state from 1641, a constitutional royalist like himself, who was killed at the first Battle of Newbury, Clarendon's admiration scarcely knew any bounds.

> If celebrating the memory of eminent and extraordinary persons, and transmitting their great virtues, for the imitation of posterity, be one of the principal ends and duties of history, it will not be thought impertinent in this place, to remember a loss which no time will suffer to be forgotten, and no success or good fortune could repair. In this unhappy battle was slain the Lord Viscount Falkland, a person of such prodigious parts of learning and knowledge, of that inimitable sweetness and delight in conversation, of so flowing and obliging a humanity and goodness to mankind, and of that primitive simplicity and integrity of life, that if there were no other brand upon this odious and accursed civil war, than that single loss, it must be most infamous and execrable to all posterity.[48]

When he came to the Parliamentarians, for obvious reasons, impartiality was much more difficult. Take, for example, Clarendon's barbed verdict on John Hampden.

> Mr Hampden was a man of much greater cunning, and it may be of the most discerning spirit, and of the greatest address and insinuation to bring any thing to pass which he desired, of any man of that time, and who laid the design deepest. . . . He made so great a show of civility, and modesty, and humility, and always of mistrusting his own judgment, and of esteeming his with whom he conferred for the present, that he seemed to have no opinions or resolutions, but such as he contracted from the information and instruction he received upon the discourses of others, whom he had a wonderful art of governing, and leading into his principles and inclinations, whilst they believed that he wholly depended upon their counsel and advice. No man had ever a greater power over himself, or was less the man that he seemed to be, which shortly after appeared to everybody, when he cared less to keep on the mask. . . . His death was no less congratulated on the one party, than it was condoled in the other. In a word, what was said of Cinna might well be applied to him: 'he had a head to contrive, and a tongue to persuade, and a hand to execute any mischief.' His death, therefore, seemed to be a great deliverance to the nation.[49]

For Oliver Cromwell, Clarendon, despite himself, showed a certain reluctant admiration, and praised the achievements, if not the man.

> Cromwell, though the greatest dissembler living, always made his hypocrisy of singular use and benefit to him; and never did anything, how ungracious or imprudent soever it seemed to be, but what was necessary to the design. . . . He could never have done half that mischief without great parts of courage, industry and judgment. He must have had a wonderful understanding in the natures and humours of men, and as great a dexterity in applying them. . . . Without doubt, no man with more wickedness ever attempted anything, or brought to pass what he desired more wickedly, more in the face and contempt of religion, and moral honesty; yet wickedness as great as his could never have accomplished those trophies, without the assistance of a great spirit, an admirable circumspection and sagacity, and a most magnanimous resolution. . . . To reduce three nations, which perfectly hated him, to an entire obedience, to all his dictates; to awe and govern those nations by an army that was indevoted to him, and wished his ruin, was an instance of a very prodigious address. But his greatness at home was but a shadow of the glory he had abroad. . . .
>
> In a word, as he had all the wickedness against which damnation is denounced, and for which hell-fire is prepared, so he had some virtues which have caused the memory of some men in all ages to be celebrated; and he will be looked upon by posterity as a brave bad man.[50]

Turning from the portraits of individuals to his general observations on a whole people, the Scots, we find that Clarendon indulged his prejudices on a correspondingly grander scale. 'Vermin', 'that foreign contemned nation' are among the choice epithets which rushed from Clarendon's pen when he turned to social life, religion, and politics north of the border. With immense disdain he spoke of,

> the numerous proud and indigent nobility of Scotland (for of the common people, who are naturally slaves to the other, there can be no wonder) [who] concurred in the carrying on this rebellion; their strange condescension and submission to their ignorant and insolent clergy, who were to have great authority, because they were to inflame all sorts of men upon the obligations of conscience; and in order thereunto, and to revenge a little indiscretion and ill manners of some of

the bishops, had liberty to erect a tribunal the most tyrannical over all sorts of men, and in all the families of the kingdom.

He counted it one of Charles I's great weaknesses that 'he was always an immoderate lover of the Scottish nation, having not only been born there, but educated by that people, and besieged by them always'. Conversely, Clarendon considered Cromwell's conquest of Scotland to be one of his most admirable achievements.[51]

As for puritanism, understandably perhaps, Clarendon could only see it as a subversive fanaticism, socially harmful and politically disastrous. The puritan clergy, in his view – and it was similar to Hobbes's – had much to answer for; it was they, above all, who had raised the political temperature to such a height in the 1640s, rousing men's passions and goading them into action by their inflammatory preaching.

> I must not forget, though it cannot be remembered without much horror, that this strange wildfire among the people was not so much and so furiously kindled by the breath of the parliament, as of the clergy, who both administered fuel, and blowed the coals in the houses too. These men having creeped into, and at last driven all learned and orthodox men from the pulpits had, as is before remembered, from the beginning of this parliament, under the notion of reformation and extirpating of popery, infused seditious inclinations into the hearts of men against the present government of the church, with many libellous invectives against the state too . . .
>
> There are monuments enough in the seditious sermons at that time printed, and in the memories of men, of others not printed, of such wresting and perverting of scripture to the odious purposes of the preacher, that pious men will not look over without trembling.
>
> And indeed no good Christian can, without horror, think of those ministers of the church, who by their function being messengers of peace, were the only trumpets of war, and incendiaries towards rebellion.[52]

Clearly, then, there is much that is absent in Clarendon's estimate of puritanism, but when Sir Charles Firth (see pp. 100–4) complained that Clarendon's 'History of the Rebellion has the fundamental defect that it is a history of a religious revolution in which the religious element is omitted', it is important to remember that he was using a Victorian yardstick;[53] methods of measurement have changed since then. Clarendon did not achieve the impartiality at which he aimed, but this in any case was an impossible target which he set for himself. Given his own place in the events he was describing, Clarendon's survey of the period is remarkably broad in its sweep and sometimes fairly generous in its tone. *The History of the Rebellion* emphatically is not the work of a sycophantic party historian; Clarendon was in a different class altogether from such writers as John Vicars and John Nalson. Modern verdicts on Clarendon have diverged. J. P. Kenyon, Royce McGillivray and Ronald Hutton to a large extent have been deflationary and hostile in their respective treatments of him. Clarendon's *History*, said Hutton, remains 'an exquisite perversion of the truth which exonerated himself and his friends and excoriated their enemies'.[54] Others have argued differently. Hill has praised his social insights into the period. Trevor-Roper has claimed him as a kind of precursor of the philosophical historians of the eighteenth-century Enlightenment.[55] Clarendon himself made bold claims for his *History* and took it in some novel directions. At the same time, however – and in this respect he was simply a creature of his age and its cross-currents – moralizing and providentialism were conspicuously present in what he wrote. Studying the dislodging rebellion that he had witnessed in his own lifetime in tandem with another long-term project, this time in Theology (*Contemplations and Reflections on the Psalms of David*) posed no problems for Clarendon. In the *History*, no less than the religious treatise, 'the hand and judgement of God' were unmistakably visible.[56]

Notes

1 T. Fuller, *The Church History of Britain*, ed. J. Nicholls (London, 1842), III, pp. 160, 150.
2 Quoted in Fuller, *An Appeal of Injured Innocence* (London, 1659), p. 46.
3 Puritanism continues to be a controversial subject in the twentieth century. See C. H. George, 'Puritanism as history and historiography', *PP*, 41 (1968), and M. G. Finlayson, *Historians, Puritans and the English Revolution: The Religious Factor in English Politics Before and After the Interregnum* (Toronto, 1983).
4 C. H. Firth, 'The development of the study of seventeenth-century history', *TRHS*, 3rd ser., 7 (1913), lists these early writers on the English Revolution. On the development of the press in this period see J. Frank, *The Beginnings of the English Newspaper 1620–1660* (Cambridge, Mass., 1961).

5 Quoted in H. R. Trevor-Roper, *Clarendon and the Practice of History* (Los Angeles, William Andrews Clark Memorial Library, 1965), pp. 38–9.
6 T. May, *History of the Parliament of England*, ed. F. Maseres (London, 1812), pp. xvii, xix.
7 *Ibid.*, pp. 6, 4.
8 T. May, *A Breviary of the History of the Parliament of England* (London, 1650), p. 2.
9 May, *History of the Parliament of England*, p. 15.
10 See P. Styles, 'Politics and history in the early seventeenth century', in L. Fox (ed.), *English Historical Scholarship in the Sixteenth and Seventeenth Centuries* (London, 1956); J. G. A. Pocock, *The Ancient Constitution and the Feudal Law: A Study of English Historical Thought in the Seventeenth Century* (Cambridge, 1957, 2nd edn, 1987); C. Hill, 'The Norman yoke', in *Puritanism and Revolution* (London, 1958); Q. Skinner, 'History and ideology in the English Revolution', *HJ*, viii (1965).
11 Sprigge's work was reprinted, ed. H. T. Moore (Gainsville, Florida, 1960).
12 J. Vicars, *England's Parliamentarie Chronicle* (London, 1644–6), pp. 31–2; C. Walker, *History of Independency* (1646), quoted in R. MacGillivray, *Restoration Historians and the English Civil War* (The Hague, 1974), p. 237.
13 J. G. A. Pocock (ed.), *The Political Works of James Harrington* (Cambridge, 1977), p. 310.
14 P. Zagorin, *History of Political Thought in the English Revolution* (London, 1954), p. 145.
15 E. Bernstein, *Cromwell and Communism* (London, 1930), pp. 192–211; A. L. Morton, *The English Utopia* (London, 1952), pp. 75–6; C. B. Macpherson, 'Harrington's opportunity state', *PP*, 17 (1960); Pocock, *The Ancient Constitution and the Feudal Law*, p. 141.
16 C. Hill, 'James Harrington and the people', in *Puritanism and Revolution*, p. 300. See also F. Raab, *The English Face of Machiavelli* (London, 1964) and J. G. A. Pocock, 'James Harrington and the Good Old Cause', *JBS*, ix (1970).
17 J. C. Davis, *Utopia and the Ideal Society: A Study of English Utopian Writing 1516–1700* (Cambridge, 1981), p. 213.
18 Tawney's essay is now reprinted in J. M. Winter (ed.), *History and Society: Essays by R. H. Tawney* (London, 1978).
19 Pocock, *The Political Works of James Harrington*, pp. 198, 201, 203.
20 Davis, *Utopia and the Ideal Society*, p. 212. See also C. Blitzer, *An Immortal Commonwealth: The Political Thought of James Harrington* (New Haven, Conn., 1960).
21 J. Rushworth, *Historical Collections* (London, 1659). The dedication was later suppressed.
22 For a brief account of Rushworth's career as a bureaucrat see G. E. Aylmer, *The State's Servants: The Civil Service of the English Republic* (London, 1973), p. 260.
23 J. Nalson, *Impartial Collection of the Great Affairs of State from the Beginning of the Scotch Rebellion in the Year 1639 to the Murder of King Charles I* (London, 1682–3), pp. i–iii, iv, vi, xxii, xxv, lxxvii–viii.
24 See Pocock, *The Ancient Constitution and the Feudal Law*, ch. 8.

25 W. Dugdale, *Short View of the Late Troubles in England* (London, 1681), preface.
26 *Ibid.*, pp. 391, preface, pp. 62, 649–50.
27 F. Tonnies (ed.), *Hobbes, Behemoth or the Long Parliament*, 2nd edn with an introduction by M. M. Goldsmith (London, 1969), p. 45.
28 *Ibid.*, p. xiv.
29 Macpherson, *The Political Theory of Possessive Individualism* (Oxford, 1962). On Hobbes as a historian see R. MacGillivray, 'Thomas Hobbes's History of the English Civil War: a study of Behemoth', *J. Hist. Ideas*, xxxi (1970), and J. G. A. Pocock, 'Time, history and eschatology in the thought of Thomas Hobbes', *Politics, Language and Time: Essays on Political Thought and History* (London, 1972). R. P. Kraynack, *History and Modernity in the Thought of Thomas Hobbes* (Ithaca, New York, 1990), and F. Levy, 'The background of Hobbes's Behemoth', in D. R. Kelley and D. H. Sacks (eds), *The Historical Imagination in Early Modern Britain: History, Rhetoric and Fiction 1500–1800* (Cambridge, 1997), pp. 243–66.
30 Macpherson, *The Political Theory of Possessive Individualism*, p. 65; Tonnies, *Hobbes, Behemoth or the Long Parliament*, pp. 4, 25, 110, 126.
31 Tonnies, *Hobbes, Behemoth or the Long Parliament*, pp. 77, 125, 112.
32 Quoted in M. M. Goldsmith, *Hobbes's Science of Politics* (London, 1966), p. 241.
33 Tonnies, *Hobbes, Behemoth or the Long Parliament*, pp. 95, 46, 49–50.
34 O. L. Dick (ed.), *Aubrey's Brief Lives* (Harmondsworth, 1982), p. 235.
35 S. I. Mintz, *The Hunting of Leviathan* (Cambridge, 1962), p. 47. See also D. Johnston, *The Rhetoric of Leviathan: Thomas Hobbes and the Rhetoric of Cultural Transformation* (Princeton, NJ, 1987).
36 Tonnies, *Hobbes, Behemoth or the Long Parliament*, p. 58.
37 *Ibid.*, p. 1.
38 On the opposition to Hobbes see J. Bowle, *Hobbes and his Critics* (London, 1951), and P. Zagorin, 'Clarendon and Hobbes', *JMH*, LVII (1985), pp. 593–616. Clarendon's hostility to Hobbes obscured the fact that they had much in common. Both were fundamentally conservative and disdainful of democracy. Clarendon, like Hobbes, could trim to the prevailing political wind. He was subsequently evasive, for example, on the stance he took at the time of Strafford's attainder.
39 A. J. Grant (ed.), *English Historians* (London, 1906), p. xx.
40 C. H. Firth discussed the composition and structure of Clarendon's *History* in three articles published at the turn of the century (*EHR*, xx (1904), pp. 26–54, 246–62, 464–83). The best rounded study is B. H. G. Wormald, *Clarendon, Politics, Historiography and Religion 1640–1660* (Cambridge, 1964). On Clarendon's writing there is now M. W. Brownley, *Clarendon and the Rhetoric of Historical Form* (Philadelphia, 1985).
41 C. Hill, 'Lord Clarendon and the Puritan Revolution', in *Puritanism and Revolution*, p. 214; R. Hutton, *The Restoration: A Political and Religious History of England and Wales 1658–1667* (paperback edn, 1987), pp. 284, 134.
42 G. Huehns (ed.), *Clarendon: Selections*, with an introduction by H. R. Trevor-Roper (Oxford, 1978), pp. 2–3, 5–6. The standard edition of Clarendon is by

W. D. Macray (six vols, Oxford, 1888), but for greater convenience all quotations in this chapter from the *History of the Rebellion* have been taken from *Clarendon: Selections*.

43 *Clarendon: Selections*, pp. 1–3.
44 *Ibid.*, pp. 6–7, 316–17.
45 *Ibid.*, pp. 100–1.
46 *Ibid.*, pp. 147.
47 *Ibid.*, pp. 103, 115–16, 118.
48 *Ibid.*, pp. 49–50.
49 *Ibid.*, pp. 166, 167, 170.
50 *Ibid.*, pp. 305–6, 355–8.
51 *Ibid.*, pp. 123–4, 317, 358.
52 *Ibid.*, pp. 253–4.
53 C. H. Firth, *Essays Historical and Literary* (Oxford, 1938), p. 119.
54 J. P. Kenyon, *The History Men* (London, 1983), pp. 29–30, 33, McGillivray, *Restoration Historians*, p. 224, Hutton, *Restoration*, p. 284. See also R. Hutton, 'Clarendon's History of the Rebellion', *EHR*, xcvii (1982), *passim*.
55 H. R. Trevor-Roper, *Clarendon and the Practice of History* (Los Angeles, William Andrews Clark Memorial Library, 1965), p. 48.
56 See M. Finlayson, 'Clarendon, Providence and the Historical Revolution', *Albion*, xxii (1990), pp. 607–32.

3

The eighteenth century: the political uses of history

There are persons so over-run with prejudice, so involved or rather immersed in Party, that it is next to impossible that they should always distinguish between truth and falsehood. Men whose eyesights are thus darkened and contracted can never see far before them. The extremities of Parties are the scandals and excrescences of human nature. (Laurence Echard, *Appendix to the History of England* (London, 1720), p. 36)

Clarendon occupies a special position in the historiography of the English Revolution. Chronologically, his *History of the Rebellion* belongs, as we have seen, to the seventeenth-century literature of the subject and to the active and commonly angry debate among contemporary observers and participants. But Clarendon, like Burnet, as we shall see (p. 42) has a place, too, in the eighteenth-century historiography of the Revolution, since although his work was written between the 1640s and 1670s, in line with the wishes of its author who advised a lengthy delay until passions had cooled, it was not actually *published* until 1702–4. It was brought out, therefore, in the reign of Queen Anne, Clarendon's own grand-daughter, and was ushered into the world with a preface by Clarendon's son, the Earl of Rochester. Rochester presented his father's work 'rather as an instruction to the present age than a reproach upon the last'. Its publication, in short, was designed to support Tory historical orthodoxy, and the appearance of the first volume (1702) came at the very time when Toryism was apparently in the ascendant. The appearance of the *History of the Rebellion*, Rochester argued, could be delayed no longer.

In an age when so many memoirs, narratives, and pieces of history come out as it were on purpose to justify the taking up of arms against that king,[1] and to blacken, revile, and ridicule the sacred majesty of an anointed head in distress; and when so much of the sense of religion to God, and of allegiance and duty to the crown is so defaced that it is already within little more than fifty years since the murder committed on that pious prince by some men made a mystery to judge on whose side was the right and on which the Rebellion is to be charged.

In the sermon-like dedication to Queen Anne in Volume Three, Rochester, by now out of office and in opposition, drew a stark contrast between 'the peace and the plenty of this kingdom [under Charles I] and in so short a space of time the bloody desolation of it by a most wicked rebellion'. He went on to elaborate his disgust even more pointedly. Charles I was

brought by unaccountable administrations on the one hand and by vile contrivances on the other into the greatest difficulties and distresses throughout all his kingdoms; then left and abandoned by most of his servants whom he had himself raised to the greatest honours and preferments, thus reduced to have scarce one faithful, able counsellor about him to whom he could breathe his conscience and complaints, and from whom he might expect one honest, sound, disinterested advice; after this how he was obliged to take up arms and to contend with his own subjects in the field for his crown, the laws, his liberty, and life; there meeting with unequal fortune how he was drawn from one part of the kingdom and from one body of an army to another, till at last he was brought under the power of cruel and merciless men, imprisoned and arraigned, condemned and executed like a common malefactor.[2]

More of a Tory than his father, Rochester helped to ensure that Clarendon's more subtle masterpiece would be denounced by the Whigs as partisan, Tory history. The early eighteenth-century reception given to the publication of the *History of the Rebellion* showed, in fact, how controversial a subject the English Revolution still remained.

The *History* sold well and quickly became influential. 'It had such a torrent of currency at first', wrote John Oldmixon, 'that it bore down all before it.' It had other effects too. The appearance of Clarendon's *History* stimulated, for example, the printing of *The*

History of His Own Time by Bishop Gilbert Burnet (1643–1715). This came out – between 1724 and 1734 – like Clarendon's *History* through the good offices of the author's son (this time a Whig). It concentrated overwhelmingly on the post-Restoration period, and in its brief treatment of the preceding decades showed no inclination to cover matters which had already been 'fully related by other historians'. Burnet had more to say about his native Scotland than about England. But he offered some pithy judgements on James I ('no king could die less lamented or less esteemed than he was') and on his son ('His reign both in peace and war was a continual series of errors. . . . He died greater than he lived'). No defender of regicide or regicides, however, Burnet was harsh on Cromwell – a usurper in whom 'the enthusiast and dissembler' struggled for precedence – and cool towards Monck.[3]

The connections between politics and history were far too strong to allow Civil War studies to lapse into a mere academic debate. In Queen Anne's reign, Whig and Tory groupings acquired cohesion and greater political meaning, though not always with complete consistency or with uninterrupted continuity. One should be wary of using too rigid and mechanistic a model, but the party divisions, none the less, were there, and the study of history increasingly took on an explicit and pronounced present purpose. Ancient Greece and Rome provided a storehouse of lessons for the eighteenth century. So, too, did the Norman Conquest. But it was the upheavals of the seventeenth century – the Civil Wars and 1688 – which were appealed to most often for political instruction. Reprints of *Eikon Basilike* appeared. Sermons, too, kept alive the memory of the recent past, especially those High Church outpourings preached on the anniversary of the execution of Charles I – designated a public fast day by Parliament in 1681. In stark contrast, there were also rumours of profane annual feasting and rejoicing by the Calves' Head Clubs on that day. Whig and Tory interpretations of the English Revolution became an essential ingredient in the subject matter of eighteenth-century politics and eighteenth-century religious controversy. When writing about this period of history, noted Gibbon in 1762, 'every writer is expected to hang out a badge of party and is devoted to destruction by the opposite faction'.[4]

Take, for instance, the debate which raged in the early years of the eighteenth century between Edmund Calamy (1671–1732) and John Walker (1674–1747). The debate focused on one aspect of the religious history of the English Revolution, the respective fortunes of opposition clergy during the Interregnum and at the Restoration, and it indicates the importance of the two religious extremes of Whigs and Tories in maintaining the temperature of party strife. This particular debate was initiated between 1702 and 1713 when Calamy published his account of ejected and silenced divines. In this work Calamy, himself the son of an ejected minister, discussed those puritan clergy who had been removed from their livings after 1660. It was obvious where his Whig sympathies lay and the authors of the Restoration settlement were vigorously denounced for fatally undermining the unity and welfare of the Church. But this was seventeenth-century history with an eighteenth-century message, as Matthews reminds us in his commentary on Calamy's work.

> It was impossible for the publication of such opinions to pass unnoticed in an age so given to controversy as that of Queen Anne. Calamy had invaded the very storm centre of contemporary party politics. To reflect on the Settlement of 1662 was to reflect on the Church of 1702, and that in the eyes of the High Churchmen and Tories was to lay sacrilegious hands upon the ark of the covenant. A nonconformist apologist stood condemned not only as a Whig but also as one who still believed in the obligation of the Solemn League and Covenant and was therefore only waiting an opportunity to re-enact the persecution of the Interregnum. Churchmen were bound to reply to the challenge offered to them and their response was profuse and bitter.[5]

John Walker, a Tory high churchman, emerged as the most conspicuous of Calamy's opponents, publishing in 1714 his *Sufferings of the Clergy*, a book which countered Calamy's evidence by documenting the deprivations of loyal Anglicans during the Interregnum. Like Calamy's account, Walker's book was specifically related to his own times. As Matthews says:

> The events Walker wrote of could not be withdrawn from the heat of party politics into the cool atmosphere of detached historical study. Tory history was an inseparable part of Tory dogma and a primary factor in its creation. The ruling men of the Interregnum had foully

outraged the two sanctities of the Tory creed, the Church and the Crown. . . . The historical writing that resulted from this outlook was of the pragmatic order, directed more to the making of history than to its impartial study.[6]

Tory political historiography, whose cause Rochester had been serving when he published Clarendon's *History*, was quickly reinforced – deliberately or unintentionally is unclear – by a *History of England* by Laurence Echard (1670?–1730), issued between 1707 and 1718. On James I, for example, Echard had this to say:

> It is true there were some heats between him and his Parliaments about the prerogative, and it happened then, as it does in most feuds, that things were carried to great extremities. Yet impartial writers think that considering his majesty's circumstances he was not well used, and that if the House had been freed from half a dozen popular and discontented members the disturbances would soon have ended.[7]

And when he came to the unhappy reign of Charles I, he made it clear how, in his view, the troubles had arisen.

> On the other side, beside the disgusts and waverings of the nobility and great men, the people proceeded to unprecedented liberties which naturally led them into many errors and dangerous paths and precipices, so that they assumed to themselves a power of censuring and intermeddling with such matters of state and religion as were unquestionably above their sphere and capacity.[8]

Echard, like so many who contributed to the discussion of this period, saw himself as an entirely truthful, unbiased historian. 'While there are such things in the world as Truth and Honesty', he wrote, 'undoubtedly there may be an impartial historian.' But in the contentious age in which he lived, Echard's professions of neutrality, even if they were true, were unlikely to be taken very seriously, and the well-meaning archdeacon provoked a storm of opposition from Whig and dissenting circles.[9]

Edmund Calamy, Walker's adversary, for example, rallied to the defence of the reputation of the puritans which he believed had been sullied by Echard's harsh treatment.

> You are too severe upon the puritans who, when you have found all faults with them you can, were generally men of great piety and true

to the interest of their country, and therefore favoured by our greatest patriots, though run down by zealous ecclesiastics, who thought
allowing others to differ from them tended to their own diminution.
. . . Methinks you more than once discover a great tenderness to the
papists. They seem to pass for a harmless sort of people. . . .

Arbitrary power, which is what so many in this reign [Charles I's]
were so much afraid of, to you appears a mere bugbear, and the dreading it you represent as a great weakness.[10]

A more extensive and heated indictment of what was seen
to be Echard's blatant Toryism (and, by extension, Clarendon's)
came from the Whig publicist John Oldmixon (1673–1743) in
his *Critical History of England*. His preface explicitly connected
past history with present politics. 'What can be more necessary',
Oldmixon asked, 'than to set people right in that which most
concerns them, their religious and civil liberties, and justify the
proceedings of the present age by those of the past?' Echard,
according to Oldmixon, had maliciously misrepresented the
Parliamentarians.

[He] treats them as so many rebels, and vindicates or extenuates all
King Charles I's invasions of the rights and liberties of the subject [as
though] . . . all our fathers and [all that] we had said and done for
liberty spiritual and temporal was unsaid and undone and the statutes
and ordinances of the Parliament in 1640 et seq and the Convention
of 1688 represented as so many acts of sedition and rebellion.[11]

Comparing the adjectives used to describe the opposing sides in the
war, Oldmixon concluded that:

The partiality is so strong that 'tis ridiculous, and there is not the like
in History from that of Herodotus to Mr Echard's . . . Mr Echard has
one of the prettiest ways of softening things that I ever met with. Thus
he melts down tyrannical proceedings into disobliging measures, and
he can turn to the other hand when he pleases, and then impeach-
ments and remonstrances are disturbers of parliament, the Rochellers
rebels, the Book of Sports a pious intention, Bishop Juxon a won-
derful treasurer, puritans cheats though not whoremasters, etc. Innu-
merable are the instances of this kind in him, too tedious and hateful
to repeat. Yet he closes the chapter with saying 'Thus with all sim-
plicity and fidelity we have gone so far'.

The reader will find so many panegyrics on Bishop Laud that if he
had really been a saint and a martyr, as he represents him, he could

45

not have said more of him; whereas there's nothing so certain in his character as Pride, Cruelty, Bigotry, and invincible Obstinacy.[12]

All Echard's sly attempts to disguise the fact that the English Revolution was a necessary defence of the ancient constitution and of the Englishman's civil and religious liberties were completely vain. The truth, Oldmixon persevered, could still be seen despite the Tory smokescreen.

> The laws and customs delivered down to us from our British and Saxon fathers, justified the practices of those brave English heroes who have always stood in the gap when our constitution has been in danger. . . .
>
> It had been impossible for the Archdeacon to have run himself into so many mistakes and errors if before he began his history he had not listed himself on the side of ceremony and severity, arbitrary power and oppression, if he had not resolved to follow such blind guides as Heath, Nalson, etc. . . . 'Tis impossible by this writer's history to conceive any idea of these times. One would imagine by his writings that the republic consisted of a parcel of thieves, cowards, blockheads, atheists and scoundrels, that their power was tyranny and the people of England slaves in the very height of liberty; that in the midst of strict justice nothing was heard of but robberies and rapes, and in the strictest practice of religion, impiety and profaneness everywhere triumphed; that at a time when trade was flourishing, poverty and beggary made the nation desolate, and when the English name and credit were the envy and dread of the world that the kingdoms and states around us looked upon us with contempt or detestation; in a word that the government of England was as much neglected and despised abroad as it had been in the reigns of King James and King Charles I. Why does he and his party invent things thus? But because they had not the power to plunder, persecute, torture and enslave their honest neighbours as in the days of Laud, Wren, Neile, etc.[13]

Oldmixon dismissed the seventeenth-century sections of Echard's work as a warped and very imperfect copy of Clarendon's *History of the Rebellion* (partly in his view a forgery by its Tory editors), and he proceeded after the corrective exercise of the *Critical History* to present his own view of the English Revolution in his *History of England during the Reigns of the Royal House of Stuart*. Published in 1730, it was dedicated to 'all true Englishmen, lovers of our present happy constitution' which in the previous century had been attacked by 'the tyranny of the High Commis-

sion court' and by all those who favoured 'the boundless prerogative of the crown, the slavish obedience of the subject, and the blessings of arbitrary power and servitude'. After looking at Oldmixon's
own account, however, his readers would be able to see,

> the facts of the four Stuarts' reigns in a true light, that the glorious
> principles and practices of your ancestors might no longer lie under
> the reproach of rebellion. . . . It will appear plain enough by the
> history of the Stuart kings that they were continually making breaches
> in this constitution and endeavouring utterly to subvert it . . . while
> their opponents were the only true sons of the Commonwealth, good
> Protestants and good Englishmen, adhering to their birthright, their
> religion, liberties and properties which those princes and their adher-
> ents in so many instances invaded and violated.[14]

Oldmixon ingeniously claimed that he himself was above party.
He was a faithful servant and admirer of the constitution. The only
'Party' were the Tories who, in their efforts to undermine the
constitution and justify absolutism, had in Queen Anne's reign
brought forth the distorted and worthless histories of Clarendon
and Echard.

> Perhaps I may myself be thought guilty of that passion and prejudice
> and be thought misled by the same weakness I condemn in others.
> It is therefore necessary to consider what is or ought to be understood
> by the word Party. And I wish what I have to say on that subject
> were worth the reader's attention, for if my conceptions are right,
> and I must think they are till I am better informed, I cannot justly
> be deemed a Party-man, or pass under that censure with men of
> reason and candour, however appearances may at first sight make
> against me. . . .
>   If this Constitution is founded in the Protestant religion, a due and
> impartial execution of the laws, a just and equal administration of
> affairs, then all contrary courses are contrary to the Constitution, and
> he who adheres to it cannot be said to be of a Party because the Con-
> stitution is the whole, and those are only Party-men who divide from
> it by setting up an arbitrary, partial, unequal, illegal government, and
> interest separate from that of the public.[15]

Whether or not this period was one of such complete Whig
supremacy in politics as older historians believed, Whiggish versions of history certainly came to the fore at this time in an attempt
to regain initiatives lost in the reign of Queen Anne. Oldmixon's

robust narrative coincided with the appearance of another like-minded but more moderate work. This was the *Impartial History of England* written by the émigré Huguenot supporter of William III, Paul de Rapin Thoyras (1661–1725). Originally written in French for a European audience by a man who was no great admirer of England, the work appeared in Tindal's English translation between 1726 and 1731, and a further six editions demonstrated its popularity. Rapin's work was the most fashionable history of its vintage, and was unrealistically hailed for a time as positively the only 'impartial' history. Certainly its author cast his net widely and took careful stock of the work of previous historians including Rushworth, who although invaluable for his documents was admittedly in his interpretation too disparaging of the King.

> He therefore that undertakes to write at this time the history of Charles I must endeavour to discover the truth in even the most partial historians and be extremely careful to avoid the continual snares they lay for their readers to favour the cause they maintain. One must know what was their design in writing, what system they followed, and the artifices they used to engage in their principles such as make but few reflections in reading a history and are apt to be easily drawn into the prejudices of the historian.[16]

Yet although Rapin frankly admitted that 'the King and the Parliament were both very much in the wrong, though not always nor on the same occasions', none the less it is his censures of Charles I which come through most clearly in his version of events.

> If it is not supposed that Charles I from the beginning of his reign to the time of this last parliament, had formed a design to establish in England an arbitrary government it will be almost impossible to understand his history, and particularly this second part. But upon this supposition, which to me appears incontestable, all difficulties vanish. It is not surprising to see the King's council, his ministers, favourites, the Star chamber, High Commission, judges of the realm, in a word, all persons in public employment, intent upon one single point, I mean the stretching of the royal authority as far as lay in their power. It is not surprising to see the implacable hatred of the House of Commons to the King's ministers, and particularly to those who were most trusted by his Majesty, and believed the chief authors of the public evils. . . .

[For the King] sincerity, as appears in his history was not his favourite virtue. He made frequent use of mental reservations, concealed in ambiguous terms and general expressions, of which he reserved the explication at a proper time and place. For this reason, the Parliament could never confide in his promises, wherein there was always either some ambiguous term, or some restriction that rendered them useless. This may be said to be one of the principal causes of his ruin, because giving thereby occasion of distrust, it was not possible to find any expedient for a peace with the Parliament. He was thought to act with so little sincerity in his engagements that it was believed there was no dependence on his word.[17]

Certainly not uncritically Whiggish in interpretation, none the less it was as a Whig historian that Rapin was regarded, and it was as a Whig that he was attacked by the Jacobite Thomas Carte (1680–1754). Carte did this first of all in his *Defence of English History against the Misrepresentations of Mr Rapin de Thoyras* (London, 1734), and later, and at much greater length, in his *General History of England* (London, 1747–55). Rapin, declared Carte in an intermediate publication,

writing his *History* abroad, had no opportunity either of consulting persons better versed in our antiquities than himself, or of searching into any of our records and repositories of public papers. Being likewise a foreigner unacquainted with our constitution he was in no respect qualified to give us the civil history of this nation.[18]

In contrast with this foreign meddler in English history, Carte proudly proclaimed himself on the title-page of his *General History* as an *Englishman*, and his preface advertised the laborious research which he had carried out. Carte's own picture of the early seventeenth century involved a denunciation of puritanism and of the unreasonableness of the parliamentary opposition to Charles I. Elizabeth, he wrote, 'left that turbulent sect of men [the puritans] in a condition that enabled them to distress her successor throughout all his reign and in that of his son, to subvert the monarchy as well as the episcopacy, liturgy, and the whole constitution of the Church of England'.[19] Moving to Charles I's reign, his comments on the Grand Remonstrance are indicative of his general approach to this period.

They had been for near a twelvemonth hammering out a Remonstrance of what they called that state of the kingdom, and the King having settled Scotland in quiet it was thought necessary to keep up jealousies in England by filling it with a bitter recapitulation of all the irregular or disagreeable steps taken since his Majesty's accession, absolutely false in some particulars, misrepresented in more, and exaggerated in all with the utmost virulence . . . the whole was calculated to infuse jealousies into the people, for which purpose it was afterwards printed.[20]

As such rivalries make clear, Whigs and Tories clashed in the field of historical interpretation as they did in the turmoil of party politics. But one should not oversimplify. The parties themselves were not fixed and monolithic; the disagreement between 'old' and 'new' Whigs is a case in point. Nor do party labels neatly fit all historians of this period. One such exception was White Kennett (1660–1728), Bishop of Peterborough. Kennett contributed a volume covering the period 1625–1702 to a *Complete History of England* which was published in 1706. Accused of Whiggery in the eighteenth century – and with some justification – his modern biographer is nevertheless inclined to see him as a Tory historian whose 'historical writing often became a mask to cover a commentary upon current events'.[21] Kennett's volume was severely factual and chronological, it quoted extensively from Clarendon, and was published anonymously; 'no prudent writer would set a name to the history of his own times, for it is impossible to please or to be thought impartial till posterity find out his plain and honest dealing.' Kennett's attempts to apply scholarly standards to his historical writing and his generous assessment of Archbishop Laud, for example, make the conventional Whig label seem inappropriate.

> Another popular outcry against Archbishop Laud and the bishops directed by him was innovation in matters of religion; few people being willing to distinguish between arbitrary alterations and the restoring an antecedent decency and order, which latter was undoubtedly the good archbishop's meaning. . . . [Laud, faced with] such a heap of accusations, made such an admirable defence against them that the innocence of this prelate and the malice of his enemies are hardly to be matched in any account of the primitive persecutions.[22]

Kennett had earlier (in 1704) vindicated Charles I's reputation in his sermon, *A Compassionate Enquiry into the Causes of the*

Civil War, a fascinating work which not only put forward Whig notions about the ancient constitution but also defended the King at the same time from all charges that he was attempting to subvert it.

> The evil of this day we now deplore in fasting and mourning was an unnatural Civil War that overturned the best constitution in the world, that made our whole island an Aceldama, a field of blood, and through heaps of rapine and slaughter proceeded to the deplorable death of the martyr of this day, one of the most virtuous and most religious of our English princes. [We must try to discover] how and why this evil came upon us as it did this day that seeing and understanding the cursed causes of it we may be better able to atone for the past iniquities and the more careful to prevent the like fatal effects for the future.[23]

Kennett proceeded to lavish fulsome praise on English liberties and the ancient constitution, but argued that Charles I was unjustly suspected of attempting to overthrow them.

> We of this happy nation have certainly the best constitution in the world, the sovereignty of the prince, the rights of the nobility, the liberties of the people, all so balanced and bearing upon one another that no government on this side Heaven can be more wisely contrived while it stands even upon its true balance. . . .
>
> Far be it from any honest heart to think that [Charles I] out of ambition or sinister ends ever proposed to injure the birthright of his subjects or to alter the constitution received from his ancestors. No! his clemency and justice, his honour and conscience were upon too high a principle for such ill designs. But it is possible that the influence of others may bring a suspicion upon princes when they themselves are innocent and then in many cases a suspicion artfully improved shall work up as much mischief as the real guilt would do. . . .
>
> If we trace back the history of former ages we shall [all] along find that the body of the English people had the spirit of a free people; that they would not by any means put their necks into a yoke nor their feet into chains, nor would they bow down their backs to any illegal burden.[24]

As Kennett's example shows, Whig and Tory versions of the past were at times just as complicated as eighteenth-century political warfare and could, on occasions, take the same unexpected turns. In the 1730s, for instance, the political rivalry between Walpole and the Whigs and Bolingbroke and the Tories came to acquire a curious historiographical dimension, the long-term result of which was to reduce the partisan character of the feudal interpretation of the English past. Here in the 1730s we find Tory politicians espousing the basic tenets of Whig historiography, while in retaliation Whigs hurled back a hastily assimilated version of Tory historical principles![25]

At first glance astonishing and inexplicable, this intriguing episode in the political use of history makes sense when we appreciate that what the Tory Bolingbroke was doing was to use the Whig appeal to a free past as a weapon in his assault on the corrupting and enslaving efforts of Walpole's Whig administration. Turning Whig theories of history on their head, Bolingbroke was arguing in his *Remarks on the History of England* (London, 1730), that the present was not better than the past but *worse*. With Tories making such impertinently novel use of Whig propaganda, what was left to Walpole and the Whigs but to detach the Tory version of the past – Brady, Spelman, and the rest – from Tory politics and proclaim it as their own modernized Whiggism? This they did, first as a religious argument in the Convocation controversy which raged for two decades after 1697, and then for strictly political purposes in the 1730s when faced with Bolingbroke's historiographical gymnastics. So, using Robert Brady's high-Tory arguments, Walpole the Whig countered the Tory Bolingbroke's Whig history by arguing that English liberties and freedom were not ancient at all; they had not existed since time immemorial. They were recent, and were in fact the product only of the seventeenth-century constitutional and religious struggles. Walpole's administration, therefore, did not represent a retreat from the ancient constitution.

> The very reverse is true of our government, which was bad in the beginning, made better by degrees and is brought to perfection at last. . . . To bring the government of England back to its first principles, is to bring the people back to absolute slavery; the primitive purity of our constitution was that the people had no share in the government, but were the villeins, vassals, or bondmen of the lords, a sort of cattle bought and sold with the land.[26]

Lord Hervey agreed with this pessimistic interpretation of the English past in his essay *Ancient and Modern Liberty Stated and Compared* (London, 1734); not until the Glorious Revolution was liberty achieved and firmly guaranteed. No wonder then that such Whigs in politics but Tories in history should find Rapin – decidedly Whig in the usual sense – unacceptable and denounce him as a Tory.

It was, more accurately, as a Whig historian that Rapin was denounced in mid-century by the cosmopolitan Scot, David Hume (1711–76). Originally attracted by Rapin's historical method, his anti-clericalism, and apparent detachment from party disputes, Hume's opinion changed. Greater familiarity bred contempt, and his *History of Great Britain* came, in fact, to be specifically directed against Rapin's Whig treatment, which he caricatured thus: 'Charles I was a tyrant, a papist and a contriver of the Irish massacre; the Church of England was relapsing fast into idolatry; puritanism was the only true religion, and the Covenant the favourite object of heavenly regard.'[27]

But, just as White Kennett had been unconventional in his combination of party and history, so Hume was not a Tory historian in the usual sense. 'Mr Hume in his *History*', wrote Voltaire, 'is neither Parliamentarian nor Royalist, nor Anglican or Presbyterian: he is simply judicious.'[28] Hume saw himself as a philosopher/historian *above* party. In a sense it was largely by chance that he became a Tory historian, and the fact owed less to Hume himself than to the way his standpoint was distorted both by contemporary supporters and by later Whig opponents. Duncan Forbes has shown the complex combination of Whig and Tory elements which existed side by side in Hume's historical interpretation – an easier feat to accomplish at this point in the century than earlier, coming as it did after the historiographical confusions of the 1730s. Hume identified himself wholly with neither camp. Using a formula that would also describe White Kennett, Hume tried to claim that the bias of his book on the Stuarts, which was the first of his complete history to appear, was 'Tory as to persons and Whig as to things'. He observed that the publication of his work met with a chorus of opposition from all sides, from 'English, Scotch and Irish, Whig and Tory, churchman and sectary, freethinker and religionist, patriot and courtier. [All] united in their rage against the man who had presumed to shed a generous tear for the fate of Charles I and the Earl of Strafford.'[29] Faced with this general criticism, highly disconcerting in the short term, Hume could at least console himself with the thought that his impartiality had been widely recognized! Given its context, however, Hume's *History* is extremely moderate in tone; he wrote not in order to supply new Tory ammunition but, rather, as Dr Forbes suggested, to further 'the abolition of the "dangerous" distinction of Whig and Tory'.[30] The central theme in his *History* is that without authority, freedom cannot exist, and by stressing this axiom Hume sought to educate the Whigs in political moderation, and to teach them that government is established to provide justice and not liberty. Resistance to established authority could not be excused.

Hume tried to achieve this process of political re-education by arguing, contrary to the orthodox Whig view, that there simply was no clearly defined ancient constitution in seventeenth-century England, and that it was its very lack of precision which helped to cause the Civil Wars.

> The uncertain and undefined limits of prerogative and privilege had been eagerly disputed during that whole period; and in every controversy betwixt prince and people, the question, however doubtful, had always been decided by each party in favour of its own pretensions. ... [Yet] nothing will tend more to abate the acrimony of party disputes than to show men that those events which they impute to their adversaries as the deepest crimes, were the natural, if not the necessary result of the situation in which the nation was placed during any period.[31]

A philosophical historian rather than blindly pro-Tory in the conventional sense, Hume none the less felt obliged to refute the extravagant claims made by uncritical exponents of the Whig interpretation of the seventeenth century.

> The Whig party for the course of near seventy years has almost without interruption enjoyed the whole authority of government, and no honours or offices could be obtained but by their countenance and protection. But this event which in some particulars has been advantageous to the state, has proved destructive to the truth of history, and has established many gross falsehoods which it is unaccountable how any civilised nation could have embraced with regard to its domestic occurrences. Compositions the most despicable, both for style and matter,

have been extolled and propagated and read as if they had equalled the most celebrated remains of antiquity (such as Rapin Thoyras, Locke, Sidney, Hoadley, etc.). And forgetting that a regard for liberty, though a laudable passion, ought commonly to be subordinate to a reverence for established government, the prevailing faction has celebrated only the partisans of the former who pursued as their object the perfection of civil society, and has extolled them at the expense of their antagonists who maintained those maxims that are essential to its very existence. But extremes of all kinds are to be avoided; and though no-one will ever please either faction by moderate opinions, it is there we are most likely to meet with truth and certainty.

The more I advance in my undertaking [he had written earlier] the more I am convinced that the history of England has never yet been written, not only for style, which is notorious to all the world, but also for matter, such is the ignorance and partiality of our historians. Rapin, whom I had an esteem for, is totally despicable.[32]

Hume's political sympathies, then, were by no means completely clear-cut, but there was much in his interpretation which was Tory in standpoint. Cromwell was contemptuously written off as a mere 'fanatical hypocrite'. Hume's rationalist attitude to the doctrinal puritans, too, was extremely hostile, and although he recognized the constitutional importance of political puritans, in dealing with them he could never overcome his conviction that religious enthusiasm was only an expression of human weakness and a source of much discord and misery.

'Tis however probable, if not certain, that they were generally speaking the dupes of their own zeal. . . . So congenial to the human mind are religious sentiments that, where the temper is not guarded by a philosophical scepticism, the most cool and determined, it is impossible to counterfeit long these holy fervours without feeling some share of the assumed warmth. And on the other hand, so precarious and temporary is the operation of these supernatural views that the religious extasies, if constantly employed, must often be counterfeit, and must ever be warped by those more familiar motives of interest and ambition, which insensibly gain upon the mind. This indeed seems the key to most of the celebrated characters of that age. Equally full of fraud and ardour, these pious patriots talked perpetually of seeking the Lord, yet still pursued their own purposes; and have left a memorable lesson to posterity, how delusive, how destructive that principle is by which they were animated.[33]

By contrast, Hume did indeed, as he admitted, 'shed a generous tear' for Charles I and Strafford.

> As a monarch, too, in the exterior qualities he [Charles I] excelled; in the essential he was not defective. His address and manner, though perhaps inclining a little towards stateliness and formality, in the main corresponded to his high rank, and gave grace to that reserve and gravity which were natural to him. . . . But the high idea of his own authority, with which he had been imbued, made him incapable of submitting prudently to the spirit of liberty which began to prevail among his subjects. His politics were not supported with such vigour and foresight as might enable him to subdue their privileges and maintain his prerogative at the high pitch to which he had raised it.[34]

Although at first some were baffled by the inconsistencies of his moderate Toryism/sceptical Whiggism, it was as a Tory historian that Hume was taken up, and the revisions made to subsequent editions of his work provided increasing justification for so doing. But although Whig and radical opposition to Hume's *History* appeared in different forms, for a variety of reasons it was slow in undermining its influence. It was not until Thomas Babington Macaulay took up his pen that the Whig interpretation was given its supreme statement and Hume began to be superseded.

In the meantime, however, one of the earliest and most extreme attacks on the new statement of Tory history came from Catharine Macaulay (1731–91) in her large-scale *History of England*, published between 1763 and 1783. Released at first in eight quarto volumes running to almost 3500 pages, it spanned the years 1603 to 1689. Three volumes were devoted to the key mid-century decades. An octavo edition followed, as did a French translation. The *History* was reissued in weekly parts to further widen its circulation. Remarkable as the first serious female historian, as an educationalist, as a believer in the perfectability of mankind, and as an avowed republican, Catharine Macaulay belongs to that line of 'Real Whigs' or neo-Harringtonians (as opposed to those Whigs in office) who transmitted the seventeenth-century republican ideology of Milton, Harrington, Neville, Nedham and others to the political world of the following century. Like other radicals of the eighteenth century, no less than in the English Revolution, she looked back longingly to the pre-Norman Yoke period of Anglo-Saxon freedom. (Symbolically in the 1770s she lived at Alfred

House, Bath, a residence whose front portico was adorned with a bust of the great Saxon monarch.)[35]

Her *History* was carefully researched and well written. She made extensive use of her own well-stocked library of Civil War tracts, the Thomason collection acquired by the British Museum in 1762, as well as recently published editions of parliamentary journals. She availed herself of the manuscript of the Memoirs of the Life of Colonel Hutchinson (unpublished until 1810) and, unusually for a historian of her time, she read Winstanley.[36] The early volumes of the *History* brought upon their author the general acclaim of Whig and radical circles and of the dissenting academies. Well-known contemporaries as varied as Horace Walpole, William Pitt, Joseph Priestley, and Benjamin Franklin all sang her praises.[37] The 'celebrated Mrs Macaulay' seemed at first to be well on the way to achieving her aim of refuting Hume's interpretation and of rivalling him in popularity. Unlike Hume, she combined reason with religion. A statue, representing her as Dame Thucydides, was commissioned by one of her most ardent admirers, and still today adorns the public library in Warrington. A contemporary portrait hangs in the relative obscurity of Beningborough Hall, North Yorkshire. Twentieth-century interest in Mrs Macaulay has been increasing and has been expressed most recently in Bridget Hill's book-length study of *The Republican Virago*.[38]

Neo-Harringtonian certainly in her emphasis on economic factors – 'industry and commerce had enabled them [the Commons] to make the full advantage of their new privilege by large purchases' – Mrs Macaulay stressed and justified the revolutionary character of seventeenth-century events. The English Civil War was England's finest hour.

> With regret do I accuse my country of inattention to the most exalted of their benefactors: whilst they enjoy privileges unpossessed by other nations they have lost a just sense of the merit of the men by whose virtues these privileges were attained; men that with the hazard and even the loss of their lives attacked the formidable pretensions of the Stuart family and set up the banners of liberty against a tyranny which had been established for a series of more than 150 years. . . . Neglect is not the only crime committed against these sacred characters. Party prejudice, and the more detestable principle of private interest, have painted the memoirs of past times in so false a light.[39]

The events of 1688, by contrast, stimulated the politics of faction. Far from 'glorious', they were the source – as she saw it – of much subsequent political corruption. The main outlines of Mrs Macaulay's interpretation are clear enough: the Stuarts were the aggressors, not to mention 'the criminal ambition of the Tudors', the ancient constitution the thing contested for, and the Parliamentarians its true champions.

> [James I] was himself the only dupe to an impertinent, useless hypocrisy. If the laws and constitution of England received no prejudice from his government, it was owing to his want of ability to effect a change suitable to the purpose of an arbitrary sway. Stained with these vices and sullied with these weaknesses, if he is ever exempt from our hatred, the exemption must arise from motives of contempt.

Pardoning Charles I, however, was even less excusable.

> [Charles I] had conceived an ineffable contempt for popular privileges with the most exalted notions of sublime authority in princes. Concessions he looked upon as derogations to the honour of a king, and opposition in subjects as such a flagrant breach of divine and moral laws that it called down from Heaven a sure and heavy vengeance on the aggressor. . . . [Under his misrule] England carried the face of a conquered province. The liberties and properties of the subject lay prostrate at the mercy of a rash imperious monarch, a rapacious insolent minister, and a designing bigoted priest; the prisons were daily filling with patriots.

Her denunciation of Strafford contrasts vividly with her account of the praiseworthy John Hampden who 'combated this new state monster, Ship money'.[40]

Although no democrat at any point – as Bridget Hill shows her confidence in the supine people was ultimate rather than immediate – the radical republicanism in her account became more pronounced as her *History* proceeded. Those moderate Whigs who had been impressed by the tone and contents of the first two volumes were embarrassed or shocked to find Catharine Macaulay in the later instalments revealing herself plainly as a 'Real Whig' and Wilkesite and defending regicide at a time when the cry of 'Wilkes and Liberty' was resounding in the London streets. She later *claimed* in the preface to Volume VI (published in 1781) that she had 'shed many tears' over the fate of Charles I, but if so she had obviously wiped them dry by the end of Volume IV in time to justify the execution of the King. Charles I's deplorable conduct, Mrs Macaulay argued, had removed from his subjects the necessity of obeying him.

> His trust and right to government from that period are forfeited, the tie of allegiance is dissolved, and the law and constitution being rendered incapable of affording the subject protection, he is no longer bound by their forms and dictates and may justly by the right of self-preservation take every profitable means to secure himself from the lawless power and enterprises of the tyrant.[41]

Views such as these, boldly and unrepentantly put forward, convinced most of Mrs Macaulay's readers beyond all doubt that hers was not the safe, respectable Whig account of seventeenth-century history that was needed to displace Hume. Catharine Macaulay's influence as a political historian declined even in the course of the publication of her eight volumes though it lasted longer in the more congenial settings of revolutionary America and France.[42] Her importance in the social history of English feminism rivals her significance as a historian. Her *History of England* became a minority taste, and in this restricted sense the work continued to cater for the interests of a small, like-minded coterie of Commonwealthmen until it was itself superseded in the 1820s.

Notes

1 Examples include the *Reliquae Baxterianae* which appeared in 1696, while the memoirs of the republican Edmund Ludlow followed two years later.
2 Clarendon, *History of the Rebellion* (Oxford, 1702–4), III, dedication.
3 *Memoirs of the Press* (London, 1742), p. 36. Quoted in J. P. Kenyon, *Revolution Principles: The Politics of Party 1689–1720* (Cambridge, 1977), p. 80; G. Burnet, *History of His Own Time*, ed. D. Allen (London, 1986), pp. 5, 15, 14–28, 31. On Burnet see T. E. S. Clarke and Hilda Foxcroft, *A Life of Gilbert Burnet Bishop of Salisbury* (Cambridge, 1907), and C. H. Firth, 'Burnet as a historian', in *Essays Historical and Literary* (Oxford, 1938), pp. 174–209.
4 H. T. Dickinson, *Liberty and Property: Political Ideology in Eighteenth-Century Britain* (London, 1977), *passim*. For the Charles I anniversary sermons see Kenyon, *Revolution Principles*, pp. 61–82; Helen W. Randall, 'The rise and fall of a martyrology', *Huntingdon Library Quarterly*, x (1946–7), pp. 135–67; B. S. Stewart, 'The cult of the Royal Martyr', *Church Hist.*, xxxviii (1969), pp. 175–87; and Dickinson, *Liberty and Property*, pp. 130–1. For the

(apparently mythical) Calves' Head Clubs see Kenyon, *Revolution Principles*, pp. 76–7. The Gibbon quotation appears in the introduction by Duncan Forbes to Hume's *History of Great Britain: The Reigns of James I and Charles I*, ed. D. Forbes (Harmondsworth, 1970), p. 43. On the political background of this period see G. Holmes, *British Politics in the Age of Anne* (London, 1967); G. Holmes (ed.), *Britain After the Glorious Revolution 1689–1714* (London, 1969); R. Willman, 'The origins of "Whig" and "Tory" in English political language', *HJ*, xvii (1974); H. T. Dickinson, 'The eighteenth-century debate on the Glorious Revolution', *Hist.*, lxi (1976); H. T. Dickinson, 'The eighteenth-century debate on the sovereignty of Parliament', *TRHS*, 5th ser., 26 (1976); and J. C. D. Clark, *English Society 1688–1832: Ideology, Social Structure and Political Practice During the Ancien Regime* (Cambridge, 1985).

5 A. G. Matthews, *Calamy Revised* (Oxford, 1934), p. xix.

6 A. G. Matthews, *Walker Revised* (Oxford, 1948), p. xi. Walker's attack on Calamy continued in 1719 with the publication of *The Church and the Dissenters Compared as to Persecution*, to which Calamy replied in 1727 with his *Continuation of the Account*. Daniel Neal's *History of the Puritans* (London, 1732–8) was similarly defensive.

7 L. Echard, *History of England* (London, 1707–18), I, p. 980.

8 *Ibid.*, II, p. 8.

9 Deborah Stephen puts forward a very different argument about this writer as the title of her article ('Laurence Echard, Whig historian', *HJ*, 32 (1989), pp. 843–66) makes clear. This is an extraordinary claim, even making every allowance for the instabilities of early eighteenth-century politics. Echard's own writing, no less than the responses it provoked, firmly resists Stephen's conclusion. Laird Okie in his *Augustan Historical Writing* (Lanham, Maryland, 1991), pp. 32–9, joins the present author in aligning Echard with the Tories.

10 Calamy, *A Letter to Mr Archdeacon Echard upon Occasion of His History of England* (London, 1718), pp. 11, 66, 62.

11 J. Oldmixon, *Critical History of England* (London, 1724–30), I, pp. iii–iv.

12 *Ibid.*, I, pp. 170, 220.

13 *Ibid.*, II, pp. ii, 128, 217–18.

14 J. Oldmixon, *History of England During the Reigns of the Royal House of Stuart* (London, 1730), pp. iv, vii, viii.

15 *Ibid.*, p. vii.

16 P. Rapin, *Impartial History of England* (London, 1784), I, p. 464. On Rapin see Nelly Girard d'Albissin, *Un Précurseur de Montesquieu: Rapin Thoyras, premier historien français des institutions anglaises* (Paris, 1969), and H. R. Trevor-Roper, 'A Huguenot historian: Paul Rapin', in Irene Scouloudi (ed.), *Huguenots in Britain and Their French Background 1550–1800* (London, 1987).

17 Rapin, *Impartial History of England*, pp. 599, 800.

18 T. Carte, *A General Account of the Necessary Materials for an History of England* (London, 1738), p. 2.

19 T. Carte, *General History of England* (London, 1747–55), III, p. 703, IV, p. 1.

20 *Ibid.*, IV, pp. 383, 403.

21 Kennett was attacked for his Whiggery by Roger North in his *Examen or an Inquiry into the Credit and Veracity of a Pretended Complete History, viz. Dr White Kennett's History of England* (London, 1740); G. V. Bennett, *White Kennett* (London, 1957), p. 173. With cruel irony, Bennett – the historian of an eighteenth-century controversialist – himself died in 1987 in the midst of another controversy (concerning his attack on the leadership of the Archbishop of Canterbury in the preface to *Crockford's Directory*).

22 W. Kennett, *Complete History of England* (London, 1706), pp. 85, 141.

23 *Ibid.*, pp. 1, 2.

24 *Ibid.*, pp. 16, 18, 20.

25 I. Kramnick, 'Augustan politics and English historiography: the debate on the English past, 1730–35', *Hist. and Theory*, vi (1967), and the same author's *Bolingbroke and his Circle: Politics and Nostalgia in the Age of Walpole* (Cambridge, Mass., 1968). See also W. A. Speck, 'Political propaganda in Augustan England', *TRHS*, 5th ser., 22 (1972), esp. pp. 24–7, and H. T. Dickinson, *Liberty and Property: Political Ideology in Eighteenth-Century Britain* (London, 1977), p. 140 *et seq.*

26 *London Journal*, 740 (1 September 1733), quoted in Kramnick, 'Augustan politics', p. 41.

27 D. Hume, *History of Great Britain* (London, 1793), viii, p. 321.

28 M. Belgion, *David Hume* (London, 1965), p. 5.

29 D. Hume, *Essays, Moral, Political and Literary* (London, 1903), p. 611.

30 Introduction to Hume, *History of Great Britain: The Reigns of James I and Charles I*, ed. D. Forbes (Harmondsworth, 1970), p. 33. The text in this reprint is the comparatively rare first edition of 1754, originally designed to stand by itself and only later integrated into a complete history. See also D. Forbes, *Hume's Philosophical Politics* (Cambridge, 1975), which contains a stimulating discussion of Hume's *History*, and E. E. Wexler, *David Hume and the History of England* (Philadelphia, 1979). The inter-relationship between Hume's work as a philosopher and as a historian is considered in J. P. Wright, *The Sceptical Realism of David Hume* (London, 1983), and in G. P. Morice (ed.), *David Hume: Bicentenary Essays* (Edinburgh, 1977).

31 Hume, *History of Great Britain*, ed. D. Forbes, pp. 396, 391.

32 Hume, *History of Great Britain*, viii, p. 323; quoted in H. R. Trevor-Roper, 'Hume as a historian', in D. F. Pears (ed.), *David Hume: A Symposium* (London, 1963), p. 90.

33 Hume, *History of Great Britain*, ed. D. Forbes, pp. 502–3.

34 Hume, *History of Great Britain*, ed. D. Forbes, pp. 328–9. J. B. Black in his useful book *The Art of History* (London, 1926), p. 113, contrasted the abusive adjectives with which Hume described the Parliamentarians and puritans with his sympathetic treatment of the Royalists.

35 Caroline Robbins, *The Eighteenth-Century Commonwealthmen* (New York, 1968); J. G. A. Pocock, 'Machiavelli, Harrington and English eighteenth-century ideologies', in *Politics, Language and Time* (London, 1972). Bridget Hill, *The Republican Virago: The Life and Times of Catharine Macaulay* (Oxford, 1992), p. 321.

36 Hill, *Republican Virago*, pp. 48, 181.

37 *Ibid.*, p. 40. Entrenched male prejudice, however, formed part of the critical response. The (male) reviewer in the *Monthly Review* of the first volume of her *History* observed 'we would by no means recommend such a laborious competition to the practice of our lovely countrywomen . . . The soft and delicate texture of a female frame [was not] intended for severe study . . . Intense thought spoils a lady's features', quoted in Hill, *Republican Virago*, p. 35.

38 Hill, *Republican Virago, passim.* See also Lynne E. Withey, 'Catharine Macaulay and the uses of history: ancient rights, perfectionism and propaganda', *JBS*, xvi (1976), and L. M. Donnelly, 'The celebrated Mrs Macaulay', *William and Mary Quarterly*, 3rd ser., vi (1949).

39 Catharine Macaulay, *History of England from the Accession of James I to That of the Brunswick Line* (London, 1763–83), I, p. viii.

40 *Ibid.*, I, pp. 267, 350, 365. *Ibid.*, II, pp. 481, 220.

41 *Ibid.*, IV, pp. 433–4.

42 Hill, *Republican Virago*, pp. 195, 216. She was fêted in America in 1784/85 as she visited Boston, Philadelphia, New York, and Mount Vernon, Virginia.

4

The French Revolution and English history

I have lived to see thirty millions of people, indignant and resolute, spurning at slavery, and demanding liberty with an irresistible voice; their king led in triumph, and an arbitrary monarch surrendering himself to his subjects. – After sharing in the benefits of one Revolution, I have been spared to be a witness to two other Revolutions, both glorious. – And now methinks, I see the ardour for liberty catching and spreading; a general amendment beginning in human affairs; the dominion of kings changed for the dominion of laws, and the dominion of priests giving way to the dominion of reason and conscience. (Richard Price, *A Discourse on the Love of our Country* (1789), in A. Cobban (ed.), *The Debate on the French Revolution* (London, 1950), p. 64)

Why was the French Revolution so bloody and destructive? Why was our revolution of 1641 comparatively mild? Why was our revolution of 1688 milder still? (T. B. Macaulay, *Edinburgh Review*, lv (1832), p. 560)

Catharine Macaulay died, already past the peak of her fame, in 1791. Her final publication, written only a matter of months earlier, was a repudiation in pamphlet form of Edmund Burke's *Reflections on the Revolution in France*.[1] Like many others at the time, Mrs Macaulay interpreted events in France in the light of what had happened in England in the seventeenth century. She had visited France in 1777–8 and relished the radical implications of the Enlightenment. She probably entertained Mirabeau during his visit to London in 1784–5; certainly he was instrumental in bringing about the French translation of her *History* in the early 1790s.[2] Englishmen in their Revolution had exerted the sovereignty of the people and thrown off the chains of the past. Now France, it seemed, was belatedly and beneficially moving in the same direction; the millennium was apparently fast approaching.

In connecting the revolutionary experience of late eighteenth-century France with that of England in the seventeenth century Catharine Macaulay was characteristic of many of her contemporaries; it was the nearest and ostensibly most suitable yardstick available, and all the more relevant since the centenary celebrations of 1688 were still fresh in the mind. Initially at least, therefore, the effect of the French Revolution on historical thinking was not to stimulate a new interpretation of English events in the seventeenth century in the light of later, different experience. The very opposite in fact took place. A confidently understood and assimilated Revolution in English history was the classic model with which a later example could be compared. Burke himself had done the same as Catharine Macaulay (though with completely different conclusions) and had been provoked into print by the address delivered on 4 November 1789 to the Society for Commemorating the Revolution in Great Britain by the veteran dissenting minister, Richard Price. For Price, 1688 was 'a great work [but] by no means a perfect work'. In itself the English constitutional settlement had not gone far enough, though it had provided guidelines and opportunities for the future which later Revolutions, first in America and currently in France, were acting upon. His address concluded with a stirring, rallying cry as relevant to his own countrymen as to those of France:

> Be encouraged all ye friends of freedom, and writers in its defence. The times are auspicious. Your labours have not been in vain. Behold kingdoms, admonished by you, starting from sleep, breaking their fetters, and claiming justice from their oppressors. Behold, the light you have struck out, after setting America free, reflected to France, and there kindled into a blaze that lays despotism in ashes, and warms and illuminates Europe.
>
> Tremble all ye oppressors of the world. Take warning all ye supporters of slavish governments, and slavish hierarchies. Call no more (absurdly and wickedly) Reformation, innovation. You cannot now hold the world in darkness. Struggle no longer against increasing light and liberality. Restore to mankind their rights; and consent to the correction of abuses, before they and you are destroyed together.[3]

The debate on the French Revolution to which Catharine Macaulay's pamphlet was an early contribution was a debate about principles, not about the actual circumstances of revolutionary France (on which most English interventionists – Burke included – were far from knowledgeable). It therefore had historiographical implications. It was a debate about rights and obligations and about the power and sanction of the past. It thus challenged accepted eighteenth-century traditions of using history. Burke upheld and restated those traditions, insisting on the controlling hand of the past, and of past agreements, over the present. Though no stranger to the concept of 'natural law', general 'natural rights' claimed by radicals, he insisted, were non-existent; the only real rights were specific and historic. While some radicals continued on the same wavelength by insisting that they were laying claim to no more than their ancestral rights as freeborn Englishmen, others more boldly eliminated history from their political thinking altogether. Reason itself was a sufficient guide.[4]

James Mackintosh moved down this road in his *Vindiciae Gallicae* (1791).

> It is not, therefore, that we have been free but because we have a right to be free that we ought to demand freedom. Justice and liberty have neither birth nor race, youth nor age. . . . Let us hear no more of this ignoble and ignominious pedigree of freedom.

Tom Paine in *Rights of Man*, first published in 1791 and distributed nation-wide in pamphlet form a year later, went even further.

> Every age and generation must be as free to act for itself, *in all cases*, as the ages and generations which preceded it. The vanity and presumption of governing beyond the grave is the most ridiculous and insolent of all tyrannies. Man has no property in man; neither has any generation a property in the generations which are to follow.[5]

There is no doubt that the French Revolution stimulated the growth of English radicalism. Veteran radicals like Cartwright, Price and Wyvill took up their pens, the Revolution Society and the Society for Constitutional Information acquired a new lease of life, and new bodies such as the London Corresponding Society and its provincial counterparts sprang into being.[6] By no means all English radicals, however, were republicans, the social basis of the radical movement was restricted (the labouring poor were never effectively won over to the cause), and by 1793 the expansive phase of radicalism was over.[7] By then the tide of the French Revolution was working *against*, not for, the radical movement in England. The September massacres, the execution of Louis XVI and Marie Antoinette, the Reign of Terror, and above all the outbreak of the Revolutionary War fundamentally affected the position of English radicals. Unrepentant radical supporters of the French Revolution remained in England after 1793 but they were fewer, more extreme, and increasingly hounded and repressed by an alarmed government. Fear of revolution in England far exceeded the actual threat of revolution.[8]

William Godwin (1756–1836), Mary Wollstonecraft's husband, provides an interesting historical and historiographical case study of these years. His own career illustrates the development of radicalism and reaction, the centrality of the French Revolution as a catalyst, and the implications of connecting the revolutionary experience of France and England. Godwin's main achievement is his *Enquiry Concerning Political Justice*, an unwieldy philosophical treatise first published in 1793. Conceived as a reasoned, rather than a passionate, response to Burke's *Reflections*, its quickly won fame was quickly lost and it was stranded like a whale by the changing tide of events of the 1790s. Godwin, ex-dissenting minister and philosophical anarchist, became the scapegoat of the English loyalist reaction to the French Revolution and he was denounced as the slavish disciple of Rousseau and Helvétius working only for a revolution in England. (Godwin's novel *Caleb Williams* (1794) – which horrified Prime Minister Pitt – concerned the witch-hunting that pursued a man who tried to tell the truth.) Godwin's briefly brilliant reputation was eclipsed, and not even repeated borrowings from his feckless son-in-law Shelley in the post-war period could save him from prolonged financial embarrassment.[9]

But Godwin, though a radical, was no revolutionary. *Political Justice* extolled reason, education, improvement, and fair treatment, not upheaval and mob rule.[10] Revised editions of the text increased its moderation and caution. Godwin was tentative, even confused about 'rights', opposed to violence, and critical of the proletarian strivings of the London Corresponding Society.[11] Godwin's ideal society was for the future, not for the present, and he recognized that it required slow and careful preparation.

> Hasty and undigested tumults may take place under the idea of an equalisation of property; but it is only a calm and clear conviction of justice, of justice mutually to be rendered and received, of happiness to be produced by the desertion of our most rooted habits, that can introduce an invariable system of this sort. Attempts without this preparation will be productive only of confusion. Their effect will be momentary, and a new and more barbarous inequality will succeed. Each man with unaltered appetite will watch his opportunity to gratify his love of power or his love of distinction by usurping on his inattentive neighbours.[12]

Godwin's intriguing response to the French Revolution was matched by his no less distinctive stance on the English Revolution of the mid-seventeenth century, and even the impressive bulk of *Political Justice* is overshadowed by the four volumes and 2,400 pages of his *History of the Commonwealth of England* (1824–8).[13] This was the first full-length study of England's experiment in republican government, the first systematic effort to fill (as Godwin termed it) 'this chasm in our annals'. Moreover, Godwin insisted on the distinctiveness of the English Revolution; it was not to be understood as an earlier version of the same kind of upheaval later experienced by France. 'The history of the Commonwealth of England', he wrote, 'constitutes a chapter in the records of mankind totally unlike any other that can elsewhere be found.'[14] Based on extensive research in the order books of the Council of State and in the Thomason tracts, Godwin's work aimed 'to remedy this defect, to restore the just tone of historical relation on the subject, to attend to the neglected, to remember the forgotten and to distribute an impartial award on all that was planned and achieved during this eventful period'.[15] His study was more temperate, less blatantly partisan than Catharine Macaulay's, but none the less Godwin held it to be an irrefutable truth that 'the opponents of Charles I fought for liberty and that they had no alternative'.[16] The early part of his work did full justice to 'the founders of the Commonwealth' – Coke, Selden, Hampden, and Pym – and he concluded here that 'the liberties of Englishmen are perhaps to no man so deeply indebted as to Sir Edward Coke'.[17]

Godwin prided himself on being a compassionate human being and not just a coldly clinical historian.

> I have no desire to be thought to look upon such transactions with indifference. I have no desire to be regarded as having no sentiments or emotions when anything singularly good or singularly evil passes under my review. I wish to be considered as feeling as well as thinking.[18]

Godwin's hostility to Charles I was undisguised, but he was political realist enough to appreciate that the King's execution was a grave tactical error.

> It is not easy to imagine a greater criminal than the individual against whom sentence was awarded. Charles I, to a degree which can scarcely be exceeded, conspired against the liberty of his country. . . . [Yet his execution] instead of breaking down the wall which separated him from others gave to his person a sacredness which never before appertained to it. . . . I am afraid that the day that saw Charles perish on the scaffold rendered the restoration of his family certain.[19]

On Cromwell – always an embarrassment to republican historians – Godwin was less severe than Mrs Macaulay. To her the Protector had appeared 'the most corrupt and selfish being that ever disgraced an human form'. No single individual in the whole of her *History* received such a hostile press.[20] Godwin, however, although he could never really forgive Cromwell for what inevitably seemed like his betrayal of the Good Old Cause – 'Cromwell was drunk with the philtre of his power' – nevertheless paid tribute to his many qualities. Cromwell was

> a man of great virtues, sincere in his religion, fervent in his patriotism, and earnestly devoted to the best interests of mankind. . . . His reputation as a man born to rule over his fellow men increased every day, and the awe and reverence of the English name that he inspired into all other states can find no parallel in any preceding or subsequent period of our history. . . .
>
> The character of Cromwell has been little understood. No wonder. The man who has so many enemies will be sure to be greatly misrepresented. . . . [But] he governed a people that was hostile to him. His reign, therefore, was a reign of experiments. He perpetually did the thing he desired not to do and was driven from one inconsistent and undesirable mode of proceeding to another. . . .[21]

Godwin's highest praise was reserved for the Commonwealth years 1649–53 and he applauded the republicans for creating order and stability in the aftermath of Civil War. Based on talent and virtue the English Republic – if not a direct political precedent for his own times – was certainly a source of moral and intellectual inspiration.[22] But it should come as no surprise to find that the critic of the London Corresponding Society was hardly expansive and enthusiastic in his treatment of the Levellers or that one whose own religious faith had been shattered should quickly dismiss the Diggers. 'Scarcely indeed worthy to be recorded, except so far as their proceedings may tend to illustrate the character and temper of the age, these men called themselves the Diggers'.[23]

Hard on the heels of Godwin's *History* came another radical contribution to the reassessment of the English Revolution, J. T. Rutt's edition of the 1650s diary of the MP Thomas Burton. Rutt (1760–1841), radical, Unitarian friend of Priestley and Gibbon Wakefield, and member of Cartwright's Society for Constitutional Information and later of the Society of the Friends of the People, used the opportunity to emphasize the importance of the Commonwealth period.

> It was distinguished by the patriotic deeds of men, whom knowledge, energy and discretion had eminently qualified to dispute the claims of the crown to an unlimited and irresponsible authority. Such had been too long the extravagant pretentions of that royal race which an absurd notion of hereditary right . . . had entailed on the acquiescing people of England.[24]

The year 1830 saw another revolution in France and this in turn stimulated renewed thinking about and comparisons with England's own century of revolution.[25] Here the key figure is T. B. Macaulay (1800–59). A fuller discussion of this celebrated historian's contribution belongs more properly to chapter five. Here Macaulay's writings of the years 1830–2 – the crisis years before the Reform Act – in which he attempted comparisons between the French and English Revolutions will be specifically considered.

Macaulay produced two writings on the subject. The first – unfinished and unpublished at the time – was his projected *History of Napoleon and the Restoration of the Bourbons*, recently discovered in the archives of Longmans the publishers.[26] The second was a review essay on Mirabeau published in the *Edinburgh Review* in 1832, the proud year of the Great Reform Act.

The first, if completed, would have been Macaulay's earliest book-length publication and in it the young historian took the opportunity afforded by a study of Napoleon to engage in general, comparative reflections on the nature of despotism and revolution. The English Revolution of the mid-seventeenth century, Macaulay argued, was essentially moderate and was untainted by the kind of excesses which characterized the French Revolution of 1789.

> The Royalists were overcome by the Presbyterians; but we had nothing like the massacres of September. The Presbyterians were overcome by the Independents; but we had nothing like the vengeance inflicted by the Mountain on the Gironde. Extraordinary judicatures were established in England; but the revolutionary tribunal of Paris often sent to the scaffold in one day five times as many victims as were condemned after our civil war by all the high courts of justice. The English nobles were at the most violent crisis of the civil dissensions, deprived of their political power by the soldiers; but the nation looked on that proceeding with disgust. The peers retained their property, their titles, and a large share of public respect. Ceremonious honours were paid to them by the revolutionary government; and they at length resumed their political functions with the general approbation of the people. The same venerable institutions which had curbed the monarchy, curbed also the revolution which overthrew the monarchy, and the military sovereignty which succeeded to the revolution. The same spirit which had saved the five members from the vengeance of the king saved Lilburne from the vengeance of the commonwealth, and Mordaunt from the vengeance of the protector. Cromwell found himself thwarted in all his arbitrary projects by parliaments and juries. He was less absolute than Napoleon, because the English republicans had been less violent than the Jacobins, because the government of the Stuarts had been milder than that of the Bourbons. The recoil was moderate, because the compression had been moderate.[27]

The comparison between the two military statesmen – Cromwell and Napoleon – begun here was pressed further as Macaulay's *History* continued and the essential differences between them underlined. The disparity between the English and French situations was even greater when Macaulay addressed the restorations

of 1660 and 1814. In England 'Charles II was recalled by a parliament which spoke the sense of the whole people of England.
. . . There was nothing in the circumstances of that event which
could wound the national pride'.[28] By contrast, the return of the
French monarchy in 1814 was an enforced external solution dic-
tated by the European powers which had defeated Napoleon.

The *Edinburgh Review* essay of 1832 carried the same discussion forward – at times in the very same words – by introducing
the French Revolution of 1830 into the comparison of French and
English revolutionary situations. Nothing could shake Macaulay
from his conviction that the French Revolution of 1789 had been
'the most horrible event recorded in history – all madness and
wickedness, absurdity in theory and atrocity in practice'. It had
been 'bloody and destructive' whereas English revolutions led by
able statesmen had been 'undertaken for the purpose of defending,
correcting and restoring – never for the purpose of destroying'.[29]
Seventeenth-century Englishmen in any case were less oppressed
than eighteenth-century Frenchmen and had been educated in the
school of liberty. By the Reform Act of 1832 'the work of three
civil wars has been accomplished by three sessions of parliament'.
Thankfully France in its revolution of 1830 had moved closer to
the English model and away from its own violent, destructive precedent of 1789. Charles X had done worse things than Louis XVI,
yet he fled and his life was safe. His ministers were imprisoned, not
executed. The law was stronger than the insurgents. 'If we compare
the present state of France with the state in which she was forty
years ago how vast a change for the better has taken place.'[30]

This was Macaulay's verdict – opinion is the wrong word to
describe such forceful views – in 1832. He was compelled to revise
it, however, in the light of events in France in 1848 (another year
of revolution) and 1851 (the coup d'état of Louis Napoleon). 'What
good have the revolutions of 1848 done? Or rather what harm have
they not done? Here is France worse than in 1788 after seventy
years of revolutions.'[31] It seemed that France, after all, was just
incapable of catching up with England whose seventeenth-century
revolutions had settled her main constitutional issues for all time.
English history, Macaulay was forced to conclude, was a much
more congenial subject than French history.

Notes

1 *Observations on the Reflections of the Right Hon Edmund Burke on the Revolution in France in a Letter to Earl Stanhope.* Burke's *Reflections* had appeared in October 1790.
2 Bridget Hill, *The Republican Virago: The Life and Times of Catharine Macaulay* (Oxford, 1992), pp. 207, 216.
3 Quoted in A. Cobban (ed.), *The Debate on the French Revolution 1789–1800* (London, 1950), p. 64. See also H. T. Dickinson, 'The eighteenth-century debate on the Glorious Revolution', *Hist.*, lxi (1976), esp. pp. 40–4.
4 See Marilyn Butler (ed.), *Burke, Paine, Godwin and the Revolution Controversy* (Cambridge, 1984).
5 Quoted in H. T. Dickinson, *Liberty and Property: Political Ideology in Eighteenth-Century Britain* (London, 1977), p. 241; quoted in Cobban, *Debate on the French Revolution*, p. 171. See also A. Goodwin, *The Friends of Liberty: The English Democratic Movement in the Age of the French Revolution* (London, 1979).
6 H. T. Dickinson, *British Radicalism and the French Revolution 1789–1815* (London, 1985); Goodwin, *Friends of Liberty, passim*; P. A. Brown, *The French Revolution in English History* (London, 1918).
7 Butler, *Burke, Paine, Godwin*, p. 10.
8 The subject is sketched in M. I. Thomis and P. Holt, *Threats of Revolution 1789–1848* (London, 1977), and more subtly examined in I. R. Christie, *Stress and Stability in Late Eighteenth-Century Britain: Reflections on the British Avoidance of Revolution* (Oxford, 1984).
9 On Godwin see H. N. Brailsford, *Shelley, Godwin and their Circle* (London, 1913); D. Locke, *A Fantasy of Reason: The Life and Thought of William Godwin* (London, 1980); P. H. Marshall, *William Godwin* (New Haven, Conn., 1984).
10 There is a modern edition of Godwin's *Enquiry Concerning Political Justice*, ed. I. Kramnick (Harmondsworth, 1976). See also the perceptive essay on this text in W. Stafford, *Socialism, Radicalism and Nostalgia: Social Criticism in Britain, 1775–1830* (Cambridge, 1987), pp. 121–45.
11 Godwin, *Friends of Liberty*, pp. 44–8.
12 Quoted in Cobban, *Debate on the French Revolution*, pp. 388–9.
13 Not surprisingly, perhaps, the four-volume epic was not a great commercial success and Godwin's publisher resisted the suggestion of a sequel. (J. Morrow, 'Republicanism and public virtue: William Godwin's *History of the Commonwealth of England*', *HJ*, 34 (1991), p. 647.)
14 W. Godwin, *History of the Commonwealth of England* (London, 1824–8), I, pp. vi, 1.
15 *Ibid.*, I, p. vi.
16 *Ibid.*, I, p. ix.
17 *Ibid.*, I, p. 9.
18 *Ibid.*, I, p. vii.
19 *Ibid.*, II, pp. 689–92.
20 Quoted in R. C. Richardson (ed.), *Images of Oliver Cromwell: Essays for and by Roger Howell Jr* (Manchester, 1993), p. 109.

21 Godwin, *History of the Commonwealth of England*, IV, pp. 599, vii, viii, 587, 597.
22 Morrow, 'Republicanism and public virtue', pp. 649, 654, 658.
23 Godwin, *History of the Commonwealth of England*, III, pp. 62–80, 82.
24 J. T. Rutt (ed.), *The Diary of Thomas Burton* (London, 1828), preface. Rutt also issued, in 1829, an edition of Edmund Calamy's autobiography.
25 See Hedva Ben-Israel, *English Historians on the French Revolution* (Cambridge, 1968). N. Gash, 'English reform and French Revolution in the General Election of 1830', in R. Pares and A. J. P. Taylor (eds), *Essays Presented to Sir Lewis Namier* (London, 1956), pp. 258–88.
26 T. B. Macaulay, *Napoleon and the Restoration of the Bourbons*, ed. J. Hamburger (London, 1977).
27 Macaulay, *Napoleon*, pp. 44–5.
28 *Ibid.*, pp. 66–7. For French historians' views of Napoleon at this time see J. K. Burton, *Napoleon and Clio: Historical Writing, Teaching and Thinking During the First Empire* (Durham, NC, 1979); P. Geyl, *Napoleon For and Against* (London, 1949); S. Mellon, *The Political Uses of History: A Study of the Historians of the French Restoration* (Stanford, CA, 1958).
29 *Edinburgh Review*, lv (1832), pp. 560, 572.
30 *Ibid.*, p. 562.
31 Quoted in Macaulay, *Napoleon*, p. 35.

5

The nineteenth century: from party polemics to academic history

Drawn to the subject by a conviction that prejudice had too deeply coloured the minds of those that had already dealt with it for their work to be in any respect final or satisfactory, and armed with a determination to be above all things open-minded and fair, he made up his mind to grapple with the whole material accessible. . . . It is not too much to say that Gardiner found the story of the first Stewarts and Cromwell legend and has left it history. (E. York Powell, 'Samuel Rawson Gardiner', *English Historical Review*, xvii (1902), pp. 276, 278)

Histories of the Stuart past generated so much discord during the nineteenth century in part because the Victorians saw a parallel between the religious controversies of the seventeenth century and the sectarian strife of their own age. Few problems troubled Victorian politics as persistently as religious dissent. (Timothy Lang, *The Victorians and the Stuart Heritage: Interpretations of a Discordant Past* (Cambridge, 1995), p. 54)

In the long run French revolutions reinforced existing convictions and prejudices rather than changed Englishmen's minds about their own history. Writing in 1832 and dreading the outcome of reform, the Tory J. W. Croker (1780–1857) was adamant that all revolutions (including the foolhardy one on which England seemed determined to embark in that very year) were evil. Events in France in 1789 and 1830 had not led him to revise his fundamentally hostile view of what had taken place in England in the seventeenth century.

Whatever excuse, then, a lover of the constitution may take for the Hampdens, the Pyms, the Russells, and the Spensers of that day, there can be none, of that kind at least, for their mischievous imitators and degenerate descendants. . . . In 1642, as now, the great body of the nation was sound and firm in the great principles of monarchy; but a handful of agitators was enabled to dominate that majority – to triumph in a civil war – to overthrow the constitution – and to shed on the scaffold the blood of the clergy, the peerage and the king.[1]

Tory versions of history, despite the assaults of Catharine Macaulay, Godwin, and the like, were still alive and well. David Hume's influence survived well into the nineteenth century, and his *History* was reprinted, re-edited, brought up to date by Smollett, and even expurgated. (The title page of one such bowdlerized version edited by a clergyman in 1816 proclaimed that Hume's work had been 'revised for family use with such omissions and alterations as may render it salutary to the young and unexceptional to the Christian'.)

Catharine Macaulay and Godwin were insufficiently Whiggish in the orthodox sense to overshadow Hume's *History*. His influence, therefore, still continued and survived two further, more conventionally Whig, rejoinders from George Brodie and Henry Hallam, just as it had earlier survived the publication of T. H. B. Oldfield's *Representative History of Great Britain and Ireland* (1816) and Lord John Russell's *Essay on the History of the English Government and Constitution* (1821).

The Scottish lawyer Brodie brought out his *Constitutional History of the British Empire from the Accession of Charles I to the Restoration* in 1822. Despite its misleading title his work was a staunchly Whig account of English domestic history (with chapters on Scotland and Ireland) deliberately, and in the event unduly optimistically, intended to demolish Hume. The latter, Brodie argued in his preface

> embarked in his undertaking with a predisposition unfavourable to a calm enquiry after truth, and being impatient of that unwearied research which, never satisfied while any source of information remains unexplored or probability not duly weighed, with unremitting industry sifts and collates authorities, he allowed his narrative to be directed by his predilections, and overlooked the materials from which it ought to have been constructed. . . . Mr Hume's view of the government and of public opinion – on which is founded his defence of the unfortunate Charles I and his minister Strafford – appears to me altogether erroneous.[2]

Brodie's view of the Stuarts, in contrast to Hume's, was extremely hostile. Under Elizabeth limited monarchy had existed and 'the grand constitutional principles were clearly defined as well as recognized'. Under the Stuarts, however, government proceeded in new and arbitrary directions. Brodie put forward an exceedingly low estimate of Laud and Strafford, but proclaimed that the name of John Hampden 'will be illustrious so long as patriotism and private virtue are venerated by men'. Under Charles I the grievances of his subjects were numerous and genuine, and the courage with which the King faced his execution, Brodie argued, should not make later generations forget his deep guilt and constant hypocrisy.[3]

> Accustomed from his earliest years to intrigue and dissimulation he seems, like his father, to have regarded hypocrisy as a necessary part of 'king-craft'. He had reconciled his conscience to the most uncandid protestations, and had studied divinity in order to satisfy himself on the lawfulness of taking oaths to break them. Though he loved the Church of England only as a prop to his own power, he had latterly endeavoured to persuade himself that, by upholding it, he was rendering a service to religion; and he was now surrounded by a clergy who, regarding the ecclesiastical establishment with reverence, partaking in no small degree of the feeling of self-interest, were ready to assure him (and well did they practise the lesson they taught) that a pious fraud which promoted such an object was not only justifiable, but commendable in the sight of God. . . . His whole government and all his measures . . . had been subversive of parliament, the privileges of the people, and in short of the law of the land, on which alone was founded his right to govern; and yet, like his two grand criminal ministers, Laud and Strafford – whose own correspondence, in the absence of all other proof, would indisputably establish their guilt – he averred on the scaffold that he had always been a friend to parliaments and the franchises of the people.[4]

The Whig standpoint was expressed just as clearly, though more moderately, in Henry Hallam's *Constitutional History of England* published in 1827. 'The Whigs', Hallam (1777–1859) roundly declared, 'appear to have taken a far more comprehensive view of the nature and ends of civil society; their principle is more virtuous, more flexible, to the variations of time and circumstance, more congenial to large and masculine intellects.'[5] So for this reason Hallam opposed the moves directed by the Stuarts towards absolutism in state and church. He was full of praise, therefore, for the Long Parliament which 'restored and consolidated the shattered fabric of our constitution'.

> But those common liberties of England which our forefathers had, with such commendable perseverance, extorted from the grasp of power, though by no means so merely theoretical and nugatory in effect as some would insinuate, were yet very precarious in the best periods, neither well defined, nor exempt from anomalous exceptions, or from occasional infringements. Some of them, such as the statute for annual sessions of parliament, had gone into disuse. Those that were most evident could not be enforced; and the new tribunals that, whether by law or usurpation, had reared their heads over the people, had made almost all public and personal rights dependent on their arbitrary will. It was necessary, therefore, to infuse new blood into the languid frame, and so to renovate our ancient constitution that the present era should seem almost a new birth of liberty. Such was the aim, especially, of those provisions which placed the return of parliaments at fixed intervals, beyond the power of the crown to elude.

But of all the reforms carried through by the Long Parliament in its early stages, the one which warmed Hallam's heart most was the abolition of the court of Star Chamber.

> Thus fell the great court of Star Chamber, and with it the whole irregular and arbitrary practice of government, that had for several centuries so thwarted the operation and obscured the light of our free constitution, that many have been prone to deny the existence of those liberties which they found so often infringed, and to mistake the violations of law for its standard.[6]

Hallam favoured all lovers of liberty, all those who believed in the ideal of 'the mixed government of England by King, Lords and Commons'.[7] His was party history of a more academic kind than had so far been current, but it was a shade too legalistic to become really influential, and for the most part he was too balanced rather than partisan to become the standard author in succession to Hume. He took Clarendon to task for the inconsistencies and half-truths of his *History* – 'a strange mixture of honesty and dis-ingenuousness' he called it[8] – yet, when he felt it was appropriate, Hallam was just as capable of criticizing Parliamentarians and republicans. He challenged the views of Mrs Macaulay and Godwin no less than he attacked those advanced by Hume. Hallam's early legal training, in fact, influenced his whole approach to history and was very evident, for example, when he discussed the political justice of the Civil War and the relative merits of the two opposing sides.[9] In the same way there were political limits beyond which Hallam himself was not prepared to go in the nineteenth century, and, though a Whig, he opposed the Reform Act of 1832.

So although Hallam had a respectful audience, although his *Constitutional History*, like his other major works, remained in print throughout the nineteenth century, his impact was not great enough to displace Hume from popular esteem. Even less calculated to achieve this object were the lightweight and anecdotal *Memoirs of the Court of Charles I* published in 1833 by Lucy Aikin (1781–1864). Only, in fact, with Lord Macaulay did a Whig historian appear on the scene who effectively combined popular appeal with party emphasis. Macaulay's historical interventions of the years 1830–2 have already been noted. He had become politically identified with the Whigs by the 1820s and as a writer was much influenced by Sir Walter Scott. Macaulay perfected a brilliant style which was undoubtedly part of the explanation of his phenomenal success. (It has been aptly described by a modern historian as 'a virtuoso's instrument played not to interpret the music but to glorify the performer'!)[10] He aimed deliberately at a wide audience. 'I shall not be satisfied', he wrote to Napier, editor of the *Edinburgh Review*, 'unless I produce something which shall for a few days supersede the last fashionable novel on the tables of young ladies'.[11] He certainly set out to supersede Hume as the leading historian of England and debunked him unmercifully.

> Hume is an accomplished advocate. Without positively asserting much more than he can prove, he gives prominence to all the circumstances which support his case; he glides lightly over those which are unfavourable to it; his own witnesses are applauded and encouraged; the statements which seem to throw discredit on them are controverted; the contradictions into which they fall are explained away; a clear and connected abstract of their evidence is given. Everything that is offered on the other side is scrutinized with the utmost severity; every suspicious circumstance is a ground for comment and invective;

what cannot be denied is extenuated, or passed by without notice; concessions even are sometimes made: but this insidious candour only increases the effect of the vast mass of sophistry.[12]

Hume's 'sophistry' needed to be replaced by a more balanced account, which Macaulay first of all began to provide in his essays. An early statement of his views on the Stuarts was published in 1824 in *Knight's Quarterly Magazine*,[13] and in the following year, with his essay on Milton, Macaulay triumphantly began a long and successful association with the Whig mouthpiece, the *Edinburgh Review*.

[Milton] lived at one of the most memorable eras in the history of mankind, at the very crisis of the great conflict between Oromasdes and Arimanes, liberty and despotism, reason and prejudice. That great battle was fought for no single generation, for no single land. The destinies of the human race were staked on the same cast with the freedom of the English people. Then were first proclaimed those mighty principles which have since worked their way into the depths of the American forests, which have roused Greece from the slavery and degradation of two thousand years, and which, from one end of Europe to the other, have kindled an unquenchable fire in the hearts of the oppressed, and loosed the knees of the oppressors with an unwonted fire. . . .

[In England, the puritans,] those who roused the people to resistance, who directed their measures through a long series of eventful years, who formed, out of the most unpromising materials, the finest army that Europe had ever seen, who trampled down King, Church, and Aristocracy, who, in the short intervals of domestic sedition and rebellion, made the name of England terrible to every nation on the face of the earth, were no vulgar fanatics. . . . We do not hesitate to pronounce them a brave, a wise, an honest and a useful body.[14]

His essays on Hallam, Sir James Mackintosh, and Lord Nugent's *Memorials of Hampden* presented the same Whig standpoint which Macaulay was to elaborate later at greater length in his *History of England* (1848–61).

And now began [in 1627] that hazardous game on which were staked the destinies of the English people. It was played on the side of the House of Commons with keenness, but with admirable dexterity, coolness and perseverance. Great statesmen who looked far behind them and far before them were at the head of that assembly. They were resolved to place the King in such a situation that he must either conduct the administration in conformity with the wishes of his Parliament, or make outrageous attacks on the most sacred principles of the constitution. . . .

[Of Charles I's many faults] faithlessness was the chief cause of his disasters, and is the chief stain on his memory. He was, in truth, impelled by an incurable propensity to dark and crooked ways. It may seem strange that his conscience, which, on occasions of little moment, was sufficiently sensitive, should never have reproached him with this great vice. But there is reason to believe that he was perfidious, not only from constitution and from habit, but also on principle.[15]

Macaulay, active himself in Whig political circles, was preeminent among historians of his age, and he supplied an attractive and satisfying alternative to Hume in the changed political climate of 1832 and after. In a political speech in 1839 he declared:

I entered public life a Whig and a Whig I am determined to remain. . . . It seems to me that, when I look back on our history, I can discern a great party which has, through many generations, preserved its identity; a party often depressed, never extinguished; a party which, though often tainted with the faults of the age, has always been in advance of the age; a party which, though guilty of many errors and some crimes, has the glory of having established our civil and religious liberties on a firm foundation; and of that party I am proud to be a member. . . . It was that party which, in the reign of James I, organised the earliest parliamentary opposition, which steadily asserted the privileges of the people, and wrested prerogative after prerogative from the Crown. It was that party which forced Charles I to relinquish the ship money. It was that party which destroyed the Star Chamber and the High Commission Court. It was that party which, under Charles II, carried the Habeas Corpus Act, which effected the Revolution, which passed the Toleration Act, which broke the yoke of a foreign church in your country, and which saved Scotland from the fate of unhappy Ireland. . . . To the Whigs of the seventeenth century we owe it that we have a House of Commons. To the Whigs of the nineteenth century we owe it that the House of Commons has been purified.[16]

At first glance it may seem unfair to use a political speech as evidence of Macaulay's historical thinking. In fact, however, electioneering of this sort was freely imported into his essays and into the *History*. Macaulay's firm beliefs in the idea of progress, in parliamentary government, civil liberty, and toleration, directly conditioned his whole attitude to the past and the way in which he wrote about it. But Macaulay cannot be classified as a Whig historian in the narrow party political sense. J. W. Burrow has done well to remind us that the *History of England* was not the mere vindication of a political party but a work which proclaimed 'the sectarianism of English respectability'.[17] Timothy Lang has recently argued that Macaulay's *History of England* needs to be read as 'a Liberal response to the religious disputes that dominated English politics from the passing of the Reform Act of 1832 to the furore over "papal aggression" in the early 1850s'.[18] Nor should his *History* be dismissed as an uncritical hymn of praise to Victorianism. Probing work on Macaulay by Hamburger and Pinney has done much to enlarge our understanding of Macaulay's complex psychology, and to expose some of the subtleties, frailties, even neuroses which lay behind the unruffled composure of the famous historian's public image.[19] None the less, with the avoidance of revolution in Britain in 1848 vindicating the wisdom of the Great Reform Act, Macaulay was increasingly complacent and confident by the time he wrote his *History* and contemplated the seventeenth-century past from the elevated standpoint of his own age. As he proclaimed at the beginning of the first chapter of his *History of England*:

> Unless I greatly deceive myself, the general effect of this chequered narrative will be to excite thankfulness in all religious minds, and hope in the breasts of all patriots. For the history of our country during the last hundred and sixty years is eminently the history of physical, of moral, and of intellectual improvement. Those who compare the age on which their lot has fallen with a golden age which exists only in their imagination may talk of degeneracy and decay; but no man who is correctly informed as to the past will be disposed to take a morose or desponding view of the present.[20]

The success of his *History* reflected the mood of relief and self-congratulation after England's avoidance of revolution in 1848. But the *History* had didactic purposes related to the changing social foundations of politics in the early Victorian age. 'The *History* being intended to train a citizenry for participation in and progression of a future England', says Owen Dudley Edwards, 'its author was vigilant in his desire to save the future masters from error'.[21] Properly understood, however, Macaulay's main achievement was that he enlarged the Whig interpretation of history from one that was the restricted property of a party to one that was subscribed to by the nation.[22]

Macaulay's epic *History*, written with unsurpassed vigour, flamboyance, and exaggeration, though it belonged to a Whig tradition which continued, in another sense came at the end of an era in historiography; only twenty years after the appearance of the last volume of his *History* the work was being criticized as 'unhistorical'.[23] After Macaulay, English historical scholarship in general was never quite the same again. For from the middle of the nineteenth century the nature of historical research and writing, following the German model, was noticeably changing and was becoming more academic and scientific in character. (Macaulay himself to all intents and purposes ignored these developments in German historiography, and, significantly, when he reviewed von Ranke's *History of the Popes* he had virtually nothing to say about the writer's methodology.) The contrast between 'literary' and 'scientific' history, of course, was not absolute; 'scientific' history too, in the nature of things, still involved subjectivity, despite the contrary claims of its practitioners. But none the less there was a difference between the two varieties of history, albeit one of *degree* rather than of kind.[24]

The more detached, more scientific approach to historical study in England was made possible first by the increased accessibility of primary source material, and second by developments in the training of historians stemming from the establishment of history as an academic discipline in its own right at the universities. The creation of separate Schools of History at Oxford in 1871, with William Stubbs as Regius Professor, and at Cambridge in 1873 helped to give the subject a firmer foothold, although it did not mean that the two universities from this date began to turn out a steady stream of professional historians. The colleges and most of the students saw history as part of a general education, well-suited for politicians, administrators, and empire-builders. The 'history for its own sake' line taken by a Regius Professor like Stubbs was at first unsympathetically received.[25] Other changes were more immediately productive. The resources of the British Museum, for example, were made more readily available to historians through systematic cataloguing. A related move was begun in 1856 with the publication of the first calendars of state papers. The new Public Record Office was opened in 1862 and the Historical Manuscripts Commission was launched seven years later. The publication of source material by such bodies as the Camden Society (founded 1838) and the Chetham Society (founded 1843) was a step in the same general direction. The *English Historical Review*, the first journal of its kind in this country, began publication in 1886. The result of developments such as these was that painstaking research, based squarely on manuscript as well as on secondary material, was coming to be regarded as the essential element in the historian's business. J. B. Bury's 1902 inaugural lecture at Cambridge on 'The Science of History' accurately reflected this state of affairs. And by that date the professionalized study of History was firmly on the academic map of provincial universities like Manchester where Professor T. F. Tout held sway.[26]

As far as the historiography of the English Revolution is concerned, the influence of these developments was obvious. A noticeable change occurred in the style of writing; one has only to contrast Macaulay's pages with the restrained and detailed scholarship of S. R. Gardiner (see pp. 91–5). The emergence of more scientific history, in fact, produced a profound change in the nature of the debate on the English Revolution. The polemical element, the party political flavour, receded, and since then the debate, for the most part, has been predominantly academic in tone.

Looking back, we can see that a move had been made in the direction of more critical, more scientific history by John Lingard (1771–1851) and there are some grounds for regarding him as the 'English Ranke'.[27] Lingard concerns us only briefly here since although he published a general *History of England from the First Invasion of the Romans to the Accession of William and Mary* (1819–30), his original researches were confined mainly to the sixteenth century rather than to the period of the English Revolution. Lingard, a Catholic priest, was the first English historian to look at Tudor policy from an international point of view, and by exploiting previously untapped European sources in the archives of Rome and Simancas he endeavoured to correct some of the most glaring distortions in the English Protestant/nationalist view of the English past. But although his religious purpose at times obstructed his scholarly objectives, and although his later volumes on the Stuarts reveal mildly Whiggish opinions, none the less Lingard did consciously *try* to be objective about the past and to aim at scientific accuracy. He was no uncritical partisan either of Church or of party. Take, for instance, his reflections on the execution of Charles I.

> Such was the end of the unfortunate Charles Stuart, an awful lesson to the possessors of royalty, to watch the growth of public opinion, and to moderate their pretensions in conformity with the reasonable desires of their subjects. . . . But while we blame the illegal measures of Charles, we ought not to screen from censure the subsequent conduct of his principal opponents. From the moment that war seemed inevitable, they acted as if they thought themselves absolved from all obligations of honour and honesty. They never ceased to inflame the passions of the people by misrepresentation and calumny; they exercised a power far more arbitrary and formidable than had ever been claimed by the king.[28]

Lingard's views on historical method, which involved an explicit rejection of 'philosophical history', were put forward most clearly in the preface to the last revision of his *History* which he undertook in 1849.

> In disposing of the new matter derived from these several sources, I have strictly adhered to the same rules to which I subjected myself in the former editions; to admit no statement merely upon trust, to weigh with care the value of the authorities on which I rely, and to watch with jealousy the secret workings of my own personal feelings and prepossessions. Such vigilance is a matter of necessity to every writer of history, if he aspire to the praise of truthfulness and impartiality. He must withdraw himself aloof from the scenes which he describes and view with the coolness of an unconcerned spectator the events which pass before his eyes, holding with a steady hand the balance between contending parties, and allotting to the more prominent characters that measure of praise or dispraise which he conscientiously believes to be their due. Otherwise, he will be continually tempted to make an unfair use of the privilege of the historian; he will sacrifice the interests of truth to the interests of party, national, or religious, or political. His narrative may still be brilliant, attractive, picturesque; but the pictures which he paints will derive their colouring from the jaundiced eye of the artist himself, and will therefore bear no very faithful resemblance to the realities of life and fact.[29]

For the final revision of his *History* Lingard made use of Carlyle's *Letters and Speeches of Oliver Cromwell* (1845), or at least of 'the letters and speeches themselves, not the running commentary with which the editor has accompanied them in language most glowing and oracular. . . . I feel no disposition to fall down before the idol, and worship him at the command of his panegyrist.'[30] In some ways Carlyle deserved Lingard's rebuke; Cromwell emerged from his pages as a Heaven-sent hero of a kind, as the author saw it, that his own generation in the nineteenth century badly needed. But despite all appearances, it could be argued that Carlyle too, perverse and idiosyncratic though he was, like Lingard moved away from party history and took a short step towards a more critical, scientific approach to the seventeenth-century past.

Judged by later standards, Thomas Carlyle (1795–1881) certainly would not rank as a scientific historian, and by the end of the century he was indeed much out of favour with the professionals. Seen in the context of his own times, however, Carlyle appears different from his predecessors in that, despite all his obtrusive subjectivity, his prejudices – vast though they were – were at least his own, and not those picked up in the Whig/Tory political arena. Carlyle felt a duty to use primary sources and described his researches on Cromwell as 'a mole's work, boring and digging blindly underground'.[31] But whereas later historians saw in research the main part of their scholarly activity, to Carlyle it was no more than a preliminary, sometimes disagreeable, to the main task of communicating ideas to society at large. He was always impatient to write down his conclusions even if he had still not genuinely reached them by his research. He wrote to a correspondent in 1845:

> I would very gladly tell you all my methods if I had any, but really I have as it were none. I go into the business with all the intelligence, patience, silence and other gifts and virtues that I have; find that ten times or a hundred times as many could be profitably expended there, and still prove insufficient: and as for plan, I find that every new business requires as it were a new scheme of operations, which amid infinite bungling and plunging unfolds itself at intervals (very scantily, after all) as I get along. The great thing is not to stop and break down. . . . Avoid writing beyond the very minimum; mark in pencil

the very smallest indication that will direct me to the thing again; and on the whole try to keep the whole matter simmering in the living mind and memory rather than laid up in paper bundles or otherwise laid up in the inert way. For this certainly turns out to be a truth: only what you at last have living in your own memory and heart is worth putting down to be printed; this alone has much chance to get into the living heart and memory of other men.[32]

Only to a limited extent, therefore, do Carlyle's *Cromwell* and his posthumously published *Historical Sketches of Notable Persons and Events in the Reigns of James I and Charles I* (1898) reveal their author as a critical, scientific historian in the later sense of the term. Far more positive and recognizable steps in this direction were taken by two distinguished European historians of seventeenth-century England, the one a Frenchman and the other a German. The first was François Guizot (1787–1874), liberal conservative politician and sometime professor of history who fell from power with the July monarchy in 1848. Guizot's historical writing can best be described, perhaps, as proto-scientific in character. As Professor Johnson has written in his study of the man and his background:

> It is easy to understand why Guizot appeared so outstanding. Nothing could appear more scientific than his detached and objective style. This is all the more striking when compared to that of his contemporaries. . . .
>
> No one would deny that Guizot had prejudices. He appears to be less one-sided than many of his contemporary historians because these prejudices are concealed under an air of dispassionate reason, and are hidden by a screen of erudition. But he simply did not have antipathies on the same scale as Macaulay or Michelet.[33]

But it was not only Guizot's style which appeared scientific to his contemporaries both in France and England, but also his very conception of history. J. S. Mill, for example, in 1845 declared that Guizot's great merit was that he set out to *explain* the facts of history, whereas in England the mere unearthing and presentation of the facts themselves satisfied historians.[34]

Guizot wrote extensively on seventeenth-century England, and did so with the confidence of one who had himself experienced revolutions and their hurtful consequences. First, in 1826, came his *History of the English Revolution of 1640* which was followed by studies of Oliver Cromwell, Richard Cromwell, General Monck, and others in the 1850s. Although J. W. Croker complained that Guizot tended to confuse the *Rebellion* with the *Revolution*,[35] his survey of seventeenth-century England was highly regarded both for its comprehensiveness and for its impartiality. Hallam, for instance, thought that if Guizot continued as he had begun then 'he will be entitled to the preference above any one, perhaps, of our native writers, as a guide through the great period of the seventeenth century'.[36]

Guizot was in fact the first historian to use the term 'English Revolution', and in the preface to the first instalment of his *History* published in 1826 he drew an extended comparison between affairs in England and the French Revolution of 1789. He emphasized that both events, far from being unexpected, were the natural result of historical development.

> Produced by the same causes, the decay of the feudal aristocracy, the church, and royalty, they both laboured at the same work, the dominion of the public in public affairs; they struggled for liberty against absolute power, for equality against privilege, for progressive and general interests against stationary and individual interests. Their situations were different, their strength unequal; what one clearly conceived, the other saw but in imperfect outline; in the career which the one fulfilled, the other soon stopped short. . . .
>
> In a word, the analogy of the two revolutions is such, that the first would never have been thoroughly understood had not the second taken place.[37]

Guizot elaborated his ideas on the seventeenth-century crisis in England in his pamphlet *Why Was the English Revolution Successful?* (1850). Looking at the Revolution in its broadest social aspects, Guizot concluded in a way that was reminiscent of Harrington that:

> Political and religious parties were not alone in the field. Beneath their struggle lay a social question, the struggle of the various classes for influence and power. Not that these classes were in England radically segregate and hostile one to another as they have been elsewhere. . . . But in the last hundred years, great changes had taken place in the relative strength of the various classes in the bosom of society without any analogous changes having been wrought in the government. Commercial activity and religious order had, in the

middle classes, given a prodigious impulse to wealth and to thought. ... Hence had arisen amongst them and the ranks beneath them a proud and powerful spirit of ambition, eager to seize the first occasion to burst forth. Civil war opened a wide field to their energy and to their hopes. It presented at its outset, no aspect of a social classification, exclusive and hostile: many country gentlemen, several even of the great lords, were at the head of the popular party. Soon the nobility on the one hand, and the middle class and the people on the other, ranged themselves in two masses, the one around the crown, the other around the parliament, and sure symptoms already revealed a great social movement in the heart of a great political struggle, and the effervescence of an ascendant democracy, clearing for itself a way through the ranks of a weakened and divided aristocracy.[38]

Written after his fall from office in 1848, Guizot's pamphlet reveals a writer who now had time, and added reason, to reflect on revolutions. His admiration for the English Revolution still remained. He stressed its constitutionalism, its appeal to Magna Carta, its resistance to tyranny: 'In the seventeenth century in England, royal power was the aggressor.'[39] The political solution – wholly admirable in Guizot's view – which emerged from the seventeenth-century crisis was constitutional monarchy. 'But in the seventeenth century they had neither the enlightenment nor the political virtues which this government requires.'[40] Regrettably, the Revolution which began so promisingly got out of hand. The execution of Charles I was a 'high crime', religious extremism degenerated into an arrogant fanaticism, and a thoroughly un-English republic was created. 'Revolutionists, even the ablest of them, are short-sighted. Intoxicated by the passion, or dominated by the necessity of the moment, they do not foresee that what today constitutes their triumph will be tomorrow their condemnation.'[41] As Guizot saw it, therefore, the English Revolution, immensely important though it was, was in some ways important for indirect reasons; it was a lesson, painfully learnt.

> After the great revolutionary crisis of 1640–1660, the English people had the good fortune and the merit of appreciating experience, and of never giving themselves up to extreme parties. Amidst the most ardent political struggles and violence, in which they sometimes impelled their chiefs, they always on great and decisive occasions reverted to that sound good sense which consists in recognising the

essential benefits it is desired to retain and attaching itself without wavering to them; enduring the inconveniences attendant on them and renouncing the desires which might compromise them. It is from the time of Charles II that this good sense which is the political intelligence of free nations has presided over the destinies of England. . . . Whether we look at the destiny of nations, or at that of great men – whether a monarchy or a republic is in question – an aristocratic or a democratic society, the same truth is revealed by facts; definitive success is only obtained by the same principles and in the same way. The revolutionary spirit is as fatal to the greatness it raises up as to that which it overturns. The policy which preserves states is also that which terminates and founds revolutions.[42]

Clearly, it was Guizot the failed, helpless, ousted politician as much as Guizot the historian who reached this verdict.

Not a politician himself, the second of these distinguished European historians of seventeenth-century England was more detached from his subject. Leopold von Ranke (1795–1886), the great German historian and the real founder of the new school of history in the nineteenth century, wrote his six-volume *History of England Chiefly in the Seventeenth Century* in the 1860s, and it soon appeared in an English translation in 1875. Ranke emphasized the advantages of an outsider's view of this important and controversial period of English history.

It is surely good that in epochs of such great importance for the history of all nations, we should possess foreign and independent representations to compare with those of home growth; in the latter are expressed sympathies and antipathies as inherited by tradition and affected by the antagonism of literary differences of opinion. . . . A historical work may aim either at putting forward a new view of what is already known or at communicating additional information as to the facts. I have endeavoured to combine both these aims.[43]

Not surprisingly in view of its author, Ranke's work was particularly valuable for its treatment of England's relations with the continent. And it was entirely characteristic of his careful and exacting scholarship to attach extensive documentary and historiographical appendices to his history.

But although he wrote as an outsider whose 'only concern is to become acquainted with the great motive powers and their results', this did not mean that Ranke's volumes consisted only of a colourless and neutral collection of facts. English history in general and the seventeenth-century crisis in particular were presented from a European point of view. The seventeenth century emerged from Ranke's pages as a heroic period for England, and the Revolution of 1688 as an event which served the interests of a Europe menaced by the ambitions of Louis XIV. The Civil War, he argued,

> is an event which concerns all, this shaking of the foundations of the old British state. Whether they would stand the shock or, if not, what shape public affairs would in that case assume was a question which must concern the continent also. The civilised world is still busy day by day with more or less conspicuous complications of the spiritual and political struggles arising from similar opposing principles.[44]

Particularly interested in the diplomatic and religious aspects of the seventeenth century, Ranke treated the religious controversies of the period with no less seriousness, and underlined the differences between the English Revolution and the French Revolution of 1789, of which he thoroughly disapproved. Unimpressed by Cromwell and republicanism, Ranke's charitable treatment of the Stuarts was based, in part at least, on their contribution to the unification of Great Britain which indirectly served the cause of a beleaguered Europe.

> James I had probably during his lifetime too high an idea of the strength of his opponents; Charles I certainly had too slight a one. . . . He knew neither the depth of the lawful desires of Parliament nor the purport of the opposition already begun: he cherished splendid hopes when nearest to his ruin. For he trusted chiefly to the intrinsic power of the rights and ideas for which he fought. . . . So far there was certainly something of a martyr in him, if the man can be so called who values his own life less than the cause for which he is fighting, and in perishing himself, saves it for the future.[45]

English historians, too, were active in the work of research and reinterpretation. J. R. Green (1837–83) was the oddity among them. His popular *Short History of the English People* appeared in 1874 and was novel in both its treatment and sympathies. In Green's work the 'people' held the centre of the stage, and the book as a whole was suffused with his Liberal convictions. Green believed, as his editor later wrote, that 'political history could only be made intelligible and just by basing it on social history in its largest sense'. As a schoolboy studying Charles I, 'it had suddenly burst upon him that Charles was wrong'. Green's *Short History* embodied the same sentiments. 'Modern England, the England among whose thoughts and sentiments we actually live, began however dimly with the triumph of Naseby. . . . For the last two hundred years England has been doing little more than carrying out in a slow and tentative way the schemes of political and religious reforms which the army propounded at the close of the Civil War'.[46] Green devoted more space to the early modern period than to any other. Approximately ten per cent of his pages were given over to his account of 'Puritan England'. (Roman Britain, by contrast, was dismissed in a mere two pages.) Pym and Hampden were applauded. Laud and Strafford were vilified. He took pains to offer a fresh interpretation of Cromwell that departed from the hero worship of Carlyle.[47]

Ultimately, however, it was S. R. Gardiner (1829–1902) who produced the classic, large-scale, new-style work on the period 1603 to 1656. Dr Lang has provided the fullest account of this famous, but strangely elusive historian.[48] For Gardiner, recognition was an uphill task, and he held no university appointment until 1871. His religious affiliations had kept him out of Oxford in earlier life and for years he had to submit to the drudgery of school-teaching to eke out a living. At the age of 42, having become an Anglican, he took up a post at King's College, London.[49] Lord Acton wrote an unenthusiastic review of the first instalment of his history in 1863. But tributes to him abounded by the end of the century. He had an Oxford research fellowship by 1884, was offered (and declined) the Regius Chair ten years later, and was editor of the *English Historical Review* from 1890. 'No man did more by his personal efforts to forward the progress of historical studies in England', wrote Sir Charles Firth after Gardiner's death.[50] Comparing historical knowledge of the early Stuarts before and after Gardiner's intervention, Firth continued, was like 'comparing an eighteenth-century map of Africa with a modern one. The outline of the country is the same in both, but we know where the great rivers rise, and can follow their windings'. 'With the possible exception of Stubbs's *Constitutional History*, his [Gardiner's] volumes form the most solid and enduring achievement of British

historiography in the latter half of the nineteenth century.' So wrote
G. P. Gooch a few years later.[51] And from America, too, came
glowing praise in the *Yale Scientific Monthly*. Gardiner, it was said,

> firmly grasped the profound distinction which lies at the root of all
> science, between the judgement of fact and the judgement of value,
> and knew that the validity of the first can only be secured if it is pro-
> visionally treated as an end in itself, in perfect abstraction from any
> possible application of it.[52]

It was his methodology, certainly, which was Gardiner's distinctive contribution to historical studies. Rejecting the impres-
sionism of earlier historians, such as Carlyle, and the oratorical
style and judge-like pose of Macaulay, Gardiner embarked on his
multi-volume history with the determination to be satisfied with
nothing less than the truth, and to break with the whole notion of
Whig and Tory history.

> When I first undertook to investigate the history of this momentous
> period, I felt a certain hesitation. Libraries positively bristled with the
> names of great writers who had given their thoughts to the world on
> the subject of these years. But I was not long in discovering that there
> was still room for further investigation. We have historians in plenty,
> but they have been Whig historians or Tory historians. The one class
> has thought it unnecessary to take trouble to understand how matters
> looked in the eyes of the King and his friends; the other class has
> thought it unnecessary to take trouble to understand how matters
> looked in the eyes of the leaders of the House of Commons. I am not
> so vain as to suppose that I have always succeeded in doing justice to
> both parties, but I have, at least, done my best not to misrepresent
> either. . . .
>   Certainly the politics of the seventeenth century when studied for
> the mere sake of understanding them, assume a very different appear-
> ance from that which they had in the eyes of men who, like Macaulay
> and Forster, regarded them through the medium of their own
> political struggles. Eliot and Strafford were neither Whigs nor Tories,
> Liberals nor Conservatives. As Professor Seeley was, I believe, the first
> to teach directly, though the lesson is indirectly involved in every
> line written by Ranke, the father of modern historical research, the
> way in which Macaulay and Forster regarded the development of the
> past – that is to say, the constant avowed or unavowed comparison
> of it with the present – is altogether destructive of real historical
> knowledge.[53]

Although a fine lecturer and a writer of school textbooks, Gardiner was primarily a historian's historian, and in contrast with Macaulay and Green his first ventures into publishing were miserably unsuccessful. But he persevered in the task and with the method with which he had begun. The hallmark of Gardiner's historical method was a strict adherence to chronology, taking into account only those sources relating to each moment in time which he examined in progression. The method had its obvious drawbacks, of course. Above all, it was not conducive to consistency, although in this, too, Gardiner believed that he was faithfully representing the times. But the main value of chronology, as he saw it, was that it was an antidote to bias.

> Hitherto no book has come into existence which has even professed to trace the gradual change which came over English feeling year by year. . . . Much confusion has been caused by the habit . . . of classifying events rather according to their nature than according to their chronological order, so that the true sequence of history is lost. It is needless to add that where, as too often happens, no attempt whatever is made to understand the strong points in the case of the King or the weak points in the case of his opponents, the result is a mere caricature.[54]

The method, however, was not used by Gardiner when writing his textbooks. One of these, boldly entitled *The Puritan Revolution*, was published in 1876 at a time when Gardiner's chronologically pursued *magnum opus* had only reached the year 1628. There is a kind of Jekyll and Hyde air about Gardiner.

Gardiner based the research for his great *History* securely on the primary sources and was helped in this by the work of the Historical Manuscripts Commission and by the calendaring of state papers. 'Evidence worth having must be almost entirely the evidence of contemporaries who are in a position to know something about that which they assert.'[55] Gardiner, however, was no narrow specialist, but was careful to place the Civil Wars and the reigns of the early Stuarts in a long perspective. Also, as a considerable linguist well versed in continental sources, Gardiner gave, so far as English historians were concerned, unprecedented attention to European affairs in this period.

> No one can really study any particular period of history unless he knows a great deal about what preceded it and what came after it.

He cannot seriously study a generation of men as if it could be isolated and examined like a piece of inorganic matter. He has to bear
in mind that it is a portion of a living whole.[56]

Gardiner's interpretation of seventeenth-century events, unlike
that associated with Macaulay's hammering technique, was less
obtrusive; 'The Puritan Revolution' is a convenient but inadequate
summary of his model. He avoided making summaries of general
trends and did not interrupt his chronological narrative to provide
full-length character portraits. It is no easy matter for the reader to
assemble Gardiner's views on Charles I, Strafford, and Pym. But
Gardiner, like all historians, could not leave himself out of account.
There was naturally a subjective as well as an objective element in
his method and interpretation, and this was systematically exposed
by the American historian R. G. Usher. 'In reality', Usher concluded, 'Gardiner has done exactly what he blamed Macaulay for
doing: he has decided a great issue in history, which was by no
means clear to the men of the time, by applying to it his later
knowledge.'[57] His own convictions got in the way of his research
and conclusions. Usher, too, criticized Gardiner for the inconsistencies into which his historical method led him; his many volumes
demonstrated his intellectual growth as a historian but did not
provide the reader with a considered and structured account of a
controversial period of English history. Even if the chronological
method was accepted at face value as Gardiner's strategy for
preparing the original volumes of his *History* as they had rolled
one by one from the press, why in 1884 when a new ten-volume
edition was issued covering the years 1603–42 had Gardiner
not taken the opportunity to revise and remove the most glaring
inconsistencies?

Others pushed criticism to unreasonable lengths (see p. 100).
'The late Professor Samuel Gardiner', later pronounced the anti-
Victorian Lytton Strachey, 'could absorb facts, and he could state
them; but he had no point of view; and the result is that his book
on the most exciting period of English history resembles nothing
so much as a very large heap of sawdust'.[58] But Gardiner's method
had simply exposed the central frailty of the assumptions on which
scientific history was based. With or without a strictly chronological method, complete objectivity was an impossible goal for the

historian to attain. Gardiner's Liberal Nonconformist background could hardly fail to make an impact on his historical writing. That he was for many years a member of the millenarian Irvingite sect, a great admirer of Gladstone, and himself a descendant of Oliver Cromwell, all helped to shape his historical perception and purposes. Notwithstanding his protestations to the contrary, therefore, Gardiner wrote about the seventeenth-century past with late Victorian politics and religion in mind. Indeed a recent commentator goes so far as to say 'Gardiner's epic becomes a parable of the Gladstonian Liberal as Hero. It is peopled with splendid statesmen and eminent Victorians'. To facilitate and foster the new democracy of the age Gardiner, like other Liberals, recognized the need to heal the rift between Anglicanism and Dissent. 'Gardiner hoped to remove the historical source of this rivalry', says Dr Lang, 'by presenting an image of the past which would demonstrate that modern England was neither Anglican nor Puritan but rather an amalgam of these two antagonistic traditions.'[59] What emerged, then, from Gardiner's account of seventeenth-century England was a record of a struggle for political and religious liberty with the House of Commons as the Chief Protagonist. 'The interest of [English] history in the seventeenth century lies in the efforts made to secure a double object – the control of the nation over its own destinies, and the liberty of the public expression of thought, without which parliamentary government is only a refined form of tyranny.'[60] His national pride comes through:

> England was then, as she has always been, decidedly in advance, so far as political institutions are concerned, of the other nations of Europe. She had to work out the problem of government unaided by experience, and was entering like Columbus upon a new world, where there was nothing to guide her but her own high spirit and the wisdom and virtue of her sons.[61]

For Gardiner, the English 'nation' and 'constitution' had clear, solid identities, and it was the English nation itself which was the repository of liberty.

> The English people had never entirely relinquished their control over their own destinies, nor had ever so put themselves like sheep into the hands of any king as to suffer themselves to be tended or shorn at his arbitrary will. Not in statute or precedent, not even in the Great

Charter itself, but in the imperishable vitality of the nation, lay the fundamental laws of England.[62]

There was a certain inevitability about the Civil War, and puritanism's role was absolutely central.

> Above all, it was Puritanism which gave to those whose energies were most self-centred the power which always follows upon submission to law. Puritanism not only formed the strength of the opposition to Charles, but the strength of England itself. Parliamentary liberties, and even parliamentary control, were worth contending for.[63]

With all these resonances of the Whig interpretation, it is easy to see how the label 'Puritan Revolution', despite the oversimplification it brought with it, became permanently and irremovably attached to Gardiner's great, but quintessentially Victorian, work. Spurred on by his search for a late nineteenth-century consensus and by the imperatives of nation-building Gardiner transformed a discordant past into a past in which Oliver Cromwell and the puritans became acceptable, indeed necessary, ingredients. The unveiling of Thornycroft's statue of the Lord Protector outside the Houses of Parliament in 1899 was a further expression of the same mood and impulse.[64]

Notes

1 J. W. Croker, *Quarterly Review* (March, 1832), pp. 288, 296.
2 G. Brodie, *Constitutional History of the British Empire From the Accession of Charles I to the Restoration* (new edn, London, 1866), I, pp. vii, viii. Godwin had utilized Brodie's work when writing his own *History of the Commonwealth of England*.
3 Brodie, *Constitutional History*, III, pp. 343–4.
4 *Ibid.*, I, p. 239, II, pp. 3–21, 113, 235–6.
5 H. Hallam, *Constitutional History of England* (London, 1827, new edn, 1872), III, p. 201.
6 *Ibid.*, II, pp. 101, 98.
7 *Ibid.*, II, p. 138.
8 *Ibid.*, II, p. 79.
9 T. Lang, *The Victorians and the Stuart Heritage: Interpretations of a Discordant Past* (Cambridge, 1995), p. 41. Hallam, *Constitutional History*, II, pp. 138–50. On Hallam see P. Clark, *Henry Hallam* (Boston, Mass., 1982).
10 P. Gay, *Style in History* (London, 1975), p. 97. Macaulay's move towards the Whigs is discussed in J. Clive, *Macaulay: The Shaping of the Historian* (London, 1973).

11 Quoted in Jane Millgate, *Macaulay* (London, 1973), p. 119.
12 *The Miscellaneous Writings and Speeches of Lord Macaulay*, popular edn (London, 1889), p. 154.
13 T. B. Macaulay, 'A conversation between Mr Abraham Cowley and Mr John Milton touching the Great Civil War', *Knight's Quarterly Magazine* (London, 1824).
14 T. B. Macaulay, *Critical and Historical Essays* (London, 1852), pp. 14, 23–4.
15 T. B. Macaulay, *History of England*, Everyman edn (London, 1953), I, p. 63.
16 *The Miscellaneous Writings and Speeches of Lord Macaulay*, pp. 583–4.
17 J. W. Burrow, *A Liberal Descent: Victorian Historians and the English Past* (Cambridge, 1981), p. 93.
18 Lang, *Victorians and the Stuart Heritage*, p. 53.
19 J. Hamburger, *Macaulay and the Whig Tradition* (Chicago, 1976); T. Pinney (ed.), *The Letters of Thomas Babington Macaulay* (Cambridge, 1974–82).
20 Macaulay, *History of England*, I, p. 6.
21 O. D. Edwards, *Macaulay* (London, 1988), p. 134.
22 Burrow, *Liberal Descent*, p. 92.
23 See, for example, J. C. Morison, *Macaulay* (London, 1882). For Gardiner's strictures on Macaulay, see p. 83.
24 See Rosemary Jann, *The Art and Science of Victorian History* (Columbus, Ohio, 1985).
25 See p. 104 for some discussion of Sir Charles Firth's difficulties at Oxford. See also P. R. H. Slee, *Learning and a Liberal Education: The Study of Modern History in the Universities of Oxford, Cambridge, and Manchester, 1800–1914* (Manchester, 1986); Philippa J. A. Levine, *The Amateur and the Professional: Historians, Antiquarians and Archaeologists in Nineteenth-Century England 1838–1886* (Cambridge, 1986); Rosemary Jann, 'From amateur to professional; the case of the Oxbridge historians', *JBS*, xxii (1983); Reba Soffer, 'Nation, duty, character and confidence: History at Oxford, 1850–1914', *HJ*, xxx (1987).
26 Doris Goldstein, 'The origins and early years of the *English Historical Review*', *EHR*, ci (1987). Bury's lecture is reprinted in F. Stern (ed.), *The Varieties of History*, 2nd edn (London, 1970), pp. 209–26.
27 D. F. Shea, *The English Ranke: John Lingard* (New York, 1969).
28 F. Jones, 'John Lingard and the Simancas archives', *HJ*, x (1967); T. P. Peardon, *The Transition in English Historical Writing* (New York, 1933), pp. 280–3; J. Lingard, *History of England*, 6th edn (London, 1855), VIII, pp. 119–20.
29 Lingard, *History of England*, I, p. 6.
30 *Ibid.*, I, p. 5.
31 A. Carlyle (ed.), *New Letters of Thomas Carlyle* (London, 1904), I, p. 244.
32 *Ibid.*, II, pp. 10–11. See L. M. Young, *Thomas Carlyle and the Art of History* (Philadelphia, 1939).
33 M. C. Connor, *The Historical Thought of François Guizot* (Washington, DC, 1955); D. Johnson, *Guizot: Aspects of French History 1787–1874* (London, 1963), p. 327.
34 Johnson, *Guizot*, p. 330.
35 *Ibid.*, p. 366.
36 H. Hallam, *Constitutional History of England* (London, 1872), I, p. vii.

37 F. Guizot, *History of the English Revolution of 1640* (London, 1867), pp. xvi–xvii.
38 *Ibid.*, p. 8.
39 *Ibid.*, p. 3.
40 *Ibid.*, p. 5.
41 *Ibid.*, p. 15.
42 *Ibid.*, pp. 49, 78.
43 L. von Ranke, *History of England Chiefly in the Seventeenth Century* (London, 1875), I, pp. xi, xiv. See C. E. McClelland, *The German Historians and England* (Cambridge, 1971), ch. 6; G. G. Iggers, *The German Conception of History* (Middletown, Conn., 1968); and L. Krieger, *Ranke: The Meaning of History* (Chicago, 1977).
44 Ranke, *History of England*, II, p. 330.
45 *Ibid.*, II, pp. 552–3.
46 J. R. Green, *A Short History of the English People* (London, 1889), pp. xiii, vi, 559.
47 See A. Brundage, *The People's Historian. John Richard Green and the Writing of History in Victorian England* (Westport, Conn., 1994), esp. ch. 6.
48 Lang, *Victorians and the Stuart Heritage*, ch. 4.
49 *Ibid.*, p. 147. Lang offers the best account of Gardiner's affiliation to and subsequent disengagement from the Irvingite sect.
50 D. Woodruff (ed.), *Essays on Church and State by Lord Acton* (London, 1952), pp. 438–9; C. H. Firth, 'Dr S. R. Gardiner', *Proceedings of the British Academy* (1903–4), p. 295; *Quarterly Review*, cxcv (1902), p. 535. See also P. M. B. Blaas, *Continuity and Anachronism: Parliamentary and Constitutional Development in Whig Historiography and in the Anti-Whig Reaction between 1890 and 1930* (The Hague, 1978), pp. 40–3, 149–50, 152–3; and J. P. Kenyon, *The History Men: The Historical Profession in England Since the Renaissance* (London, 1983), esp. pp. 214–22.
51 G. P. Gooch, *History and Historians in the Nineteenth Century* (London, 1952), p. 335. The book was first published in 1913.
52 H. B. Learned, 'Samuel Rawson Gardiner', *Yale Scientific Monthly* (June 1902).
53 S. R. Gardiner, *History of England 1624–8* (London, 1875), I, preface; S. R. Gardiner, *History of England 1603–42*, new edn (London, 1893–6), I, p. vi.
54 S. R. Gardiner, *History of England 1628–37* (London, 1877), I, preface.
55 S. R. Gardiner, *What Gunpowder Plot Was* (London, 1897), p. 4.
56 Quoted in C. H. Firth, 'Samuel Rawson Gardiner', *Quarterly Review*, cxcv (1902), p. 550.
57 R. G. Usher, *A Critical Study of the Historical Method of S. R. Gardiner* (Washington University Studies, III, pt 2, no. 1, 1915), p. 74. See also D. M. Fahey, 'Gardiner and Usher in perspective', *J. Hist. Studs.*, I (1968), pp. 137–50.
58 L. Strachey, *Portraits in Miniature and other Essays* (London, 1931), pp. 169–70. Quoted in Lang, *Victorians and the Stuart Heritage*, p. 139.
59 Lang, *Victorians and the Stuart Heritage*, p. 141. See also J. S. A. Adamson, 'Eminent Victorians: S. R. Gardiner and the liberal as hero', *HJ*, 33 (1990), p. 657.

60 S. R. Gardiner, *The First Two Stuarts and the Puritan Revolution 1603–1660*, 8th edn (London, 1888), p. v.
61 Gardiner, *History of England 1603–42*, II, p. 197.
62 *Ibid.*, VIII, pp. 84–5.
63 S. R. Gardiner, *History of the Great Civil War 1642–49* (London, 1893), I, p. 9.
64 R. Howell, 'Who needs another Cromwell? The nineteenth-century image of Oliver Cromwell', in R. C. Richardson (ed.), *Images of Oliver Cromwell. Essays for and by Roger Howell Jr* (Manchester, 1993), p. 96. See also Lang, *Victorians and the Stuart Heritage*, ch. 5, *passim*.

6

The twentieth century:
the nineteenth-century inheritance
and its development

[Gardiner's works] cover the period from 1603 to 1656 with unexampled thoroughness. Even after the lapse of fifty years it is difficult to add substantially to or to make more than minor corrections of this narrative. (Godfrey Davies, *The Early Stuarts 1603–1660* (Oxford, 1937, 2nd edn, 1959), p. 418)

But in England the revolutionary passions were stirred by no class in its own material interest. Our patriots were prosperous men, enamoured of liberty, or of religion, or of loyalty, each for her own sake, not as the handmaid of class greed. This was the secret of the moral splendour of our Great Rebellion and our Civil War. (G. M. Trevelyan, *England under the Stuarts* (12th edn, London, 1925), p. 196)

The criticism of Gardiner's historical method made by R. G. Usher in 1915 was carried to much greater lengths by an anonymous correspondent in the *Times Literary Supplement* in 1919. This writer, whose tone became increasingly irascible week by week as the correspondence developed, denounced Gardiner as 'a subtle and dangerous partisan. The truth is that nothing he says can be trusted. Every reference note should be checked.'[1] Leading academic historians like A. P. Newton, A. F. Pollard, and C. H. Firth rallied to the defence of Gardiner's reputation. Without the latter's pioneering efforts, they argued, the state of knowledge of seventeenth-century history would have been immeasurably poorer. 'It is an ungrateful act', one of them said, 'to kick down the ladder whereby you have climbed.'[2] Appropriately, it was Sir Charles Firth (1857–1936) who took the lead in vindicating Gardiner against this violent attack, and on this occasion, as on others, he proved himself a true disciple. In the obituaries he wrote for the *Quarterly Review* and for the *Proceedings* of the newly formed British Academy, he helped to ensure that Gardiner received the honour that was due to him as one of the leading English historians.

For years before Gardiner's death Firth had been his friend and amanuensis. As Gardiner wrote in the preface to the revised edition of his *History of the Great Civil War*:

> I wish it were possible for me to give adequate expression to my sense of the obligation under which I am to Mr Firth. He has generously allowed me to draw on his vast stores of knowledge concerning the men and things of this period and has always been ready to discuss with me any point of importance as it arose, often very considerably modifying the opinion at which I had originally arrived.[3]

Firth was the obvious choice to continue Gardiner's history from the point where he had broken off in 1656, and he did so specifically at Gardiner's request. The result was *The Last Years of the Protectorate 1656–58* published in 1909. This in turn was eventually carried forward in *The Restoration of Charles II* published as recently as 1955 by Firth's own friend and former student Godfrey Davies.[4] By this process of apostolic succession, therefore, the Gardiner tradition was ensured of a long, continuous life. In an obituary notice the *American Historical Review* accurately claimed that Davies 'did much to maintain the central tradition regarding [seventeenth-century English history] against eccentric revisions from writers of the left and of the right'.[5]

It was not that Firth's view of history and of the seventeenth century was simply an exact replica of Gardiner's. Firth, certainly in later life, did not share Gardiner's own religious convictions and, appropriate to one drawn from a well-known family of Sheffield metalmasters, he gave more emphasis to social and economic aspects than his predecessor had done. Firth, too, far excelled Gardiner in his broad and intimate knowledge of English literature – significantly he played a prominent part in the foundation of the English School at Oxford – and his style was undoubtedly superior.[6] Firth was inferior to Gardiner, however, as a linguist and as a lecturer, and his historical knowledge was in some ways less wide-ranging. 'I am conscious that I do not possess either the comprehensive knowledge or the perfect equipment which he [Gardiner] brought to his task.' So Firth wrote in the preface to *The Last Years of the Protectorate*. But Firth thought that Gardiner's early writings at times adhered too rigidly and mechanically to a chronological sequence. Far from exactly modelling himself on Gardiner, therefore, in this respect, Firth wrote his history of the years 1656–8 in the conviction that 'it seemed to me as important to show the temper of the time as to narrate the events'.[7] Firth's capacity for generalization was even more clearly revealed in his short study of *The Parallel Between the English and American Civil Wars* (1910). And Firth was not averse to publishing historical works of an unashamedly topical nature. His study of *The House of Lords During the Civil War* (1910) appeared at the height of Lloyd George's struggle with the upper house, and it expressed the hope that the evidence concerning seventeenth-century parliaments would serve 'for the instruction of their descendants'.

But such differences apart, Firth acknowledged Gardiner as his mentor and continued, extended, and, in his *Oliver Cromwell and the Rule of the Puritans in England* (1900), popularized Gardiner's model of the seventeenth-century crisis.[8] In Firth's view of the Civil War, puritanism was still at the heart of things, as he made abundantly clear in his critical comments on Clarendon's neglect of the religious factor (see p. 35). Firth's scientific method, too, had some of Gardiner's weaknesses, as W. S. McKechnie pointed out in a perceptive review of his book on the House of Lords.

> His interests reveal themselves as centring round principles and tendencies rather than families or individuals. Carefully suppressing, so far as that is possible, all personal prejudices or predilections of his own, he strives to allow the bare facts to speak for themselves subject to such colour as they may receive from the estimates of contemporaries.

The result of this method, McKechnie argued, was to some extent deceptive; conclusions seemed to emerge of their own accord whereas in fact, of course, it was the author who had established them.[9]

Trained at Oxford, where he was much influenced by Stubbs as Regius Professor, and remaining there for most of his academic career, Firth's earliest work was of an editorial kind. He brought out, for example, critical editions of the *Memoirs of Colonel Hutchinson* in 1885 and of *The Life of the Duke of Newcastle* in the following year. Firth's chief contribution as an editor, however, was in publishing *The Clarke Papers* – which he had himself discovered – in four Camden Society volumes between 1891 and 1901. (William Clarke was an influential member of the republican secretariat, and his papers are a tremendously important source for the military campaigns of the period, the relations between Parliament and the army, and for the events leading up to the Restoration in 1660.) Besides this important editorial work Firth was later an extremely active member of the Royal Commission on Public Records and contributed no fewer than 275 articles to the *Dictionary of National Biography*.

Firth had a keen interest in historiography, as the chapters on Raleigh, Milton, Clarendon, and Burnet in his *Essays Historical and Literary* make clear. In 1904 he contributed three detailed articles to the *English Historical Review* which established the way in which the final version of Clarendon's *History of the Rebellion* had been constructed from originally separate works (see p. 38 n. 40). Also in 1904 he supplied an important critical introduction to an edition of Carlyle's *Letters and Speeches of Oliver Cromwell*, while in 1913 he published a useful general survey of 'The development of the study of seventeenth-century history'.[10] Firth's major work in the field of historiography was his *Commentary on Macaulay's History of England*, which Godfrey Davies edited for publication in 1938. The book consisted of a series of Firth's lectures, the purpose of which had been,

> not merely to criticize the statements made by Macaulay and the point of view adopted by him, but also to show the extent to which his conclusions had been invalidated or confirmed by later writers who had devoted their attention to particular parts of his subject, or by the new documentary materials published during the last sixty years.[11]

By systematically examining such aspects as the genesis of Macaulay's *History*, his historical method, his use of authorities, and his treatment of particular subjects and characters, Firth tried to place Macaulay in perspective and to provide his students with a model of the critical method which they themselves should learn to practise.

Apart from his editorial work, his general surveys of the Civil War and Interregnum, and his writings on historiography, Firth had a special interest in military history. His well-known study of *Cromwell's Army* made its appearance in 1902, and at the time of his death he was still working on his *Regimental History of Cromwell's Army*. Firth approached military history in the broadest possible way. 'A civil war is not only the conflict of opposing principles', he wrote in the preface to *Cromwell's Army*, 'but the shock of material forces.'[12] Firth's chief concern was to explain Parliament's military superiority, and he became deeply involved, therefore, with questions of military organization, with discipline, pay, religion, and politics.

Firth became Regius Professor of History at Oxford in 1904 and did much to improve research facilities and the professional training of historians at the university. His intentions were announced in his inaugural lecture, *A Plea for the Historical Teaching of History* (1904), which caused such a stir that the aggrieved college tutors, resentful of Firth's haughty attack on their work and values, petitioned against it. Firth's difficulties stemmed from the anomalous position of history at Oxford as well as from his own defects of character. Although established as a course of study at the university, few of its students in fact went on to become historians themselves. These problems Firth set out to remedy by providing instruction in the handling of sources, and by encouraging postgraduate research.[13]

Godfrey Davies (1892–1957) was one of Firth's students, and with his book on the Restoration, he reached the point at which Gardiner himself had originally aimed when he launched his massive narrative history. Davies began his teaching career at Oxford, his own *alma mater*, but moved to America in 1925 to take up appointments first at the University of Chicago and then, from 1930, more congenially at the Huntington Library, San Marino, California. Besides his book on *The Restoration of Charles II*, Davies collaborated on Firth's *Regimental History of Cromwell's Army* (1940). In 1937, the year of Firth's death, he published *The Early Stuarts 1603–1660* in the Oxford History of England series, a work which in many ways was a summary of

Firth's and Gardiner's volumes. Davies's book was a densely packed factual narrative, and the clearest statement of his overall view of the period is found not in the text itself but in the introduction. 'The keynote of the seventeenth century', he wrote, 'was revolt against authority. Modern times as distinct from the Middle Ages had begun under the Tudors and were now developing rapidly'. However, Davies went on to say that:

> In some ways the 'Great Rebellion' is a better label than 'Puritan Revolution' for the movement that led to the execution of Charles I and the establishment of the protectorate. It is true that most puritans sided against the king, that the parliamentary commissions ran in the name of the king and parliament and thus afforded their holders a somewhat transparent screen against being called rebels, and that a war concerned mainly at the start with political sovereignty rather changed its character and became a crusade for religious freedom. Nevertheless the struggle, though at no time a class war, was to a large extent a revolution by the middle classes against personal government. They had been growing steadily in power under the Tudors when they had been allowed to participate in government at the will of the sovereign. Now they were no longer content merely to register approval of royal edicts.[14]

Davies collaborated with William Haller in editing *The Leveller Tracts 1647–53* (1944), and his *Essays on Later Stuart History* were published posthumously in 1958.

Other writers, too, acknowledged an obligation to Firth and Gardiner and followed their lead. One such historian was F. C. Montague (1858–1935) whose textbook on the period 1603–60 in a multi-volume *Political History of England* was first published in 1907.[15] Another was Sir J. A. R. Marriott (1859–1945), who in 1930 brought out a book called *The Crisis of English Liberty*. Marriott, whose own main research interests were not in this field, in his preface acknowledged a special debt to Gardiner and Firth. But Gardiner especially would have been horrified at the use to which his findings were being put. Gardiner firmly believed that the mingling of past and present was anti-historical; Marriott's approach to the seventeenth century was unashamedly present-minded.

> History, it has always seemed to me, is something more than a mere record of the past; it must necessarily represent the past as seen through the medium of the present. Consequently, each generation

must look at the past from a fresh angle. True of all periods, this is pre-eminently true of the history of the seventeenth century and of those who look back upon it from the twentieth. For this reason. The seventeenth century was confronted by problems which we thought it had permanently solved. Unexpectedly, they have in these latter days re-emerged; they are still, it seems, living issues; they still stir the blood of those who mingle in public affairs. . . .

I regretfully recognize that this avowal will cost me the good opinions of some 'orthodox' historians, and that I shall be accused of the deadly sin of 'reading history backwards'. But all history, save contemporary history, must, in a sense, be read backwards.[16]

As Marriott saw it – and as well as being a historian he had first-hand political experience as a Conservative MP – twentieth-century England faced much the same kind of crisis of liberty as seventeenth-century England had done.

This much is clear that under conditions greatly altered and in forms not always recognizable, devices adopted by the Stuart kings in their contest with parliament and in their relations with the judges are today making an unwelcome re-appearance. . . .

Recent tendencies have thus invested the history of the seventeenth century with new and arresting significance. It may not then be amiss to con once more the lessons which that period is pre-eminently calculated to teach.[17]

Twentieth-century Englishmen found themselves swamped by an ever-growing volume of legislation and confronted by a 'new despotism' in which the position of the central government and its experts was becoming daily more unassailable.

Yet another writer whose writings in a way helped to perpetuate Gardiner's influence in the twentieth century was G. M. Trevelyan (1876–1962). But Trevelyan, like Marriott and unlike Firth and Davies, could hardly be classified as Gardiner's disciple in the conventional sense; in his style of writing and view of the social function of history he owed far more to his great-uncle Macaulay. 'I have not been an original but a traditional kind of historian', Trevelyan wrote in his autobiography.

The best that can be said of me is that I tried to keep up to date a family tradition as to the relation of history to literature, in a period when the current was running strongly in the other direction towards history exclusively 'scientific', a period therefore when my old-fashioned ideas and practice have had, perhaps, a certain value as counterpoise.[18]

And he could take for granted as a matter of fact the consensus about the seventeenth-century national past over which the Victorians had earlier struggled. In his famous textbook *England Under the Stuarts* (1904) Trevelyan tried to bring together Gardiner's research and Macaulay's style. The American historian W. C. Abbott (a former research student of Firth's at Oxford), in one of the few serious academic reviews which the book received, saw its value as a work of popularization even though it made 'no great original contribution to knowledge'. 'That it bears any such relation to the seventeenth century as the work of Professor Gardiner bears to the period 1603–1660 or that of Bishop Stubbs to the constitutional development of England before 1485 no one could seriously maintain.'[19]

Despite his rejoinder to Professor J. B. Bury's 1902 Cambridge inaugural lecture on 'The Science of History', Trevelyan did not oppose 'scientific' history in any wholesale and indiscriminate way. As a student at Cambridge he developed a deep respect and admiration for Lord Acton. In the bibliography of *England Under the Stuarts* he described Ranke's work on England as 'one of the great histories of our country, too much neglected'. In the same book, Trevelyan spoke of Gardiner as '*the* authority on the period for both general readers and students', Firth's *Cromwell* was listed as 'the highest authority on the subject', while his *Cromwell's Army* was praised as 'the best book and the most learned authority on the military side of the war'.[20] It was not scientific history as such which Trevelyan attacked, but the excesses committed in its name, its harmful effects on style and therefore on history's role as a social educator, and, by no means least, its German origins. As he wrote in the second edition (1919) of his essays:

> If the first and most important essay [The Muse of History] was received better than I hoped at the time of its publication [1913], it will scarcely be regarded with more disfavour now, seeing what a dance German 'scientific' history has led the nation that looked to it for political prophecy and guidance. The wheel has indeed come full circle. Treitschke worship and Kultur are at a discount, and

Englishmen need no longer apologise for the free traditions of their own history and of their own great national historians.[21]

Historians like Carlyle, Macaulay, and indeed Sir Walter Scott, formed an important part of this national heritage, and it was wrong to ignore or reject them. Scott, he claimed in his inaugural lecture at Cambridge in 1927, 'did more for history, I venture to think, than any professed historian in modern times'. In the same lecture he praised Carlyle.

> The past was full of passion and passion is therefore one element in historic truth. Sympathy is a necessary part of understanding. Carlyle helped as much as Gardiner to elucidate the forgotten truth about the English Puritan era and the character and career of Cromwell about whom generations of dispassionate historians, Whig as well as Tory, had unerringly missed the point.[22]

Trevelyan's work, therefore, attempted to combine what was best in the two schools of history, although in the last analysis, like Macaulay, it was his literary style which was its hallmark. His style, however, was simpler, less complex and ornate than Macaulay's. *England Under the Stuarts* was a textbook, but as J. H. Plumb has remarked, 'surely no textbook has ever before or since been written with such gusto'.[23] Continuing in the 'family tradition', Trevelyan revived not only the art of narrative, but also in a frank and explicit way the Whig interpretation of the seventeenth century. 'The historian's bias', Trevelyan wrote, 'may sometimes help him to sympathize with the actual passions of people in the past whose actions it is his business to describe. Clio should not always be cold, aloof, impartial.'[24] In the pages of *England Under the Stuarts*, therefore, the idea of a Puritan Revolution, a struggle for liberty, was presented forcefully and vividly.

> England has contributed many things, good and bad, to the history of the world. But of all her achievements there is one, the most insular in origin, and yet the most universal in effect. While Germany boasts her Reformation and France her Revolution, England can point to her dealings with the House of Stuart. . . . At a time when the continent was falling a prey to despots, the English under the Stuarts had achieved their emancipation from monarchical tyranny by the act of the national will; in an age of bigotry, their own divisions had forced them into religious toleration against their real wish; while

personal liberty and some measure of free speech and writing had been brought about by the balance of two great parties. Never perhaps in any century have such rapid advances been made towards freedom.[25]

The 'Glorious' Revolution of 1688/9, of course, occupied an honoured place in Trevelyan's vision of seventeenth-century England – as in Macaulay's – and he devoted a separate study to it in 1938. But the Civil War period, too, had a share in this 'glorious' achievement and belonged to the same basic struggle for constitutional liberty. In Trevelyan's view the Civil War was fought over ideas and principles.

> For it was not, like the French Revolution, a war of classes. . . . It was a war not of classes or of districts, but of ideas. Here there was a nobler speculative enthusiasm among the chiefs and their followers, but less readiness to fight among the masses of the population, than in other contests that have torn great nations. The French Revolution was a war of two societies; the American Civil War was a war of two regions; but the Great Rebellion was a war of two parties.

Predictably, perhaps, he was less at ease with the Interregnum and with the power politics of Oliver Cromwell. It was no easier, however, for this descendant of a seventeenth-century Royalist family to say anything very positive about 'the second Stuart despotism' contrived by Charles II and James II. After the Civil Wars of the 1640s no further high point was reached until 1688.[26]

This concern for liberty was one of the central motifs of Trevelyan's voluminous output. It conditioned his historical approach, and even helped to determine the subjects he chose to deal with. It was not fortuitous that Trevelyan wrote on Wyclif, on Italian unification, and on seventeenth-century England. Such was Trevelyan's identification with the Whig tradition, in fact, that when Herbert Butterfield's book *The Whig Interpretation of History* appeared in 1931, it was widely taken as a thinly veiled attack on Trevelyan himself though his name was not specifically mentioned in the text.

Trevelyan's liberal, patriotic interpretation of seventeenth-century England was restated, more briefly, in his *History of England* (1926), and in his *English Social History* (1944). In the first of these two general works he declared:

The English Civil War was not the collapse of an out-worn society in a chaos of class hatred and greed, but a contest for political and religious ideals that divided every rank in a land socially sound and economically prosperous.

The causes of the war were not economic and were only indirectly social. Nevertheless the old aristocratic connection was apt to favour the King while the world that had arisen since the Reformation was apt to favour Parliament.

Trevelyan, too, made his contribution to perpetuating the hoary myth that 'all the Roman Catholics were for the King and more particularly for the Queen who was the real head of their party'.[27]

Trevelyan's *English Social History*, so patriotic, like Laurence Olivier's rousing film of *Henry V* made in the same year, that it can almost be regarded as an integral part of the war effort, repeated the same basic interpretation of the Civil War that he had first outlined forty years earlier.

> The Cromwellian revolution was not social and economic in its causes and motives; it was the result of political and religious thought and aspiration among men who had no desire to recast society or redistribute wealth. No doubt the choice of sides that men made in politics and religion was to some extent and in some cases determined by predispositions due to social and economic circumstance; but of this the men themselves were only half conscious. . . . Every class in town and country was itself divided. . . . [The Civil War was] more ubiquitous in its scope and area than the Wars of the Roses, but fought from less selfish and material motives.[28]

Few historians, perhaps, would have disagreed with this verdict if it had been written by S. R. Gardiner in the nineteenth century at a time, for instance, when the discipline of economic history was still in an infant state. But by 1944, recollections of Victorian self-confidence and prosperity were fast receding. Vastly different conditions now prevailed. Marxism was providing an intellectual and political alternative to liberalism. The traumatic effects of the Second World War were being experienced. Thus Trevelyan's unashamedly 'old-fashioned' view of seventeenth-century English history appeared at a time when the Gardiner/Firth historical orthodoxy – and all the assumptions on which it was based – was being called into question. Some historians at least were now arguing that the crucial element in the seventeenth-century crisis was precisely those 'material motives' and their social milieu which Trevelyan had disregarded. The most prominent (though not the most radical) of these historians was R. H. Tawney.

Notes

1 *TLS*, 25 September 1919, p. 515.
2 *TLS*, 9 October 1919, p. 549. I am indebted to Mr Arthur Crook, former editor of the *TLS*, for his help in trying to establish the identity of the anonymous 'Historian'. Unfortunately this proved impossible.
3 S. R. Gardiner, *History of the Great Civil War*, rev. edn (London, 1893), I, p. vii.
4 As Firth had written Gardiner's so Davies wrote Firth's obituary for the *Proceedings of the British Academy*, xxii (1937).
5 *AHR*, lxiii (1957), p. 280.
6 Godfrey Davies published a selection of Firth's *Essays Historical and Literary* (Oxford, 1938).
7 C. H. Firth, *Last Years of the Protectorate* (London, 1909), p. vi.
8 Gardiner reviewed Firth's book, *EHR*, xv (1900), pp. 803–4.
9 *EHR*, xxvi (1911), pp. 585–6.
10 *TRHS*, 3rd ser., vii (1913).
11 C. H. Firth, *Commentary on Macaulay's History of England*, ed. G. Davies (London, 1938), p. vii.
12 C. H. Firth, *Cromwell's Army* (London, 1902), p. vii. The military history of the Civil War – which this book has chosen to pass over very quickly – has continued to be an active branch of the historiography of the subject since Firth's day. See, for example, A. H. Woolrych, *Battles of the English Civil War* (London, 1961); P. Young and R. Holmes, *The English Civil War: A Military History of the Three Civil Wars 1642–1651* (London, 1974); and R. Hutton, *The Royalist War Effort* (London, 1982).
13 C. H. Firth, *A Plea for the Historical Teaching of History* (Oxford, 1904), pp. 15, 19. Firth's difficulties at Oxford, which depressed him greatly, are examined in an excellent article by J. P. Kenyon on 'Sir Charles Firth and the Oxford School of Modern History 1892–1925', in A. C. Duke and C. A. Tamse (eds), *Clio's Mirror: Historiography in Britain and the Netherlands*, VIII (Zutphen, 1985), pp. 163–84.
14 G. Davies, *The Early Stuarts 1603–1660* (Oxford, 1937), p. xxii.
15 For an explicit example of Gardiner's influence on Montague see p. 491 of his book.
16 J. A. R. Marriott, *The Crisis of English Liberty* (Oxford, 1930), pp. v–vi.
17 *Ibid.*, pp. 16, 18.
18 G. M. Trevelyan, *An Autobiography and Other Essays* (London, 1949), p. 1. On Trevelyan see J. M. Hernon, 'The last Whig historian and consensus history: George Macaulay Trevelyan 1876–1962', *AHR*, lxxxi (1976); Mary Moorman, *George Macaulay Trevelyan* (London, 1980); and J. P. Kenyon, *The History Men* (London, 1983), esp. pp. 226–35.
19 *AHR*, xi (1905–6), p. 378.

20 Trevelyan's *England Under the Stuarts* went through twenty-one editions, the latest of which was in 1966.
21 G. M. Trevelyan, *The Recreations of an Historian* (London, 1919), p. 8.
22 G. M. Trevelyan, *The Present Position of History* (London, 1927), pp. 16, 7. Trevelyan published an anthology of Carlyle's writings in 1953.
23 J. H. Plumb, *G. M. Trevelyan* (London, 1951), p. 17.
24 G. M. Trevelyan, 'Bias in history', in *An Autobiography and Other Writings*, p. 77.
25 G. M. Trevelyan, *England Under the Stuarts*, 12th edn (London, 1925), pp. 1, 516.
26 *Ibid.*, pp. 228, 229. See D. Cannadine, *G. M. Trevelyan. A Life in History* (London, 1992), esp. pp. 99–101, 201–2.
27 G. M. Trevelyan, *History of England* (London, 1926), pp. 406, 407.
28 G. M. Trevelyan, *English Social History* (London, 1944), pp. 234, 253.

7

The twentieth century: social interpretations of revolution

The test of an historian is not so much the final validity of his theories as the originality of his approach, his talent in devising new and
more fruitful ways of looking at the problems of the past. . . . Because
he first posed the questions in the answers to which lie the key to historical understanding of the period, 1540–1640 will remain 'Tawney's
century' for an indefinite period to come. (Lawrence Stone, 'R. H.
Tawney', *Past and Present*, 21 (1962), p. 77)

It is the strength of Hill's work that he realizes that there is a *whole
picture*, and that the parts are intrinsically interrelated: that no aspect
can be isolated and reified as a 'topic' of its own. It is the ways in
which different elements interconnect that give them their particular
historical significance and efficacy. Moreover Hill realizes that in part
these very interconnections are artefacts of our retrospective standpoint of interest: they are the relationships in which we are interested
from a particular point of view. (Mary Fulbrook, 'Christopher Hill
and historical sociology', in G. Eley and W. Hunt (eds), *Reviving the
English Revolution* (London, 1988), p. 48)

R. H. Tawney (1880–1962), although he disagreed with Trevelyan's
political presuppositions and found his conclusions unsatisfying,
would at least have concurred with the Cambridge Regius Professor's hostile views on the cold detachment of scientific academic
study. 'There is no such thing as a science of economics, nor ever
will be', Tawney wrote in 1913. 'It is just cant, and Marshall's talk
as to the need for social problems to be studied "by the same order
of mind which tests the stability of a battleship in bad weather" is
twaddle.'[1] Tawney studied history in order to understand present
problems.

Tawney's political writings – he became, of course, one of the great intellectual fathers of the Labour movement – and his work on history shared common origins, and both were suffused with his deep-rooted Christian Socialism. Tawney's pre-First World War commonplace book shows him wrestling with historical and modern problems simultaneously. Later, *The Acquisitive Society* (1922) and *Equality* (1931) told as much about his approach to the past as about his view of the twentieth-century crisis. For Tawney, history was not a source of 'dead' information; it was first a means to understanding, and then a guide to action. Such was his capacity to proceed on two fronts simultaneously that 1913 saw the publication of Tawney's essays on 'Poverty as an industrial problem' (in the twentieth century) and on 'The assessment of wages in England by the JPs' (in the sixteenth and seventeenth centuries).[2] For Tawney himself, this blending of past and present was a gain rather than a loss. Later critics – such as Kerridge and Elton – have taken the opposite view.

Tawney was drawn to the economic and social history of pre-Revolutionary England, a field where William Cunningham had led the way, partly as a result of his dissatisfaction with a purely political approach. ('It says so much and explains so little.') His experience of Workers' Educational Association teaching also contributed. 'The friendly smitings of weavers, potters, miners, and engineers, have taught me much about problems of political and economic science which cannot easily be learned from books.' So Tawney wrote in the preface to *The Agrarian Problem in the Sixteenth Century* (1912).[3] Above all, however, Tawney developed a particular interest in the sixteenth and seventeenth centuries because he saw this as a crucial period in the emergence of capitalism and of the changing relationship between economic power and political power.

The Agrarian Problem in the Sixteenth Century was Tawney's first book, and his preoccupation with the historical origins and consequences of capitalism was as clearly expressed there as it was in all his later writings on the early modern period. Small-scale peasant farming was overcome, he argued, by the aggressive forces of a growing rural capitalism, which gained strength from the redistribution of monastic lands in the sixteenth century and achieved victory in the Civil Wars and the settlements of 1660 and 1689.

With the destruction in 1641 of the Court of Star Chamber and the Councils of Wales and of the North, an end was put to the last administrative organs which could bridle the great landed proprietors. . . . Henceforward there was to be no obstacle to enclosure, to evictions, to rack-renting, other than the shadowy protection of the Common Law; and for men who were very poor or easily intimidated, or in the enjoyment of rights for which no clear legal title could be shown, the Common Law with its expense, its packed juries, its strict rules of procedure, had little help. Thus the good side of the Absolute Monarchy was swept away with the bad. . . . For to the upper classes in the eighteenth century the possession of landed property by a poor man seemed in itself a surprising impertinence which it was the duty of Parliament to correct, and Parliament responded to the call of its relatives outside the House with the pious zeal of family affection.[4]

Having pursued a new economic perspective on the English Revolution, Tawney moved on in his next and most famous major work to explore a socio-intellectual dimension of the seventeenth-century crisis. This was *Religion and the Rise of Capitalism* (1926), a work which brought together Tawney's own religious concerns and his interest in the origins of capitalism. 'I wonder if Puritanism produced any specific attitude towards economic matters?' Tawney had asked himself in his commonplace book in September 1912.[5] His own book, written in the light of Weber's *The Protestant Ethic and the Spirit of Capitalism* (1904), was an attempt to answer the question, and a whole generation of historians was influenced by its conclusions. Professor W. H. B. Court, a student at Cambridge when Tawney's classic was first published, recalled that this

was one of the books which everyone read. It responded brilliantly in typically Tawney fashion to the mood of a time of sharp disillusion and changing social values. He linked the study of history with sociology on the one side and with social philosophy on the other and asked where changes of social values in the past had come from.[6]

Tawney's modification of the Weber thesis lay in his stress on the initial conservatism of the reformed religion; it was only in the long run, he argued, as the result of a dual relationship between puritanism and society, that the godly discipline became compatible with the religion of trade.

Puritanism was the schoolmaster of the English middle classes. It heightened their virtues, sanctified, without eradicating, their convenient vices, and gave them an inexpugnable assurance that, behind virtues and vices alike, stood the majestic and inexorable laws of an omnipotent Providence, without whose foreknowledge not a hammer could beat upon the forge, not a figure could be added to the ledger. But it is a strange school which does not teach more than one lesson, and the social reactions of Puritanism, trenchant, permanent and profound, are not to be summarized in the simple formula that it fostered individualism. . . . There was in Puritanism an element which was conservative and traditionalist, and an element which was revolutionary. . . . That it swept away the restrictions imposed by the existing machinery is true; neither ecclesiastical courts, nor High Commission, nor Star Chamber, could function after 1640. But if it broke the discipline of the Church of Laud and the State of Strafford, it did so but as a step towards erecting a more rigorous discipline of its own. It would have been scandalized by economic individualism, as much as by religious tolerance, and the broad outlines of its scheme of organization favoured unrestricted liberty in matters of business as little as in the things of the spirit.[7]

Tawney's book, written in his unmistakable style, made a seminal contribution to a historical debate which has ever since continued to attract the attention of historians, sociologists, theologians, and economists.[8]

The large-scale work on sixteenth- and seventeenth-century England which for many years Tawney was known to be writing unfortunately never saw the light of day. The project had been outlined in rough as early as 1914. The scheme was to treat:

The rise of capitalism, beginning with the end of the sixteenth century, describing the economic policy of the Tudors and first two Stuarts, the economic causes for the opposition of the middle classes to the monarchy, the growth of the sects, the economic ideas of the Levellers, Diggers, ending with the economic results of the Revolution of 1688.[9]

'But shall I ever have time?' Tawney ended. In fact, Tawney only found time to publish, in 1941, his two articles on 'The rise of the gentry 1558–1640' and 'Harrington's interpretation of his age' and to bring out, in 1958, his monograph on *Business and Politics Under James I*.[10] Even so, it was a remarkable achievement and provided glimpses, at least, of the grand survey that might have been. The Ford Lectures he gave at Oxford in 1936 were never prepared for publication.

Business and Politics Under James I: Lionel Cranfield as Merchant and Minister was a case study of those general themes in seventeenth-century history with which Tawney had been concerned throughout his academic career. Through the biography of this one influential individual Tawney explored once more that 'seductive border region where politics grease the wheels of business and polite society smiles hopefully on both'.[11] The book's historiographical significance was partly that it revealed a new facet of Tawney's attitude to capitalism. As T. S. Ashton pointed out, 'Tawney, who in his earlier works, had tended to treat merchants and financiers with distrust here comes near to presenting a capitalist turned administrator as a hero.'[12] The change surprised even Tawney himself. He wrote to William Beveridge, his brother-in-law, in 1961, explaining that he began the book

> with a prejudice against [Cranfield] as a capitalist on the make. I ended with a respect for the man who, without being over-scrupulous in business, was in courage and public spirit head and shoulders above the awful gang of courtly sharks and toadies with whom, as a minister of the crown, he was condemned to mix, and sacrificed his career for the service of the state.[13]

From a wider point of view, the historiographical importance of the book was that it brought historians away from the parliamentary opposition back to the weaknesses of the central government.

> The monarchy, in short, does not fight a losing battle against a remorseless tide of rising prices. Before it can be submerged by the advancing flood it is well on the way to drown itself. . . . Tendencies already visible before the death of James make a too exclusive emphasis on the follies and misfortunes of his son difficult to accept. Among these tendencies not the least important . . . was the decline in the prestige of the monarchy.[14]

It was in his two famous articles on Harrington and on the rise of the gentry, published in 1941, that Tawney reached out most explicitly for a theory of the Civil War, and in so doing started a long controversy which became one of the *causes célèbres* of modern historiography. Tawney's essay on Harrington enlarged on the economic explanation of the seventeenth-century crisis put forward in *Oceana*, that it was the imbalance between economic realities and political structure which produced the Civil War. Tawney stressed the relative decline of the aristocracy ('In a period of sensational monetary depreciation, the economy of many noble landowners was an obsolete anachronism'[15]) and the rise of a new class of hard-headed, business-like gentry, alert to the opportunities provided by an expanding market. Using the detailed statistical evidence provided, for example, in Savine's *English Monasteries on the Eve of the Dissolution* and in *The Domesday of Crown Lands* by S. J. Madge, Tawney charted the process whereby land was redistributed away from the one group towards the other.[16]

The theme was elaborated, with all Tawney's distinctive eloquence, in his article on 'The rise of the gentry':

> To say that many noble families – though not they alone – encountered, in the two generations before the Civil War, a financial crisis is probably not an overstatement. The fate of the conservative aristocrat was, in fact, an unhappy one. Reduced to living 'like a rich beggar, in perpetual want', he sees his influence, popularity and property all melt together. . . . [But] the conditions which depressed some incomes inflated others; and, while one group of landowners bumped heavily along the bottom, another, which was quicker to catch the tide when it turned, was floated to fortune. The process of readjustment was complex; but two broad movements can be observed, affecting respectively the technique of land management and the ownership of landed property.[17]

Tawney buttressed the rhetoric of his thesis with statistics, demonstrating first a fall in the number of manors held by the aristocracy and, second, the growing importance of medium-sized landowners.

Tawney's thesis of the rise of the gentry was supported by a young Oxford historian, Lawrence Stone, when he rashly published an article on 'The anatomy of the Elizabethan aristocracy'.[18] Backed by some impressive (though insecurely based) statistics, Stone underlined Tawney's point about the decline of the aristocracy and argued that this was largely the result of their over-expenditure.

The 'storm over the gentry' broke in 1951 with the first of two contributions from H. R. Trevor-Roper (1914–), already well-known for his biography of Laud.[19] The article was directed against Stone, and in one of the most savage and devastating attacks ever to appear in the pages of a learned journal, Trevor-Roper ruthlessly undermined the foundations (statistical or otherwise) of Stone's fragile thesis. 'An erring colleague is not an Amalekite to be smitten hip and thigh', cried Tawney, angered by the tone of the debate.[20] Stone came back with 'The Elizabethan aristocracy: a re-statement',[21] but this was as much an apology as a rejoinder, and it took some years and much laborious research before this deflated author had sufficiently regained his confidence to launch his magisterial work of mature scholarship, *The Crisis of the Aristocracy*. But soon it was not just the disciple but the master himself who was under attack from Trevor-Roper. The tone was more respectful now. *The Gentry 1540–1640* opened with a compliment.

> Perhaps no man has stimulated the study of English history in the sixteenth century more effectively than Prof. Tawney: the century from 1540 to 1640, the century which separates the Dissolution of the Monasteries from the Great Rebellion, may almost be defined, thanks to his radical reinterpretation of it, as 'Tawney's century'. All historians who have since studied that period are inevitably, even if unconsciously, affected by his reinterpretation: they can no more think of it now in pre-Tawney terms than sociologists can think of society in pre-Marxist terms.[22]

But the compliment given, Trevor-Roper, one of the most brilliant historical essayists of the twentieth century, none the less elegantly but vigorously launched his attack. He attempted to counter and discredit Tawney's notion of the rise of the gentry with a rival and persuasive alternative thesis of the decline of the 'mere gentry', middling men whose precarious wealth was drawn from land alone at a time when inflation was playing havoc with landed incomes. These 'mere gentry' were the basis of the country party which, in opposing the stranglehold of the court, ultimately overthrew Charles I, and later were the chief advocates of decentralization under the republic. Those who rose in this period were rather, on the one hand, those gentry who had access to other, more lucrative, sources of income (office-holding, trade, and the law), and on the other hand the yeomen, who combined direct intensive farming with austere living.[23] An article by J. P. Cooper ('The counting of manors', *Ec.H.R.*, 2nd series, viii, 1956) lent support to Trevor-Roper's alternative explanation of social change and revolution by completely discrediting the statistical basis of the case which Tawney and Stone had put forward.

It was not long, however, before the tables were turned, and the Trevor-Roper thesis itself came under heavy attack from Christopher Hill and the American Perez Zagorin.[24] Both these writers emphasized the extreme frailty of some of the supposedly logical connections in Trevor-Roper's argument and its entirely nonstatistical approach; using his favourite method, his long essay was mainly an exercise in rhetoric. In particular, Trevor-Roper was criticized (quite rightly) for the ease with which 'mere gentry', 'small gentry', and 'declining gentry' came together in his argument, the three terms being used virtually synonymously. Hill was no more satisfied with Trevor-Roper's identification of the Independents with the 'mere gentry'.[25] Trevor-Roper was (with equal justice) called to account for asserting that in a period when food prices were still rising, agriculture was not a route to wealth. Conversely, Trevor-Roper's critics argued, his thesis exaggerated the ease with which court fortunes could be built up. The links which Trevor-Roper postulated between economic decay and religious nonconformity were similarly unconvincing to his critics; *either* kind of religious extreme (puritanism or Catholic recusancy) would do equally well, apparently, as a refuge from decline. The American historian J. H. Hexter (1910–96) joined the chorus of critics almost simultaneously, but broadened his front to attack Tawney as well. His stylish essay 'Storm over the gentry' was first published in *Encounter* in 1958, but appeared in an extended and more scholarly form three years later as part of his *Reappraisals in History*. Both Tawney and Trevor-Roper, for different reasons, were accused of subscribing to a narrow economic determinism. Hexter's contribution, like others from the same author, tended to make the attack an end in itself, but the demolition work cheerfully completed, Hexter offered a modified version of Lawrence Stone's earlier thesis stressing, however, a *military* rather than an economic decline of the aristocracy in the century before 1640.

Tawney himself took no further part in the debate on the gentry after his postscript of 1954. His age, of course, disinclined him from so doing, but there were other reasons. Given the limited sources available to the disputants, Tawney frankly saw no additional value in the controversy, or in engaging further in a debate, the tone of which he found increasingly distressing and distasteful.[26] Tawney began the debate but did not expect or desire that his interpretation would become a stifling orthodoxy. Although he firmly believed that historians should generalize and draw out the main outlines, Tawney recognized that the only way forward in this subject, as in others, lay in further research; a new synthesis of the evidence would then become possible.

One obvious direction in which further research on the gentry could be undertaken was at the local and regional level. (These studies are examined in chapter 9.) Another was explored with commendable thoroughness in *The Crisis of the Aristocracy 1558–1640* (Oxford, 1965). Lawrence Stone (1919–), its author, graduated from Oxford and taught there until 1963 when he joined the brain drain to America and became Dodge Professor of History at Princeton. His main field of interest has been that of social structure and social process in early modern England. His books on *Social Change and Revolution in England 1540–1640* (London, 1965), *The Causes of the English Revolution 1529–1642* (London, 1972, 2nd edn, 1986), his work on English education, and his massive, multi-volume study of English marriage and divorce, all bear witness to his wide-ranging and prolific work in this area.[27] His monumental exploration of *The Crisis of the Aristocracy* took fourteen years' research to complete. A kind of companion volume, *An Open Elite? England 1540–1880*, this time computer aided, appeared in 1984.[28]

Tawney was given pride of place in the acknowledgements to his 841-page epic on aristocratic crisis.

> My greatest intellectual obligation is to the late Professor R. H. Tawney. He was always ready with information, advice, and encouragement and I owe him more than perhaps he realized, for it was his writings which first stimulated my interest in Tudor history. Above all he taught me to shun the temptation to which economic and social historians are so exposed, of taking the mind out of history. I am particularly anxious to acknowledge my dependence on his inspiration and example, since I have ultimately come to differ substantially from many of his conclusions.[29]

A vast and impressive undertaking, Stone's *Crisis of the Aristocracy* had twin objectives:

This book sets out to do two things: firstly to describe the total environment of an *élite*, material and economic, ideological and cultural, educational and moral; and secondly to demonstrate, to explain and to chart the course of a crisis in the affairs of this *élite* that was to have a profound effect upon the evolution of English political institutions. It is therefore at once a static description and a dynamic analysis; it is a study in social, economic and intellectual history, which is consciously designed to serve as the prolegomenon to, and an explanation of, political history.[30]

The 'crisis' thesis which Stone advanced combined some of his earlier ideas from the days of the gentry controversy with those of J. H. Hexter. The result was an interpretation which stressed the aristocracy's loss not just of military power but of lands and prestige. In Elizabeth's reign the real income of the peers declined sharply so that in the seventeenth century, above all, they were in a disadvantageous position as compared with the greater gentry. It was the decline in the authority and power of the aristocracy, argued Stone, which ultimately made possible the collapse of Charles I's government in 1640, since its effect was to leave the monarchy in a dangerously exposed and isolated position.

It was a provocative thesis which in the nature of things was unlikely to produce general assent, even though all reviewers paid tribute to the vast research effort involved. Alan Everitt, for instance, criticized what he found to be Stone's tendency to tie himself up in a statistical straitjacket. As a local historian he was critical, too, of Stone's insensitivity to the richness of provincial life, and expressed doubts as to whether the 'crisis' was as catastrophic as Stone argued or indeed whether it was quite so central to the outbreak of the Great Rebellion.[31] Quantification, of course, was an essential part of Stone's method, and was what chiefly distinguished it from the inspired or unfortunate sampling of the gentry controversy. What Stone offered in his book was not a few well-chosen examples to illustrate his points, but a survey of *all* the titular aristocracy with estimates of the mean net income of the peerage in 1559, 1602, and 1641.

> I think one has an obligation today to try to quantify. It is true that in the pre-statistical age of the sixteenth and seventeenth centuries, accurate figures are very hard to come by: error is enormous, and one

is dealing very probably with highly hypothetical figures if one is dealing globally. My only defence of my figures is that they are better than nothing.[32]

But as one reviewer of *The Crisis of the Aristocracy* pointed out, 'Professor Stone's confidence in his statistics appears to increase in direct relation to their distance from his original qualifying remarks'. D. C. Coleman was even more sceptical about the value of many of Stone's calculations.[33] Stone, however, stuck unrepentantly to his historical method and there was a pronounced statistical emphasis in his more recent book, *Family and Fortune: Studies in Aristocratic Finance in the Sixteenth and Seventeenth Centuries* (Oxford, 1973) and in *An Open Elite?* The latter, like *The Crisis of the Aristocracy* before it, had two objectives – to analyse a social world in its various aspects (from demography to foxhunting) and to advance a thesis. The thesis here was that there was long-term stability in the composition of the landed élite from the seventeenth to the nineteenth centuries.

Stone's final conclusions on the aristocracy were not closely in line with Tawney's views on the subject. Indeed the hallmark of Tawney's influence on other historians was not the creation of an orthodoxy to which growing numbers subscribed; Tawney, unlike Sir Lewis Namier, did not found a historical 'school'. His main legacy was not his methods or even his conclusions as such, but his stress on a questioning approach to the past and on a humane concept of economic history.[34] Tawney encouraged historians to go out in new directions and, responding to his invitation and stimulus, they have enlarged, extended, and in some cases corrected his own work on English society before the Revolution. The roll-call of historians of seventeenth-century England acknowledging an intellectual debt to R. H. Tawney is impressive and extends over a long period.[35] As a tribute to the old man on his eightieth birthday a Festschrift was prepared with F. J. Fisher as editor.[36] Jack Fisher (1908–88) himself, Tawney's friend, amanuensis and colleague, supplied an appropriate introduction on 'Tawney's century'. The other contributors included Joan Thirsk, Ralph Davis, D. C. Coleman, and Robert Ashton, all former research students of Tawney at the LSE, as well as Lawrence Stone and Christopher

Hill. Hill's contribution to the Tawney volume was on 'Protestantism and the rise of capitalism', and in its opening paragraph he paid tribute to the master's classic on that controversial subject.[37]

Hill had never been a student of Tawney's, his political opinions were more left-wing than those of the LSE professor, and it was not Tawney but T. S. Eliot who first attracted him to the study of seventeenth-century ideas and society. None the less Hill deeply admired Tawney as a historian and as a man. 'One thing that made Tawney great in my eyes', Hill has said, 'was his politics. He was a deeply committed Christian Socialist. [For him] heavenly intervention went hand in hand with human action.' But it is impossible to conceive of Tawney, Hill has argued, without Karl Marx, 'Marx because the main feature of Tawney's work is a never failing concern for the underdog in history'.[38] Hill was the young Marxist historian from Oxford, 'a fine scholar of Tudor and Stuart England', whom Tawney once defended in the 1950s from attack by an anti-communist colleague. On another occasion, Tawney said, 'I don't mind Hill being a Marxist, but I do wish he wouldn't sing the doxology at the end of every piece he writes'. 'That got right under my skin', Hill has written in some reminiscences of Tawney, 'because it showed me that to him I looked exactly what I was reacting against. I have tried ever since to keep the doxological element in my writing under control.'[39] Tawney, himself, 'a Victorian in all but essentials', was in no sense a Marxist. 'Was the Civil War a bourgeois revolution?' Tawney was once asked. 'Of course it was a bourgeois revolution. The trouble is the bourgeoisie were on both sides.'[40] Tawney took Marx and Marxism seriously but did not subscribe to its ideology.

Until the 1920s and 1930s, in any case, British socialism was not divided into separate Marxist and social democratic fronts. It was not until the break with the Labour Party in the 1920s that communism began to run a separate course in Britain and not until the crisis years of the 1930s, when the Left Book Club was campaigning for an alliance with the Soviet Union, that it began to acquire an intellectual wing. Although a ceaseless critic of social injustice, Tawney never felt a cultural alienation from his own society, nor did he feel that Stalinism was a workable or appropriate solution to Britain's social and political problems.[41] Events, however, overtook Tawney. The current of enthusiasm for Marxism in the 1930s left him to some extent out on a limb both politically and historiographically. He remained there for different reasons in the 1950s in the hysterical anti-Marxism of the Cold War.

Christopher Hill (1912–), at Balliol College Oxford for most of his career, has been one of the most prolific and bold of all historians of the English Revolution; 'the master historian of his chosen field – Hill's half century', is how one American scholar has described him.[42] Deservedly, his work has received a great deal of attention. Hill's leading – though not now dominant – position in the field of Revolutionary studies today rests both on the quality and vast quantity of his output. It is a position which was neither easily nor rapidly achieved. For a long time his Marxism came up against the solid wall of a prejudiced Establishment and undoubtedly obstructed his career development.

It would clearly be unrealistic and unprofitable to treat his books and articles produced over the last sixty years as a single unified whole. There are some common characteristics, certainly, but obviously a historian's work and method change and mature over time as his knowledge deepens. And they move in different directions. Marxism has been for Hill the most obvious of these common characteristics, but this, too, has changed greatly both in emphasis and intensity. There is a strong case, then, for treating Hill's earlier work separately rather than as part of a monolithic whole as John Sanderson did in an article published twenty years ago.[43] And it is not only the earlier work itself which needs to be considered but also the context – the world of the left-wing intellectuals of the 1930s and 1940s – in which it took shape.

The landmarks are clear enough. Hill visited Russia in 1935–36 and his earliest published articles were to a large extent the direct product.[44] Their evangelistic purpose was simply to introduce English historians, still largely committed to the Gardiner/Firth model of the 'Puritan Revolution' to the invigorating challenges of Marxist reinterpretation. Hill, therefore, summarized the views of the Soviet historians Savine, Pashukanis, Angarov, and Arkhangelsky on England's mid-seventeenth-century Revolution.

The second landmark came in Battle of Britain year 1940 with *The English Revolution 1640*, a kind of Marxist textbook which

Hill edited as a celebration of the 300th anniversary of the seventeenth-century explosion. (It was also, potentially, his political testament should he die in the Second World War.)[45] Hill's bold opening paragraph threw down the gauntlet to historians of the old school.

> The English Revolution of 1640–1660 was a great social movement like the French Revolution of 1789. An old order that was essentially feudal was destroyed by violence, a new and capitalist social order was created in its place. The Civil War was a class war, in which the despotism of Charles I was defended by the reactionary forces of the established Church and feudal landlords. Parliament beat the King because it could appeal to the enthusiastic support of the trading and industrial classes in town and countryside, to the yeomen and progressive gentry, and to wider masses of the population whenever they were able by free discussion to understand what the struggle was really about.

Discussing the capitalist penetration of agriculture and industry in this period, Hill lost no opportunity to make analogies with the modern world.

> The seventeenth century English Revolution changed the organisation of society so as to make possible the full development of all the resources of that society. A transition to socialism will be necessary to win the same result in England today.

'We have still much to learn from the seventeenth century', was Hill's provocative last sentence in this essay.[46]

Hill wrote a number of articles in the 1940s for such journals as *The Modern Quarterly*, *The Communist Review*, and for the American Marxist periodical *Science and Society*, and in them aired his dissatisfaction with the 'Puritan Revolution' model of England's seventeenth-century crisis. For Christopher Hill there was only one alternative model which could possibly replace Gardiner's. 'It is difficult to see what satisfactory synthesis could be advanced other than the Marxist view that the English Revolution was a bourgeois revolution. This interpretation can alone explain all the new facts, fit them into a coherent story which makes sense'.

> Marxism restores unity to history because it restores real, live, working and suffering men and women to the centre of the story and does

not deal merely with their abstract ideas and rationalizations. . . . Finally the Marxist approach, and it alone, can restore to the English people part of their heritage of which they have been robbed.[47]

The final landmark in these early publications had a different route to the realization of the same purpose. This was a source-book, co-edited with Edmund Dell, *The Good Old Cause: The English Revolution of 1640–1660* (1949), assembled to show the validity of the Marxist interpretation through contemporary evidence of classes and class struggle before 1640, the sects and democracy, and the Levellers and Diggers.

The chief significance of Hill's early work, then, was that it publicized Marxist ideas on the seventeenth-century crisis at a time when very little of that kind was available in English. A translation of the German Marxist historian Eduard Bernstein's *Cromwell and Communism*, it is true, had come out in 1930. Harold Laski's semi-Marxist 'essay in interpretation' on *The Rise of European Liberalism* joined it in 1936. Holorenshaw's *The Levellers and the English Revolution* was published in 1939 by the Left Book Club, the same organization which in the previous year had issued A. L. Morton's *A People's History of England*.[48] In this work Morton (1903–87), communist teacher, bookseller, and journalist, offered the first full-length Marxist history of England. 150 pages were devoted to the sixteenth and seventeenth centuries and in them Morton proclaimed:

> In spite of all that has been said to the contrary it cannot be too strongly insisted that the Civil War *was* a class struggle, *was* revolutionary and *was* progressive. A Royalist victory would have meant a dead hand imposed upon the development of the country, feudal forms devoid of real content ossified into a monarchical tyranny, the persistence of a less advanced form of social and political organisation.[49]

The Left Book Club also brought out in 1940 David Petegorsky's semi-Marxist account of *Left-Wing Democracy in the English Civil War: A Study of the Social Philosophy of Gerrard Winstanley*.[50] Maurice Dobb's *Studies in the Development of Capitalism* appeared in 1946 and was joyously hailed by fellow Marxists as 'the most important single work on British history so far produced by an English marxist'. 'This erudite work', Christopher Hill declared, 'puts the English Revolution into perspective as part of the rise of capitalism on a European scale'. R. H. Hilton, writing in the *Labour Monthly*, readily agreed.[51] Harvey Kaye in his study of *The British Marxist Historians* (Cambridge, 1984) was surely right to emphasize the seminal importance of Dobb and his book.

Seminal also for Hill and other British Marxists of this period was the Historians' Group of the Communist Party, formally established after the Second World War. Here historians such as Eric Hobsbawm, Victor Kiernan, John Saville, R. H. Hilton and others argued over and reconstructed the English past. The Historians' Group provided Hill, he later admitted, with 'the best academic training I ever got'.[52] One product – though it retained a separate existence – of the Historians' Group was the journal *Past and Present* which Christopher Hill helped to launch in 1952. Originally subtitled 'a journal of scientific history', no journal has since done more for seventeenth-century studies. R. H. Hilton and Maurice Dobb joined Hill on the original editorial board and John Morris and Eric Hobsbawm were the first editors. Hill's article on 'Puritans and the poor' appeared in the second issue of the journal in November 1952. In 1970 the *Past and Present* Society paid tribute to him by making him its President.

The Marxist-oriented *Past and Present* struggled for existence in its early years, and it would have been difficult then to predict its present position in the historical 'Establishment'.[53] For English Marxists, too, as well as for Marxist journals, the 1950s proved a critical period. Discontent with Stalinism and with the Communist Party leadership in Britain was being expressed by the Party's intellectual wing. The historians E. P. Thompson and John Saville moved into open attack in 1956, Thompson denouncing the Party's 'uncritical and inaccurate propaganda about the Soviet Union extending over a period of twenty years'. Both Thompson and Saville were suspended from Party membership as a result. The rising in Hungary, and official Communist Party reactions to it, brought the crisis to a head. The Party leadership was challenged from the branches and a massive loss of membership resulted, including many of the Party's intellectuals such as Christopher Hill.[54]

Intellectually as well as politically, the crisis of the mid-1950s must have been a traumatic and chastening experience. Certainly, the aggressive propagandist element and the doxology which Tawney had complained about have since receded in Hill's writing. *Economic Problems of the Church from Archbishop Whitgift to the Long Parliament* (Oxford, 1956), Hill's first major research work, published at the age of 44, signalled a new period in his writing and a much more flexible and sophisticated use of the Marxist model. As one (decidedly anti-Marxist) reviewer of the book trenchantly put it,

> Mr Hill is a Marxist who has come out of his trance. He does not say so himself, either because he is still a little dazed or because a candid confession would be too painful. But anyone who remembers *The English Revolution* or its companion volume [*The Good Old Cause*] can see that the spell is broken.

D. H. Pennington, a former student of Hill's, reviewing the book in *History*, took a similar line, contrasting the two Christopher Hills, the one a Marxist propagandist and the other a critical scholar. Pennington pointed to the 'undogmatic realism' of Hill's new book, its self-mockery about 'that ubiquitous class the rising bourgeoisie', and its invitation to 'ignore his occasional genuflexions [to Party dogma] and listen to the sound sense he talks'.[55] R. H. Tawney too, no doubt to Hill's immense gratification, saw *Economic Problems of the Church* opening up a new and important phase in Hill's work as a historian, and lavished praise on its thorough, penetrating and convincing scholarship.[56]

Since 1956 and *Economic Problems of the Church*, Christopher Hill's output of books and articles has been extraordinarily immense. Invariably full of insights, informative, lively, challenging, and frequently controversial, Hill's work rests on a secure mastery of the printed word in the seventeenth century. Between 1958 and 1990 no fewer than six volumes of his essays – containing eighty separate articles – have appeared and they by no means exhaust the full store from which they were selected.[57] Two widely used textbooks came from his pen in 1961 and 1967: *The Century of Revolution* and *Reformation to Industrial Revolution: A Social and Economic History of Britain 1530–1780*. The rest of his books are research works. *Society and Puritanism in Pre-Revolutionary England* (London, 1964) was a companion volume to *Economic Problems of the Church*. *Intellectual Origins of the English Revolution* (Oxford, 1965), his Ford Lectures at Oxford, has been one of Hill's most provocative books, variously regarded as one of the stimulating studies of the seventeenth-century crisis or, by a particularly cantankerous American historian, as a 'blunt instrument' from which ensued an 'historiographic disaster'.[58] A second edition, published in 1997, leaves the original text virtually intact but adds thirteen new, short chapters (115 pages) to extend and justify the original arguments with new material. Compared with this thunderbolt his *Antichrist in Seventeenth-Century England* (Oxford, 1971) was positively low-key. His *World Turned Upside Down: Radical Ideas during the English Revolution* (London, 1972), arguably his finest book, was more stirring and made a decisive contribution to the development of 'history from below' (see pp. 185–6). Hill has also brought out three unconventional biographical studies of leading individuals of the time. *God's Englishman: Oliver Cromwell and the English Revolution* (London, 1970) was as much concerned with the ways in which the great Civil War general and Lord Protector was shaped by his times as with the ways in which he imprinted himself on them. Hill's controversial *Milton and the English Revolution* (London, 1977) boldly reclaimed the poet and radical heretic from literary critics interested only in the words on the page, and placed him firmly in the contemporary revolutionary ferment on which he drew and to which he variously contributed. Hill's book on Bunyan (*A Turbulent, Seditious and Factious People: John Bunyan and his Church 1628–1688*) appeared in 1988 and was no less contextual in its strategy. Above all, Bunyan's highly specific local context was carefully established – a particularly necessary task in view of the fact that he was the first major English writer who was neither university educated nor London based. His *Holy War*, 'Bunyan's vast cosmic drama, is rooted in the politics of a small town'.[59] For Bunyan, as for so many others in this period, the Bible was a revolutionary text. Hill's *The English Bible and the Seventeenth Century Revolution* (London, 1993) explored the complex ramifications of this politico-cultural phenomenon. 'The ideas which divided the two parties in the Civil War and which divided conservatives from radicals among the victorious Parliamentarians, were all found in the Bible'.[60] Hill's most recent book – *Liberty against the Law: Some Seventeenth-Century Controversies* (London, 1996) is another of this author's contributions to 'history from below' and is best discussed in that context. (See pp. 186–7.) At the age of 85 the indefatigable Hill is preparing a new book on seventeenth-century women.

One of Hill's most consistent preoccupations has been with the need to find a satisfactory synthesis to replace Gardiner's model of the 'Puritan Revolution'.[61] His first instinct in his early writings, as we have seen, was simply to dismiss the notion out of hand. But such brusque treatment, as Hill himself came to recognize, did Gardiner less than justice. 'We all stand on his shoulders', he wrote in *God's Englishman*. In *The Century of Revolution*, writing of the historian's tendency to emphasize social and political causes of the Civil War at the expense of its religious dimension, Hill argued that 'the very idea of a Puritan Revolution is more complex than we used to think'. Nevertheless, 'the Puritan Revolution was an unfortunate concept. It suffered both from exaggeration by Gardiner's epigones and from an equally exaggerated reaction away from it by some twentieth-century historians.' 'In some recent explanations of the English Revolution', Hill wrote in *Economic Problems of the Church*, 'the material conflicts seem to me to have been presented too simply, in terms of outs versus ins, country versus court gentry, the bourgeoisie versus a "social justice" state. . . . Puritanism would not have been the historical force it was if it had been a mere economic reflex.' 'Puritan Revolution' in a real sense, Hill argued in *Change and Continuity*, put historians on the wrong tack.

> For this implied, or could appear to imply, a revolution made by Puritans in order to establish a Puritan society. It assumes an element of conscious will among an identifiable group of those who made the revolution. Most historians reject the Puritan Revolution these days, and interpret the events of 1640–60 in more sociological terms. There is no need why such interpretations need make any assumptions about purpose. The object indeed of a sociological interpretation should be to account for events which cannot be explained in terms of human intentions.[62]

Before either using or discarding the term 'Puritan Revolution', Hill has insisted, historians obviously need to be clear about what they understand by 'puritanism' and 'revolution'. And in his book of essays published under that title in 1958, Hill argued that from this point of view English historians had laboured under a double disadvantage.

> First, few of us have any experience of revolutions. The British tradition since the seventeenth century has been almost entirely gradualist: revolutions are things we learn about from books. Secondly, most of us think that we do know all about Puritanism. But too often we are thinking – whether with conscious hostility or unconscious sympathy – not of Puritanism at all but of later non-conformity. . . . So we have to make a deliberate intellectual effort to open our minds to revolutionaries, and to clear them of erroneous prepossessions about Puritans. When we are dealing with men who were simultaneously Puritans and revolutionaries the task is doubly exacting.

The whole corpus of Hill's mature work can be summed up as an attempt to come to terms with the complexities of puritanism and revolution, and with the role of ideas and ideology. One could cite the fact, for instance, that Hill has devoted two whole books (*Economic Problems of the Church* and *Society and Puritanism*) to 'some of the non-theological reasons which might lead men to oppose the Laudian regime in the English church' and indeed to the 'non-theological reasons for supporting the Puritans, or for being a Puritan'.[63]

Hill's definitions of revolution occasionally have had a circular tendency. His theories of causation and of dialectic have been less than clear, as the philosopher W. H. Dray, for one, has pointed out. 'Although Hill generally provides his readers with a wealth of data about similarities, spatio temporal coincidences, social opportunities and the like, he rather too often leaves them to work out the connection for themselves'.[64] There has been an uneasy reliance on assumed links, associations, and a blurring of the distinctions between latent preconditions and active sufficient causes. Mary Fulbrook perhaps puts her finger on it. 'Hill's particular strength', she writes, 'has been in richness of illustration and evocation rather than in rigour of theoretical testing'.[65] Causes, connections, and consequences have not always been properly distinguished. Conal

Condren, one of Hill's critics, goes further. 'Hill postulates a very general causative sequence which is neither falsifiable nor verifiable, takes no explanatory risks, and so must itself remain in the realms of faith'. Hill offers accounts, the same relentless critic continues, of 'the occasional happening which is taken to symbolise a series of highly rarified abstractions, a series of revolutions of indeterminate identity and rather long duration, and these in turn are attached to the barely discussed English Revolution'.[66]

Hill's interpretation – unrepentantly adhered to in the face of criticism – has been that the changes associated with the events of the mid-century were so momentous that 'revolution' is the only term that can describe them. 'The 1640s and 50s marked the end of medieval and Tudor England' in government, agriculture, commerce, colonial and foreign policy, industry, finance, religion, and ideas.[67] In a broadcast talk Hill said:

> I certainly think it was a revolution, and I don't think much of some recent attempts to argue the contrary – . . . . I would see the English Revolution of the seventeenth century as clearing the path for the sort of economic development which made the Industrial Revolution happen in England first.

Judged by its *consequences*, the English Revolution was a bourgeois revolution in the Marxist sense.

> I would think of what happened in the seventeenth century as being, in the marxist sense, a bourgeois revolution. I don't think that two classes lined up to fight, any more than they have done in any revolution. There were members of all classes on both sides. But what I think I understand by a bourgeois revolution is not a revolution in which the bourgeoisie did the fighting – they never do that in any revolution – but a revolution whose outcome is the clearing of the decks for capitalism.[68]

This shift in Hill's writing towards *results* (as witnessed in his book *Some Intellectual Consequences of the English Revolution* (London, 1980)) was significant for what it had to say about his changing preoccupations. The stress on *revolution*, however, is unswerving and Hill in 1998 is as committed to this central fact as he was sixty years ago.

'The word "Puritan" ', Hill has argued, 'is an admirable refuge from clarity of thought.'[69] It was used by contemporaries in a variety of ways, and no simple religious or politico-religious definition is adequate to describe its whole range of meanings. Originally it was 'a reproachful name', and its political and religious ramifications also had a pronounced social dimension. Puritanism, Hill contended in *Society and Puritanism in Pre-Revolutionary England* and elsewhere, appealed particularly to the 'industrious sort of people', 'those smaller employers and self-employed men, whether in town or country, for whom frugality and hard work might make all the difference between prosperity and failure to survive in the world of growing competition'.[70] 'There were social reasons for the puritan ministers' special emphasis on the duty of working hard, for extolling the dignity of labour.' Puritanism, then, was primarily the ideology of the large group of economically independent yeomen, artisans, and small and middling merchants. Sabbatarianism was, as much as anything, a means of conducting industrial life on a more rational and methodical basis. 'Without the backing of large numbers of humbler men, Puritanism could never have challenged the crown and the bishops: the civil war could never have been fought and won.'[71] Hill's interpretation of puritanism – and, of course, he covers far more ground than this brief summary can suggest – is interesting and important, but lingering doubts remain as to whether Hill has, first, entirely succeeded in defining accurately the socio-economic context in which puritan ideas were received and, second, shown how the puritan gentry can be accommodated in his model.

'Puritanism was perhaps the most important complex of ideas that prepared men's minds for revolution, but it was not the only one.' In his *Intellectual Origins of the English Revolution*, Hill looked at some of the others, 'particularly at those which appealed to "the middling sort", to merchants, artisans, and yeomen', and in so doing produced his most controversial work.[72] 'Within less than a decade successful war was levied against the King; bishops and the House of Lords were abolished; and Charles I was executed in the name of his people. How did men get the nerve to do such unheard of things? . . . If there was no Rousseau, perhaps there were Montesquieus, Voltaires and Diderots of the English Revolution?'[73] Hill argued that there were indeed such counterparts, and he devoted his book to looking at the ferment of ideas associated with Bacon, Ralegh, Coke, and the London scientists.

> Bacon, Ralegh, Coke, together with the many lesser figures whom we have studied in this book, helped to undermine men's traditional belief in the eternity of the old order in Church and state, and this was an immense task, without the successful accomplishment of which there could have been no political revolution. . . . Scientific utilitarianism and radical Protestantism grew up side by side in the urban centres, with support from some gentlemen but deeply rooted in the middle and lower middle class. . . .
>
> The Civil War was fought largely by Puritans, with useful support from the scientists, against (among other things) the 'inquisitorious and tyrannical duncery' of the bishops and consequent intellectual frustration. This struggle had its counterpart inside Oxford and Cambridge: only the Puritans and scientists could never have won there without support from outside.[74]

Hill's preface to *Intellectual Origins of the English Revolution* expressed the view that 'my object was not to write a definitive work, but with luck to start a discussion'. He certainly succeeded. A lively debate ensued on the jousting ground of *Past and Present* and elsewhere, which criticized Hill's view of scientific advance in England for being too insular in conception, treating England in isolation from Europe. The debate also called in question Hill's use of evidence and the connections he postulated between puritanism and science.[75] (Charles Webster's weighty and learned volume on *The Great Instauration: Science, Medicine and Reform* (London, 1975) profitably carried forward the discussion of these and other related issues.)

Hill's special province has always been that of relating ideas to society. 'Historians are interested in ideas', he has asserted, 'not only because they influence societies, but because they reveal the societies which give rise to them. Hence the philosophical truth of the ideas is irrelevant to the historian's purpose.'[76] Explicitly confronting the vexed question of the relationship between the climate of ideas, ideology, and the Revolution in his *Intellectual Origins*, Hill wrote:

> Ideas were all-important for the individuals whom they impelled into action; but the historian must attach equal importance to the cir-

cumstances that gave these ideas their chance. Revolutions are not made without ideas, but they are not made by intellectuals.[77]

Holding back, therefore, from the view that ideas are causally efficacious in themselves, Hill has none the less seen ideas as a necessary element in the chain of causation. Intellectual break-throughs, old ideas with new content, 'class' differentials in inter-preting those ideas, time-lags in securing their acceptance, have all received Hill's attention. One of the clearest statements of all this is Hill's book on *The English Bible* (London, 1993) which is wholly concerned both with the specific ways in which this central text was used and with its ubiquitous role in defining the ethos of the age. Nor has he been content to restrict himself simply to those whose ideas happened to win. The unsuccessful 'revolt within the Revolution' was the work not of a lunatic fringe but of earnest, soul-searching men, and the historian, he pleaded, ought to take it seriously.[78]

Hill himself has been one of the first to admit that 'a socio-logical approach to intellectual history carries its own risks', as does the psychological. Ideas have a history of their own and are not simply a reflection of economic conditions or needs. But equally, pedigrees of ideas can be plotted with a totally spurious precision. 'It is always easy to construct chains of causes once you know what you have to explain.' There is the danger, too, of being over- (and falsely) selective in treating the evidence. In the preface to *Intellectual Origins* Hill wrote:

> I was advancing a thesis, not attempting to sketch the intellectual history of England in the fifty years before 1640. I therefore picked out evidence which seemed to me to support my case. So, though I hope I suppressed no facts which make against me, I have often . . . omitted facts which seemed to me 'neutral'.

In *Puritanism and Revolution* there is a related statement.

> I am selecting unfairly, for in each case Perkins qualifies heavily by insisting that riches are good *as they are used*, that men must desire them to glorify God, not for themselves. And he denounces engrossers, forestallers, usurers in the traditional manner. But I suspect that many good bourgeois in the congregations of Perkins and his followers would follow the same principles of selection as I have done.

Another significant statement from Hill about his use of sources comes in *The English Bible*.

> My object in this book is to try to assess the part played by the Bible in the lives of Englishmen and women during England's revolutionary seventeenth century. . . . I have read widely but not very systematically. . . . I have done the best I can on the basis of many years of desultory general reading in and around the subject . . . in Puritan and radical writings and Anglican commentaries on the Puritan wing. For my purposes the more traditional views of Catholics and high Anglicans seemed less relevant.[79]

Hill's critics, however, have argued that although he recognized these traps, this has not prevented him from falling into them. 'The trouble is,' wrote Trevor-Roper, 'when we skim through sources looking only for such evidence as supports our case, we tend only to notice such convenient evidence: and thus in spite of our efforts to be impartial, scholarship is transformed into advocacy.' The case against Hill has been put even more forcefully by the accomplished American demolition expert J. H. Hexter, who accused him of systematic 'source-mining' to accumulate material on specific points, and then of compulsive 'lumping' of evidence together into a preconceived pattern.

> Each historian lives under an especially heavy obligation to police himself. Far from just looking for evidence that may support his thesis, he needs to look for vulnerabilities in that thesis and to contrive means of testing them. Then, depending on what he finds, he can support the thesis, strengthen its weak points, or modify it to eliminate the weaknesses in it. He should in effect always be engaged in an inner dialectic, compensating for history's limitations with respect to codified, externalized conditions of proof by being a hard master to his own mind. For a historian of great erudition and vivid imagination to fail to do this is for him to fail his colleagues, to place on them a burden that should have been his. Christopher Hill so fails his colleagues. It is too bad.[80]

It seems that venom may have taken over from reason in the way that it did over half a century ago in the debate on the historical method of S. R. Gardiner (see p. 100). Hill's method involves 'source-mining', certainly – doesn't that of any historian?

– and, to use Hexter's unhappy term, it also involves 'lumping', if by that is meant interpreting and synthesizing; most historians, in fact, want to make some sense out of history. Hill's method and approach to history, however, like anyone else's, have their limitations. There is much repetition in his work. There are unresolved problems in his theories of causation. He has relied almost exclusively on printed sources, even though ideas and attitudes are expressed in manuscripts as well as in books and often with greater immediacy, openness, and local understanding. He has been more interested in change than in continuity.

But Hexter was surely unreasonable to attack Hill's method *as such*, and in a spirited and convincing reply Hill defended not just himself, but also a view of the purpose of historical study to which most historians would probably subscribe.

> The professor's division of historians into lumpers and splitters (his elegant phrases) revives an old distinction . . . between those who try to make sense of history and those who see nothing in it but the play of the contingent and the unforeseen, who think everything is so complicated that no general statements can safely be made, who are so busy making qualifications that they forget that anything actually happened. . . .
>
> Historians whose sole concern is with tortoise watching have an enjoyable hobby which satisfies the academic's sense that he is different from the vulgar. But it is not self-evidently superior.[81]

No-one could accuse Christopher Hill of tortoise watching! And significantly even some of his recent critics end up praising him. John Morrill, for example, in a review article which highlighted Hill's weaknesses, concluded by saying,

> Christopher Hill has dwelt on the way in which some vital groups worked out their destiny in those desperate days. He may have illuminated part of the picture and left other parts in the shade. But as we all struggle to make sense of the English Revolution, we will for a long time yet owe him a massive debt. Because of him, I know many vital things about the English Revolution; but for him I might never have wanted to know anything about it.

Even more notably Alastair MacLachlan, in a pugnacious book devoted to attacking Marxist accounts of the English Revolution, ends by conceding that Hill has 'poured out books of high quality and monumental learning'. He pays tribute to Hill's enviable capacity for self-criticism and to his

> extraordinary responsiveness to changes in historical fashion and in society at large . . . The result was a Marxism that was constantly renewing itself . . . From *Sovieticus Triumphans* to *Radicalistus Agonistes* – Hill's work presented a wonderful ensemble of Marxist preoccupations and interpretations.[82]

From such an opponent this is high praise indeed. Few historians have done as much as Christopher Hill to enlarge our understanding of the social history of the English Revolution and of the changes in ideas which went with it. Few historians have shown more willingness to go on extending their research, taking account of the work (and criticisms) of others, and refining their ideas. Hill has always been ready to revisit his work and former conclusions and to atone for past fixations, myopias and neglect. His current project on seventeenth-century women is clearly the result of the guilt he now feels for largely ignoring women's part in history for so long. 'We have to undertake a bigger rethink about the past than even feminist historians have yet realized', he has said.[83] He has been no less determined, it is true, to remain unrepentant when convinced he has got it right, but in these cases he has offered more evidence and has not simply dug in his heels. (The rationale and structure of the new edition of *Intellectual Origins* are very revealing from that point of view.)[84] Taking a wider view few historians have contributed more to the development of social history as a discipline. Hill's influence, even outside the seventeenth-century field, has been considerable. (E. P. Thompson's work on the eighteenth and early nineteenth centuries demonstrates a clear intellectual debt to one who was 'Master of more than an old Oxford College'.)[85] Not surprisingly, then, the names of many of Hill's former students will figure prominently in later chapters.

Hill's influence, however, has not been a constant. In recent years Revisionists have tended to dismiss him. (See pp. 218–28.) Their students have not been encouraged to read him. In the USA several of his most recent books have been remaindered. Hardline Marxists like Norah Carlin now find Hill too tame for their liking, and say so in print.[86] Two publications above all illustrate the particular character of Hill's influence and chart the vicissitudes of his reputation. The first is his Festschrift – aptly named *Puritans and Revolutionaries* – which was presented to him in 1978. It was a splendid tribute to one of the most learned, prolific, and generous of modern historians and demonstrated incontrovertibly the decisive inspiration which Hill has provided in seventeenth-century studies; almost without exception the essays in the collection developed themes first explored by Hill himself. But there was no consensus among the contributors, and some of them noticeably disagreed with Hill's convictions and conclusions. (Nicholas Tyacke's analysis of 'Science and religion at Oxford before the Civil War' was a case in point; in it he called into question Hill's claims for the specific contribution of puritanism to the intellectual revolution and advanced instead the argument that there was only 'a negative correlation between religion and science'.) But the lack of unanimity in the volume should not surprise us. Hill, like Tawney, never wished to create a school of disciples. The second publication, issued ten years later, stands in stark contrast to the first. It was seen by its editors as a necessary reaction against what appeared to be a 'discounting of Hill's contribution to seventeenth-century studies'. Pointedly entitled *Reviving the English Revolution*, this was no Festschrift but a carefully orchestrated *defence* of this historian's achievement against his critics and of the continued relevance of his work.[87]

Notes

1 J. M. Winter and D. M. Joslin (eds), *R. H. Tawney's Commonplace Book* (Cambridge, 1972. *Ec.H.R.* Supplement, 5). See also J. M. Winter, 'R. H. Tawney's early political thought', *PP*, 47 (1970).

2 Both of Tawney's essays are reprinted in R. H. Tawney, *The American Labour Movement and Other Essays*, ed. J. M. Winter (Brighton, 1979). The most recent discussion of Tawney's socialism and his contribution to the Labour Party is A. Wright, *R. H. Tawney* (Manchester, 1987).

3 N. B. Harte (ed.), *The Study of Economic History* (London, 1970), p. 106. Also R. Terrill, *R. H. Tawney and his Times: Socialism as Fellowship* (London, 1974), pp. 39–40, D. O. Ormrod, 'R. H. Tawney and the Origins of English Capitalism', *Hist. Workshop J.*, xviii (1984), D. A. Martin, 'R. H. Tawney's normative economic history of capitalism', *R. Soc. Econ.*, xliii (1985). For the critics see E. Kerridge, *Agrarian Problems in the Sixteenth Century and After* (London, 1969), esp. p. 15, and G. R. Elton, *TLS*, 11 February 1977. The characteristically trivial, egocentric and caustic comments of A. L. Rowse, *Historians I Have Known* (London, 1995) do not merit attention.

4 Tawney, *The Agrarian Problem in the Sixteenth Century* (London, 1912), pp. 399, 400.

5 Winter and Joslin, *R. H. Tawney's Commonplace Book*, p. 29.

6 W. H. B. Court, *Scarcity and Choice in History* (London, 1970), p. 18.

7 R. H. Tawney, *Religion and the Rise of Capitalism* (London, 1926), pp. 211, 212.

8 In the historical debate on the subject opposing positions have been taken by Christopher Hill, 'Protestantism and the rise of capitalism', in F. J. Fisher (ed.), *Essays on the Economic and Social History of Tudor and Stuart England* (Cambridge, 1961), and H. R. Trevor-Roper, 'Religion, the Reformation and social change', in the book of that name (London, 1967). The economist's contribution is represented by K. Samuelsson, *Religion and Economic Action* (Stockholm, 1961).

9 Winter and Joslin, *R. H. Tawney's Commonplace Book*, pp. 80, 81.

10 These and other essays by Tawney are conveniently reprinted in J. M. Winter (ed.), *History and Society: Essays by R. H. Tawney* (London, 1978) and Tawney, *American Labour Movement*.

11 R. H. Tawney, *Business and Politics under James I: Lionel Cranfield as Merchant and Minister* (Oxford, 1958), p. 83. Menna Prestwich, *Cranfield: Politics and Profits under the Early Stuarts* (Oxford, 1966), supplements Tawney's volume.

12 T. S. Ashton, 'Richard Henry Tawney', *Proc. Brit. Acad.*, xlviii (1963), p. 477.

13 Quoted in Terrill, *R. H. Tawney*, p. 103.

14 Tawney, *Business and Politics*, pp. 140, 291.

15 Tawney, 'Harrington's interpretation of his age', reprinted in Winter, *History and Society*, p. 78.

16 See S. B. Liljegren, *The Fall of the Monasteries and the Social Changes in England leading to the Great Revolution* (Lund and Leipzig, 1924).

17 Tawney, 'Rise of the gentry', reprinted in Winter, *History and Society*, pp. 92, 94.

18 *Ec.H.R.*, xviii (1948).

19 H. R. Trevor-Roper, *Archbishop Laud* (London, 1940).

20 Tawney, 'The rise of the gentry: a postscript', in Winter, *History and Society*, p. 126. By using this metaphor, Hill has written, Tawney 'is not making a theological allusion. He wants us to see Prof Trevor-Roper as a barbarian killer from a primitive stage of Middle Eastern history'. (Review of Terrill, *R. H. Tawney*, in *Balliol Parish Magazine* (1974), p. 30.) On Trevor-Roper as a controversialist see V. Mehta, *Fly and the Fly Bottle* (London, 1962).

21 *Ec.H.R.*, 2nd ser., iv, 1952.

22 *Ec.H.R.*, Supplement 1 (1953).

23 As a social group yeomen were better covered historically than most at the time Trevor-Roper was writing. See Mildred Campbell, *The English Yeoman under Elizabeth and the Early Stuarts* (New Haven, 1940. 2nd edn, London, 1960).

24 C. Hill, 'Recent interpretations of the Civil War', in *Puritanism and Revolution* (London, 1958). P. Zagorin, 'The social interpretation of the English Revolution', *J. Ec. Hist.*, xix (1959).

25 Trevor-Roper published some second thoughts on the Independents in 'Oliver Cromwell and his parliaments', in R. Pares and A. J. P. Taylor (eds), *Essays presented to Sir Lewis Namier* (London, 1956).
26 Terrill, *R. H. Tawney*, p. 101.
27 L. Stone, 'Social mobility in England 1500–1700', *PP*, 33 (1966), 'The educational revolution in England 1560–1640', *PP*, 28 (1964), 'Literacy and education in England 1640–1900', *PP*, 42 (1969), *The University in Society* (Princeton, NJ, 1974), *The Family, Sex and Marriage in England 1500–1800* (London, 1977), *The Road to Divorce: England 1530–1987* (Oxford, 1990), *Uncertain Unions: Marriage in England 1600–1753* (Oxford, 1992), *Broken Lives: Separation and Divorce in England 1570–1857* (Oxford, 1993).
28 On *An Open Elite?* see the reviews by C. Clay (*Ec.H.R.*, 2nd ser., xxxviii (1985), pp. 452–4) and by C. W. Brooks (*EHR*, ci (1986), pp. 176–9).
29 L. Stone, *The Crisis of the Aristocracy* (Oxford, 1965), p. xviii.
30 *Ibid.*, pp. 7–8.
31 A. Everitt, 'The peers and the provinces', *Ag.H.R.*, xvi (1968).
32 *Listener* (4 October 1973), p. 450.
33 R. Ashton, 'The aristocracy in transition', *Ec.H.R.*, 2nd ser., xxii (1969), p. 311. D. C. Coleman, 'The gentry controversy and the aristocracy in crisis', *Hist.*, li (1966).
34 Critics of Stone's thesis in *An Open Elite?*, like those of *Crisis*, have again questioned the statistical validity of his findings, and pointed out that in practice his coverage is restricted to the very apex of the elite (the great territorial magnates), and that as a result upward mobility into the middling and lesser gentry is ignored. Stone's conclusion that 'the traditional concept of an open elite is dead' is, therefore, they argue, an optical illusion. L. Stone, 'R. H. Tawney', *PP*, 21 (1962), J. D. Chambers, 'The Tawney tradition', *Ec.H.R.*, 2nd ser., xxiv (1971), N. B. Harte (ed.), *The Study of Economic History* (London, 1970), p. xxviii.
35 These include A. P. Wadsworth, Julia de Lacy Mann, W. G. Hoskins, D. Brunton, D. H. Pennington, Alan Everitt, Peter Bowden, J. U. Nef, and George Yule.
36 Its unwieldy title is best relegated to a footnote: F. J. Fisher (ed.), *Essays in the Economic and Social History of Tudor and Stuart England in honour of R. H. Tawney* (Cambridge, 1961).
37 Hill in Fisher, *Essays*, pp. 35–6.
38 Quoted in V. Mehta, *Fly and the Fly Bottle* (London, 1962), pp. 163–4. In 1950 Hill was pleased to be able to record that 'Professor Tawney has himself advanced a long way from his early Fabianism in politics'. ('Historians and the rise of British capitalism', *Science and Society*, xiv (1950), p. 310 n. 10.)
39 Terrill, *R. H. Tawney*, pp. 273–4.
40 Terrill, *R. H. Tawney*, p. 244. Hill, *Balliol Parish Magazine* (1974), p. 31.
41 George Orwell described the Communism of the 1930s as 'the patriotism of the deracinated' (quoted in Terrill, *R. H. Tawney*, p. 238).
42 R. B. Schlatter, *AHR*, lxxviii (1973), p. 1054.

43 Sanderson, 'Reflections upon Marxist historiography: the case of the English Civil War', in B. Chapman and A. Potter (eds), *W.J.M.M. Political Questions* (Manchester, 1975). Hill has also been discussed extensively in H. J. Kaye, *The British Marxist Historians* (Cambridge, 1984).

44 Hill, 'Soviet interpretations of the English interregnum', *Ec.H.R.*, viii (1938), pp. 159–67, 'The agrarian legislation of the Revolution', *EHR* (1940) reprinted in Hill, *Puritanism and Revolution* (London, 1958), pp. 153–96.

45 G. Eley and W. Hunt, *Reviving the English Revolution* (London, 1988), p. 99.

46 C. Hill, *The English Revolution 1640* (London, 1940), pp. 9, 27 n. 1, 82.

47 C. Hill, *Science and Society*, xiv (1950), pp. 309–10, 320–1.

48 Henry Holorenshaw was the pseudonym chosen by the scientist Joseph Needham (J. Lewis, *The Left Book Club: An Historical Record* (London, 1970), p. 8).

49 Hill, *Science and Society*, xiv (1950), p. 313. A. L. Morton, *A People's History of England* (London, 1938), p. 222.

50 David Petegorsky (1915–56), a Canadian-born Jew, studied under Harold Laski at the LSE in the late 1930s, and his doctoral thesis formed the basis of his book. This was his only publication in the field; after the Second World War his work centred on Jewish affairs. (I am indebted to Prof. Morris Silverman of Yeshiva University, New York, for this information.)

51 Hill, *Science and Society*, xiv (1950), p. 315. R. H. Hilton, *Labour Monthly* (January 1947), pp. 29–30. The reviews indicate how inseparable the Marxist writers of this period could easily become. Both Hill and Hilton were thanked by Dobb in his preface 'for guidance concerning the Tudor and Stuart age'.

52 Quoted in L. Humber and J. Rees, 'The good old cause – an interview with Christopher Hill', *International Socialism*, 56 (1992), p. 128.

53 For some discussion of the establishment and growth of the journal *Past and Present* see C. Hill, '*Past and Present*; origins and early years', *PP*, 100 (1983), pp. 3–14, J. Le Goff, '*Past and Present*: later history', *PP*, 100 (1983), pp. 14–28.

54 This paragraph is based on H. Pelling, *The British Communist Party: A Historical Profile* (London, 1958).

55 A. Simpson, *JMH*, xxix (1957), p. 261, D. H. Pennington, *Hist.*, xlii (1957), pp. 236–8. The book was enthusiastically reviewed by the American historian W. K. Jordan in *AHR*, lxii (1957), pp. 613–14, and by Norman Sykes (*EHR*, lxxiii (1958), pp. 294–8) though he felt that the economic factors had been overplayed at the expense of the religious.

56 Winter, *History and Society*, pp. 221–8.

57 They are *Puritanism and Revolution* (London, 1958), *Change and Continuity in Seventeenth-Century England* (London, 1975), *Writing and Revolution in Seventeenth-Century England* (Brighton, 1985), *Religion and Politics in Seventeenth-Century England* (Brighton, 1986), and *A Nation of Change and Novelty: Radical Politics, Religion and Literature in Seventeenth-Century England* (London, 1990).

58 *TLS*, 28 November 1975, p. 1419.

59 Hill, *A Turbulent, Seditious and Factious People*, p. 240. Not all have been

convinced by Hill's account of Bunyan. J. C. Davis – one of Hill's recent spar-
ring partners – sees too many loose ends in Hill's interpretation which, he
insists, perversely underestimates the conservative in Bunyan (J. C. Davis,
'Puritanism and Revolution: themes, categories, methods, and conclusions',
HJ, 34 (1991), pp. 483–4).

60 Hill, *The English Bible*, p. vii.

61 Elliot Rose in his *Cases of Conscience: Alternatives Open to Recusants and
Puritans under Elizabeth I and James I* (Cambridge, 1975), p. 177 n. 1 makes
the extraordinary claim that Hill's work has *affirmed* the idea of the Puritan
Revolution.

62 C. Hill, *God's Englishman: Oliver Cromwell and the English Revolution*
(London, 1970), p. 268, Hill, *The Century of Revolution 1603–1714*
(Edinburgh, 1961), p. 75, Hill, *Economic Problems of the Church* (Oxford,
1956), pp. x, xiii, Hill, *Change and Continuity in Seventeenth-Century
England* (London, 1975), p. 279.

63 Hill, *Puritanism and Revolution*, p. vii; Hill, *Society and Puritanism in Pre-
Revolutionary England* (London, 1964), p. 9.

64 W. H. Dray, 'Causes, individuals and ideas in Christopher Hill's interpretation
of the English Revolution', in B. Y. Kunze and D. D. Brautigam (eds), *Court,
Country and Culture: Essays on Early Modern British History* (Rochester, NY,
1992), p. 25.

65 Mary Fulbrook, 'Christopher Hill and historical sociology', in Eley and Hunt,
Reviving the English Revolution, p. 48.

66 C. Condren, 'Christopher Hill on the English Revolution: a sceptical decoding
of significance', in S. N. Mukherjee and J. O. Ward (eds), *Revolution as History*
(Sydney, 1989), pp. 33, 31.

67 This interpretation is outlined most clearly in *Reformation to Industrial
Revolution* (London, 1967).

68 *Listener* (4 October 1973), pp. 448–9. Contrast C. Wilson, 'Economics and
politics in the seventeenth century', *HJ*, v (1962), and the same author's
England's Apprenticeship 1603–1763 (London, 1965). See also Joan Thirsk
and J. P. Cooper (eds), *Seventeenth-Century Economic Documents* (Oxford,
1972), p. v.

69 Hill, *Society and Puritanism*, p. 13. He will have nothing to do with the school
of thought which denies to puritanism any distinctive identity of its own. See
C. H. and C. K. George, *The Protestant Mind of the English Reformation
1570–1640* (Princeton, NJ, 1961), I. Breward, 'The abolition of puritanism',
J. Relig. Hist., vii (1974), and M. G. Finlayson, *Puritanism and the English
Revolution: The Religious Factor in English Politics before and after the
Interregnum* (Toronto, 1983). See also W. Lamont, *Puritanism and Historical
Controversy* (London, 1996).

70 Hill, *Society and Puritanism*, p. 134. Hill's work on puritanism runs
parallel at many points with that of the American historian William
Haller. See the latter's books on *The Rise of Puritanism* (New York, 1938)
and *Liberty and the Reformation in the Puritan Revolution* (New York,
1955).

71 Hill, *Society and Puritanism*, pp. 138, 135.

72 C. Hill, *Intellectual Origins of the English Revolution* (Oxford, 1965), p. 6.

Hill's work needs to be seen in relation to R. K. Merton, *Science, Technology and Society in Seventeenth-Century England* (Bruges, 1936, 2nd edn, New York, 1970).

73 Hill, *Intellectual Origins*, pp. 5, 1–2.

74 *Ibid.*, pp. 291, 294, 314.

75 H. F. Kearney and T. K. Rabb debated the subject with Hill in *Past and Present*. These essays are collected together in C. Webster (ed.), *The Intellectual Revolution of the Seventeenth Century* (London, 1974). See also A. R. Hall, 'The Scientific Revolution and the Puritan Revolution', *Hist.*, 1 (1965), and N. Tyacke, 'Science and religion at Oxford before the Civil War', in D. H. Pennington and K. Thomas (eds), *Puritans and Revolutionaries* (Oxford, 1978), and C. Webster, *The Great Instauration: Science, Medicine and Reform* (London, 1975).

76 C. Hill, *The World Turned Upside Down* (London, 1972), p. 15.

77 Hill, *Intellectual Origins*, p. 3.

78 Hill, *Antichrist in Seventeenth-Century England* (Oxford, 1971), Hill, *The Experience of Defeat* (London, 1984), Hill, B. Reay, and W. Lamont, *The World of the Muggletonians* (London, 1983). See also P. Toon, *Puritans, the Millenium and the Future of Israel* (Cambridge, 1970) and P. Christianson, *Reformers and Babylon: Apocalyptic Visions from the Reformation to the Eve of the Civil War* (Toronto, 1977).

79 Hill, *Intellectual Origins*, pp. 2, vii, Hill, *Puritanism and Revolution*, p. 230, Hill, *The English Bible*, p. vii.

80 H. R. Trevor-Roper, *Hist. and Theory*, v (1966, p. 73. See also Blair Worden's review of Hill's *Change and Continuity in Seventeenth-Century England* in *New Statesman* (24 January 1975), p. 113. Hexter, *TLS* (24 October 1975), p. 1252. See also *TLS* (28 November 1975). Hexter, more or less unrepentantly, reprinted this attack on Hill in *On Historians* (London, 1979), pp. 227–51. See W. G. Palmer, 'The burden of proof: J. H. Hexter and C. Hill', *JBS*, xix (1979), pp. 122–9. For some of Hexter's earlier forays into the demolition business see his *Reappraisals in History* (London, 1961). On Hexter see W. H. Dray, 'J. H. Hexter, neo-Whiggism, and early Stuart historiography', *Hist. and Theory*, xxvi (1987), pp. 133–49.

81 Hill, *TLS* (7 November 1975), p. 1333.

82 J. Morrill, *The Nature of the English Revolution* (London, 1993), p. 284, A. MacLachlan, *The Rise and Fall of Revolutionary England: An Essay on the Fabrication of History* (New York, 1996), pp. 127, 179, 325.

83 Hill, *A Nation of Change*, p. 246.

84 In a recent review (*THES* 28 November 1997) of the new edition of Hill's book Lisa Jardine pays tribute to Hill's importance but bemoans the 'strikingly bland and fusty' packaging given to the volume by Oxford University Press and the absence of a proper context for his interventions in debate. 'Have Hill's "enemies"', she asks, 'in the end vanquished him by making him donnishly respectable?'

85 Thompson used the phrase in his dedication to Hill of his book *Whigs and Hunters* (London, 1975).

86 Norah Carlin, 'Marxism and the English Civil War', *International Socialism*, 10 (1980), pp. 113–28.

87 Eley and Hunt (eds), *Reviving the English Revolution*. See also M. Roberts, 'A nation of prophets: England and Christopher Hill', *Hist. Workshop J.*, 27 (1989), pp. 164–73, and A. Callincos, 'Bourgeois revolutions and historical materialism', *International Socialism*, 43 (1989), pp. 113–71. Callincos argues in favour of the continued vitality of Hill's model of the English Revolution.

8

The twentieth century:
social complexities

The allegiances of individuals do not appear to have been determined by their social status or wealth. There were prosperous and declining landed gentry, merchants, and lawyers on both sides. Also it is not clear what is the relevance of social and economic motivation to individuals who changed sides or, what was more common, remained neutral in the 1640s.

Two major charges can be levelled against the participants in the 'causes of the English Revolution' debate. The first is that too many broad hypotheses have been made without sufficient factual basis. The second is that historians have not always been clear what they are trying to explain. (Barry Coward, *The Stuart Age: A History of England, 1603–1714* (London, 1980), p. 161)

Are we to conclude, then, that social interpretations of the English Revolution are bound to fail, that there is no connection between the rise of agrarian capitalism within an aristocratic and landlord shell and the mid-seventeenth-century conflicts? In my opinion, such a conclusion would be premature, to say the least. (Robert Brenner, 'Bourgeois revolution and transition to capitalism', in A. L. Beier *et al.* (eds), *The First Modern Society: Essays in English History in Honour of Lawrence Stone* (Cambridge, 1989), p. 303)

Like Karl Marx before them Tawney, Stone and Hill all boldly and controversially attempted broad social interpretations of the English Revolution. Very noticeably in the last decade they have had few direct followers. One of them, Mark Gould – sociologist and metatheorist – offered a strikingly ambitious social model of the English Revolution. His book on *Revolution in the Development of Capitalism: The Coming of the English Revolution*

(Berkeley, L. A., 1987) was designed to provide 'an examination of seventeenth-century English social structure; specifically an attempt to explain the genesis of revolution within that social structure, and to speculate on the consequences of revolution for the transformation of it'.[1] The result of the endeavour, however, was self-evidently a kind of sociology and not social history. Robert Brenner (1943–), on the other hand, writes from within the historical profession. An American Marxist, a former student of Lawrence Stone, and now – significant title – Professor of History and Director of the Center for Social Theory and Comparative History at the University of California, Los Angeles, Brenner has gone in for history on the grand scale.[2] The place of the English Revolution in the transition from feudalism to capitalism has been his principal preoccupation since the 1970s and was the underlying theme of his epic study of *Merchants and Revolution: Commercial Change, Political Conflict and London's Overseas Traders, 1550–1653* (Cambridge, 1993). Its lengthy model-building postscript – deflated by some of its more conservative reviewers – was one of the most striking features of an otherwise densely detailed book.

Relishing controversy, Brenner has called into question both traditional social interpretations and the non-revolutionary, short-term factor scenarios offered as alternatives in their place.[3] Brenner argued that the chief weakness of traditional social interpretations of the Tawney and Hill kind was

> the inability of its adherents to demonstrate that English agrarian society was reproducing both a feudal and a capitalist landed class in the seventeenth century, let alone that those classes took opposing sides in the political conflicts of that era.[4]

Social interpretations of a different kind, drawing their inspiration from the later Marx, however, have had for Brenner a powerful validity. Both in his earlier articles and in his *magnum opus* Brenner has made much of the differentiations and contradictions in the development of capitalism in England and of their relation to state formation. Following Stone and his depiction of something other than a terminal crisis of the aristocracy, Brenner argued that out of that crisis came solutions as aristocratic landlords rationalized and exploited their estates and increasingly became more commercially minded. It was 'the development of capitalism within an aristocratic landlord framework that both provides the key to the specific path of long-term political evolution in early modern England and helps to explain why this evolution did not take place without profound conflicts'.[5] The tensions between different forms of merchant capitalism (the old established 'company' merchants and the enterprising 'new' merchants heaping up profits in the unregulated trades with the American colonies and the West Indies) formed the substance of his major book which linked them integrally to the parliamentary revolution of the 1640s and the Commonwealth of the 1650s.

Brenner's book, 'a monumental exercise in *l'histoire integrale*', blended social history with political history.[6] Most of today's social historians – who have often turned their backs on past politics – are more interested, it seems, in social complexities than in overarching interpretations, and their characteristic mode of analysis tends to be thematic. They are often more concerned with structures rather than dynamics and less concerned with the whole picture. They have focused on particular social groups (on the 'middling sort' and on individual professions, for example), on particular kinds of religious experience, on the family, and on women. Through detailed painstaking research the internal features and subtleties of society in the early seventeenth century have become more clearly delineated. For a variety of reasons overviews are currently less and less fashionable. A backlash against the Marxists, distrust of sociology and its claims, and the rise of Revisionism (see pp. 218–28) have all contributed. So, unquestionably, has the growing specialization of historical research. It is no doubt significant that neither Tawney, nor Stone, nor Hill undertook a PhD as part of their training. 'I think there may be something to be said', Hill has written, 'for breaking the universal tyranny of the DPhil . . . A danger of the thesis approach is its encouragement of the classic historian's vice of continuing to learn more and more about less and less. Some never become interested in . . . wider aspects of society and its culture'.[7] Adrian Wilson and some of the contributors to *Rethinking Social History* (Manchester, 1993) have documented the failure of social history to deliver what its visionaries expected of it in the 1960s and to engage in a meaningful two-way traffic of ideas with the social sciences. One of the most conspicuous features of recent work on social history, they insist (and echo Christopher Hill in this), has been its *enclosure* since the 1970s. Too many of its practitioners, they argue, have been content to produce self-contained histories of particular topics and to confine themselves within an inappropriate, inherited periodization. *Tunnel vision*, Keith Wrightson claims in this volume, is the prevailing characteristic of such historians. Even the links between social history and economic history are less strong and interactive in practice than they ought to be.[8]

For most historians of the English Revolution today causal connections between early seventeenth-century English society and the upheavals of the 1640s remain at best a matter for debate. None would now argue that a straightforward connection between the two existed. That arch conservative G. R. Elton saw England's seventeenth-century crisis as an 'unexplained revolution' and insisted that there was no 'highroad to Civil War'.[9] Social history textbooks on this period by Keith Wrightson, J. A. Sharpe and Christopher Clay have relatively little to say on the social origins, social nature or social consequences of the English Revolution largely because of the thematic structure they adopt.[10] The American historian Perez Zagorin has rejected – on principle, it seems – all Marxist-inspired social-change explanations of the seventeenth-century crisis (see pp. 215–17). The Revisionists, as we shall see, have concentrated on the short-term factors and have shunned the teleologies of both Marxists and Whigs (see pp. 218–28). So has Jonathan Clark in his *Revolution and Rebellion: State and Society in England in the Seventeenth and Eighteenth Centuries* (Cambridge, 1986), where he foamed at the mouth against 'Old Guard' historians like Hill, reared in the climate of 1930s Marxism, and their unhelpful concept of 'revolution' (see p. 247).

One direction which social historians' research has taken has been to re-examine particular social and occupational groups in the period before, during, and after the English Revolution. The gentry, not surprisingly, continue to find their historians, though none of them seeks to revive the long dormant gentry controversy. Felicity Heal and Clive Holmes in their book *The Gentry of England and Wales 1500–1700* (London, 1994) made this clear by the long time-span and 'neutral' opening and closing dates they chose for their study. They were not chiefly concerned to explain the gentry's part in the mid-century crisis; they had more to say in fact on its immediate impact and long-term effects. But they attempted to do for the gentry at least part of what Stone did for the aristocracy by depicting the whole social, economic and cultural ethos of this group. They demonstrated regional differences in status and lifestyle and showed the gentry as both agents and victims of the changes taking place in early modern England. The 'middling sort of people' – much invoked in Christopher Hill's work – formed the subject of a collection of essays edited by Jonathan Barry and Christopher Brooks.[11] Consisting of 30–50 per cent of the population of the time but intrinsically very fragmented and miscellaneous, a precise definition of them remains elusive. But the book helpfully charted the growing usage of the term 'middle sort' from the 1620s and the increasing number of ideological expressions of 'bourgeois collectivism'.

One component of the 'middling sort', broadly defined, was the professions, and social historians have been concerned to investigate their growth and consolidation in the late sixteenth century and early decades of the seventeenth century. In 1987 Wilfred Prest – one of Hill's former students – edited a symposium on the professions which embraced the Anglican clergy, lawyers, doctors, schoolmasters, estate stewards, and the profession of arms. Already in the previous year Prest had brought out a detailed study of *The Rise of the Barristers: A Social History of the English Bar, 1590–1640*. This examined the social, geographical, and educational background, career structure, wealth, social mobility, religion, and politics of the upper branch of the legal profession. Though not specifically concerned with the outbreak of Civil War in England Prest's book bore out the notion that lawyers figured prominently in the opposition to Charles I and found that far more of them were puritan rather than high church in inclination. He underlined connections between the law and the growth of capitalism and rejected Perkin's claim that it was the later Industrial Revolution that emancipated the professions from dependency on clients of higher social rank. The English bar in this period was clearly expanding. Prest's estimate was that the proportion of barristers in English society was almost the same in 1636 as it was in 1978.[12] The lower branch of the legal profession in this period has also found its historian, and by a coincidence C. W. Brooks' volume on this subject appeared in the same year as Prest's. Brooks' findings and conclusions corresponded in a number of ways with those in *The Rise of the Barristers*. Attorneys, like those called to the bar, multiplied phenomenally in these years. Brooks suggested an approximately 900 per cent increase in their numbers between 1560 and 1640 and saw this as the accompaniment to the growing need for legal servicing of complex business transactions and to an increase in litigiousness in society. That attorneys' services enabled tenants to challenge landlords and the relatively unprivileged to defend their rights against their social superiors – and the reverse in each case as well, of course – provides an obvious link with the tension-laden society depicted by Christopher Hill.[13]

The growth of another profession no less closely associated with the mid-seventeenth-century upheavals has also been explored. Rosemary O'Day in *The English Clergy: The Emergence and Consolidation of a Profession 1558–1642* (Leicester, 1981) underlined the dramatic improvement in their educational qualifications and documented the development of a more attractive career structure. 'By the 1620s new recruitment into the church was almost entirely via the universities'. (She contrasted this with the situation earlier; in the diocese of Chester, for example, in the 1560s only one of the 282 clerics ordained was a graduate.) She had some interesting things to say, too, about the ways in which the shared educational experience, academic interests, day-to-day concerns, and ties of kinship, friendship and locality all helped to bind the clergy together into a coherent, self-conscious social group. The extent to which episcopal leadership contributed to these changes was also assessed, as were the ways in which lay patronage both facilitated and obstructed the emergence of the clergyman's profession. That a growing anti-clericalism – one element in the English Revolution – accompanied all these changes was also made clear.[14]

Scholarly interest in religion and society generally in the early seventeenth century – not just puritanism – has grown in the last two decades. Kenneth Fincham's edited collection on *The Early Stuart Church 1603–1642* (London, 1993) was chiefly a top-level, institutional view of the subject which reassessed contemporary thinking about the nature of the church and attempted to break free from the constraining effects of studying the church history of these years simply as an aspect of the causes of the English Civil Wars. That issue was not evaded here; the editor himself concluded that 'religion may have been the central discourse of 1642 yet we must acknowledge that it embodied and mediated a host of secular concerns and values'. But the agenda was more diverse and questions led in other directions or were more genuinely open-ended. Fincham's book illustrated the value of allowing the early Stuart church to be seen as 'a battleground for rival visions of English society, fought out at court, in Parliament, and in the parishes of early Stuart England'. The inadequacies of interpretations based on dichotomies of 'Anglican' and 'Puritan' or 'Arminian' and 'Calvinist' were rehearsed by some of the contributors; the need to redefine the religious spectrum of early seventeenth-century England, to establish different chronologies, and to recognize vertical as well as horizontal religious divisions in society were underlined as major priorities for today's historians.[15] Fincham's volume, it may be said, linked neatly with an earlier collection of essays on *Princes and Paupers in the English Church 1500–1800* (Leicester, 1981) edited by Rosemary O'Day and Felicity Heal. Here the primary emphasis was on the economic foundations of the church – its internal economy in fact – and with their chronological, geographical and social variations. The mid-seventeenth-century upheavals did not loom large in this book save in discussions of pre-Civil War bishops as landowners and of the reformation of parochial finances in the 1640s and 1650s.[16]

The structure, controls and sanctions of the church found a place in another collection of essays, *The Experience of Authority in Early Modern England* (London, 1996), but in other recent publications it has been puritanism that has stood in the limelight. Dr Cliffe has written at length on the puritan gentry before and during the Civil Wars, examining inter-marriage between like-minded gentry families, their role as ecclesiastical patrons, their activities and reputation as landowners, and their connections with the legal profession and with trading and colonial enterprises like the Providence Island Company. War-time damage to estates, losses through declining rent revenues and enhanced levels of taxation were also examined.[17] Even more centrally social in its discussion was the recent collection of essays edited by Christopher Durston and Jacqueline Eales on *The Culture of English Puritanism 1560–1700*

(London, 1996). This book followed Hill in recognizing the essential fluidity, 'the contested social and cultural meanings that cluster around' this elusive religious phenomenon. Such problems of definition notwithstanding, however, Jacqueline Eales insisted that the puritan origins of the Parliamentarian party of the 1640s were unmistakable and the label 'Puritan Revolution' 'entirely legitimate . . . even if it was ultimately unsuccessful'.[18] Patrick Collinson, in another essay in the collection, addressed puritanism as both a culture in its own right and as a resistant counter culture. Language, gestures, habits, preferences and priorities, and the dynamics of religiosity all came under review. Margaret Aston, in a parallel way, continued the exploration of the same inter-related theme of culture/counter culture by examining the evidence for puritan iconoclasm directed against church ornamentation and against art, both in terms of unlicensed and group initiatives in the early seventeenth century and then, from 1641, under parliamentary authorization. Martin Ingram examined the collisions and confrontations between puritans and the church courts. He was quick to recognize, however, the vacuum in public discipline which followed the collapse of the old ecclesiastical system in the early 1640s and the way in which this disadvantaged puritans no less than others. Ralph Houlbrooke surveyed the puritan 'art of dying' and its promulgation in a succession of religious treatises, spiritual biographies, and funeral sermons. The failure of the attempted cultural revolution projected by puritans in power in the 1640s and 1650s formed the subject of Christopher Durston's chapter. The attempts to impose a new puritan calendar and to extend a distinctively puritan moral code were rehearsed as were the various forms of non-co-operation and resistance provided by local office-holders and the general mass of the population. The book concluded, appropriately, with a probing discussion of what happened to puritanism after 1662 and its enforced partial transformation into dissent. John Spurr showed how uncomfortably ill-assorted the dissenters were and how different shades of conformity co-existed with the conscious preservation of continuities in the puritan tradition.

Hill and others long since recognized the social importance of the family unit to puritan organization and to the transmission of puritan culture.[19] Christopher Durston's *The Family and the*

English Revolution (Oxford, 1989) focused on what might be considered the most crucial and testing time in the history of familial relations in England. The military upheavals of the Civil War, the enforced increase in mobility for a substantial section of the male population, the competing ideologies in religion and politics, all combined in these years to challenge the organization, unity and patriarchal nature of the family. No wonder that conservative contemporary writers like Clarendon expressed alarm about what was happening. Many families were indeed divided, Durston confirmed, some permanently and irreconcilably by conflicting political allegiances in the Civil War, and by religious differences. But such cases, it seems, were far from representative. Over the country as a whole not much more than 10 per cent of gentry families were split in this way. Moreover in most cases it seems clear that after 1646 Civil War divisions rapidly healed and that by the 1650s intermarriage between former Royalists and Parliamentarians was commonplace. The resilience of family units, even in the midst of the greatest adversity, was remarkable. Such was the case, too, with the institution of marriage. Though there are some examples of husbands and wives being rent apart by Civil War 'the overwhelming majority of wives', said Durston, 'adopted without question the religious and political opinions of their husbands'. Nor did the defeat and later execution of the national patriarch Charles I engender a widespread collapse of the authority of husbands and fathers. The disrupting impact on the social order of religious extremists such as the Ranters, Durston argued, has been greatly exaggerated. There were probably few prosecutions under the draconian Adultery Act of 1650. 'The English Revolution failed to destroy the family', Durston concluded, 'but the family may have helped to destroy the English Revolution'. Paradoxically, the upheavals of the mid-century period may in some cases have helped to strengthen, not weaken, the family unit. 'It is not surprising that many individuals came to see their immediate families as bulwarks against, and refuges from, the uncertainty that surrounded them'. It was an undramatic conclusion, but it was not altogether fanciful to suggest that concern for traditional familial culture had a bearing on the circumstances which led to the Restoration of 1660. Mary Astell's complaints in her *Reflections on Marriage* (1700), Durston pointedly reminded his readers, provide an emphatic demonstration that patriarchal power in the family was as strong and entrenched as ever decades after the storms of the English Revolution.[20]

Women's part in developments before and during the English Revolution is belatedly finding its historians – guilt-ridden like Christopher Hill or otherwise – and thus forms a conspicuous example of a new awareness of the gendered refractions of the past. Until relatively recently all writing about the period of the English Civil Wars documented the activities of men and men only. The imbalance is now being actively rectified. The authentic voices of women can now be heard more clearly through the publication of collections of primary sources. Once wrongly considered isolated and exceptional it seems in point of fact that there are so many texts from which to choose. Patricia Crawford has calculated that well over five times as many books and pamphlets by women authors appeared in the 1640s and 1650s than in the whole of the previous three decades combined. Volumes providing compilations of verse and autobiographical writing as well as complete editions of the works of individual women such as the prophetess Lady Eleanor Davies are now freely available.[21] The Women Writers Project at Brown University, Rhode Island, USA, aims to publish through the Internet hundreds of such texts by the year 2000.

Women's social and economic position and roles in the mid-seventeenth-century decades have been revealingly explored in a cluster of recent books by Antonia Fraser, Mary Prior, Margaret George, Anne Laurence, Amy Erickson and Alison Plowden. Roger Thompson boldly attempted a comparative study of *Women in Stuart England and America* (London, 1974). Not surprisingly, in all of these studies women from the 'middling sort' or above stand out most clearly.[22] Susan Dwyer Amussen in *An Ordered Society: Gender and Class in Early Modern England* (Oxford, 1988) had an ambitious agenda. The wide-ranging subject matter of this book embraced marriage and family life, gender relations, sexuality, scolding, witchcraft, infanticide, poverty and vagrancy, fen drainage and its social ramifications, and the operation of justice, social controls and concepts of 'honesty' and 'credit'. Women also occupied no less space than men in Anthony Fletcher's *Gender, Sex and Subordination in England 1500–1800* (New Haven, 1995). Based on an impressively wide range of written and visual sources

the book in broad terms was a study of patriarchy and its operation in early modern England, but in exploring it Fletcher eschewed
the tendency of many feminists to treat the subject as something
undifferentiated, consistent, immoveable and monumental. Like
Judith Bennett before him, Fletcher saw patriarchy as a plural
phenomenon. In the period 1500 to 1800 – and no doubt in
others too – its undoubted survival depended on adaptation.
Women as well as men were agents in this process. 'We can find
women corroborating male constructions of them in legal
situations', says Fletcher, 'in a manner which was often more
manipulative than passive. There was nothing women could do in
this society to resist the way men insisted upon reading them, but
there was much they could do about using those readings to
their own advantage'.[23] Though the Civil Wars did not even figure
in Fletcher's index it is clear none the less that the mid-seventeenth
century was a dividing line in the experience and sensibilities
he was exploring. In the century and a half after 1660, he made
clear, a revised, reformulated patriarchy and recognizably modern
notions of masculinity and feminity were constructed and
expressed in education, social life and leisure, sexuality, and the
workplace.

The mental worlds of Stuart women, no less than their social
and economic roles and milieu, are being rigorously investigated
through their writings by feminists and others. *Half Humankind:
Contexts and Texts of the Controversy about Women in England
1540–1640* by Katherine Usher Henderson and Barbara F.
McManus (Urbana and Chicago, Ill., 1985) helped set the scene.
Sara Heller Mendelson's three case studies of the scheming Margaret Cavendish, Duchess of Newcastle, the pious Mary Rich,
Countess of Warwick, and the larger-than-life playwright Aphra
Behn appeared in 1987. Two collections of essays by literary critics
published almost simultaneously in 1992 – *Women, Texts and Histories 1575–1760* and *Women, Writing, History 1640–1740* – cast
their nets more widely.[24]

Women's religious lives and their place in the mid-century
upheavals have received a great deal of attention. Patricia Higgins
has examined the activities of women petitioners to the Long Parliament. Keith Thomas has reviewed the active participation
of women in the Civil War sects, and Ann Hughes has written a

penetrating study of Leveller wives.[25] Patricia Crawford's *Women and Religion in England 1500–1720* (London, 1994) unambiguously proclaimed a centre of interest which tied in closely with the English Revolution. Kings and bishops and their policies, however, were hardly mentioned in this book. Crawford's overriding concern was to examine 'the gendered nature of religion, beliefs, institutions and languages', still a relatively unusual undertaking, but even more distinctive in this book in that it took on a religious spectrum that extended from puritans to Roman Catholics. (Their 'patterns of piety', she demonstrated, 'had many features in common'.) Following Keith Thomas's lead she took a partly anthropological approach to her subject and, like E. P. Thompson (see p. 185), she was conscious that what she was attempting was an exercise designed to recognize the agency of women in making history, and to rescue them from the prejudice and condescension of both male contemporaries and later male historians. Much was said about the significance and roles of women in the Reformation within the home and within congregations. But it was the period of the English Revolution that formed the centrepiece of Crawford's book and the abundant available evidence enabled her to document women's roles as Civil War period writers, preachers and prophets. The dynamics of puritan family worship were explored and their long-term legacies indicated. The place of women in the creation and growth of the Quaker movement was reassessed. Individual case studies of Exeter and Bristol in the 1650s were introduced. Readers were left in no doubt that the implications of Crawford's argument for English Revolutionary studies were considerable. 'Unless historians study questions about the politics of sex, of marriage and of the family', she declared, 'all of which involve questions of power between men and women, then they will fail to understand the wider systems of power in early modern society'.[26]

Crawford's book now shares the stage with others. Hilary Hinds, a historically minded literary critic, has brought to bear a range of modern theoretical strategies from her discipline in an extended examination of prophetic writings, spiritual autobiographies and short tracts by women from the mid-seventeenth-century radical sects. Questions relating to authorship, language, style and audience were all pressed. Although feminist in inspiration the book made claims for the importance of its subject while at the same time resisting a simplistic search for 'foremothers'.[27] The 'visionary women' considered from the perspective of literary criticism in Hinds's book had already received an extended historical treatment from the American historian Phyllis Mack in a complex, pioneering book published in 1992. Over three hundred such women in the English Revolution – two-thirds of them Quakers – were identified by the author, and she explored the use of prophecy as a means of reaching an audience and gaining influence. The Quaker women's meeting, she argued, was 'a cradle not only of modern feminism but of the movements of abolitionism, women's suffrage and peace activism'.[28]

The boldness which has characterized feminist-inspired gender studies of the early modern period, like that underpinning the sociological schematization attempted by Mark Gould and that animating the reformulated Marxism of Robert Brenner, stands out from the rest of the recent literature in this field supplied by social historians. The reasons for this state of affairs have already been suggested. The social history produced in the last two decades has often lost some of the earlier radical spirit and determination – even nerve – of earlier generations. (In that respect the trend coincided with the eclipse of the Left in British politics in an extended period of Conservative Party ascendancy.) It is not that the social historians in question have openly rejected the notion of an English Revolution; indeed a few of them, like Christopher Durston in his work on the family unit, still focus on it. In the case of others, however, their longer chronologies, their thematic approaches, their particular specializations have all taken them away from direct engagement with the landmarks of Tawney's century and Hill's half-century. Their main interests lie elsewhere. Studying the interplay between economy, society and politics no longer has the appeal it once exerted. The academic training of today's social historians inclines them to shun the broad overview and synthesis and to practise a much greater specificity. Part of Hill's lasting significance in this field, therefore, may be said to consist of his resilient capacity to work on a large canvas. He has continued in publication after publication, to integrate into a coherent whole so many of the separate research contributions which their authors were content to leave in a largely free-standing state. Compared with what Tawney, Stone and Hill once offered the scale of many recent social histories of the period of the English Revolution has self-evidently contracted. It is no accident, therefore, that for many social historians themselves the most valuable linkage they have achieved is at the interface of their subject with local history.

Notes

1 Gould, *Revolution in the Development of Capitalism*, p. xiii.
2 Brenner contributed to Stone's Festschrift and dedicated his own *magnum opus* to his Princeton mentor.
3 The journal *Past and Present* raged with a controversy in the late 1970s and early 1980s sparked off by Brenner. The articles are conveniently collected together in T. Aston and C. H. E. Philpin (eds), *The Brenner Debate: Agrarian Class Structure and Economic Development in Preindustrial Europe* (Cambridge, 1985).
4 R. Brenner, 'Bourgeois revolution and transition to capitalism', in A. L. Beier *et al.* (eds), *The First Modern Society: Essays in English History in Honour of Lawrence Stone* (Cambridge, 1989), pp. 296–7.
5 *Ibid.*, pp. 303–4.
6 Review by Robert Ashton in *EHR* (1994), p. 118.
7 C. Hill, *A Nation of Change and Novelty: Radical Politics, Religion and Literature in Seventeenth-Century England* (London, 1990), p. 246.
8 See also P. Joyce, 'The death of social history', *Social Hist.* (1995), pp. 73–91.
9 G. R. Elton, 'A high road to civil war?' and 'The unexplained revolution' are both reprinted in Elton, *Studies in Tudor and Stuart Politics and Government*, II (Cambridge, 1974), pp. 164–89.
10 K. Wrightson, *English Society 1580–1680* (London, 1982), C. G. A. Clay, *Economic Expansion and Social Change in England 1500–1700* (Cambridge, 1984), J. A. Sharpe, *Early Modern England: A Social History 1550–1760* (London, 1987, 2nd edn, 1997).
11 *The Middling Sort of People: Culture, Society and Politics in England, 1550–1800* (London, 1994).
12 Prest's book was the opening volume to appear in the Oxford Studies in Social History series. His earlier book on *The Inns of Court under Elizabeth I and the Early Stuarts 1590–1640* came out in 1972.
13 C. W. Brooks, *Pettyfoggers and Vipers of the Commonwealth: The 'lower branch' of the Legal Profession in Early Modern England* (Cambridge, 1986).
14 O'Day, *English Clergy*, pp. 6, 132, chs 12 and 14 *passim*.
15 Fincham, *Early Stuart Church*, pp. 22, 1.
16 These are the essays by Felicity Heal on 'Archbishop Laud revisited: leases and estate management at Canterbury and Winchester before the English Civil War' (pp. 129–52), and by Rosemary O'Day and Ann Hughes on 'Augmentation and amalgamation: was there a systematic approach to the reformation of parochial finance?' (pp. 167–94).
17 Paul Griffiths, Adam Fox, and Steve Hindle (eds), *The Experience of Authority in Early Modern England* (London, 1996). J. T. Cliffe, *The Puritan Gentry: The Great Puritan Families of Early Stuart England* (London, 1984), and

Puritans in Conflict: The Puritan Gentry during and after the Civil Wars (London, 1988).

18 Durston and Eales (eds), *Culture of English Puritanism*, p. 185.

19 C. Hill, *Society and Puritanism in Pre-Revolutionary England* (London, 1964), ch. 13 'The spiritualisation of the household', L. L. Schucking, *The Puritan Family* (London, 1969), A. Macfarlane, *The Family Life of Ralph Josselin a seventeenth-century Clergyman* (Cambridge, 1970).

20 Durston, *The Family*, pp. 148–9, 69–70, 130, 33–56, 58, 156–7, 173, 166, 173. See also Ilana Krausman Ben Amos, *Adolescence and Youth in Early Modern England* (New Haven, 1994).

21 Germaine Greer *et al.* (eds), *Kissing the Rod: An Anthology of Seventeenth-Century Women's Verse* (New York, 1988), Elspeth Graham *et al.* (eds), *Her Own Life: Autobiographical Writings by Seventeenth-Century Englishwomen* (London, 1989), Charlotte F. Otten (ed.), *English Women's Voices 1540–1700* (Miami, Florida, 1992), Suzanne Trill *et al.* (eds), *Lay by your Needles Ladies, take the Pen: Writing Women in England 1500–1700* (London, 1997), Esther S. Cope (ed.), *Prophetic Writings of Lady Eleanor Davies* (New York, 1995).

22 Antonia Fraser, *The Weaker Vessel: Woman's Lot in Seventeenth-Century England* (London, 1984), Mary Prior (ed.), *Women in English Society 1500–1800* (London, 1985), Margaret George, *Women in the First Capitalist Society: Experiences in Seventeenth-Century England* (Brighton, 1988), Anne Laurence, *Women in England 1500–1700: A Social History* (London, 1994), Amy L. Erickson, *Women and Property in Early Modern England* (London, 1993), Alison Plowden, *Women All on Fire: The Women of the English Civil War* (Stroud, 1998).

23 Fletcher, *Gender, Sex and Subordination*, pp. xvi, xix, 123, 283–96.

24 Sara Heller Mendelson, *The Mental Worlds of Stuart Women: Three Studies* (Brighton, 1987), Clare Brant and Diane Purkiss (eds), *Women, Texts and Histories 1575–1760* (London, 1992), Isobel Grundy and Susan Wiseman (eds), *Women, Writing, History, 1640–1740* (London, 1992).

25 Patricia Higgins's essay forms part of B. Manning (ed.), *Politics, Religion and the English Civil War* (London, 1973), pp. 179–222. Keith Thomas's was first published in *PP*, 13 (1958) and is reprinted in T. Aston (ed.), *Crisis in Europe 1560–1660* (London, 1965), pp. 317–40. Ann Hughes, 'Gender and politics in Leveller literature', in Susan D. Amussen and M. A. Kishlansky (eds), *Political Culture and Cultural Politics in Early Modern England* (Manchester, 1995), pp. 162–88.

26 Crawford, *Women and Religion in England*, pp. 10, 76, 98, 160–84, 3.

27 Hilary Hinds, *God's Englishwomen: Seventeenth-Century Radical Sectarian Writing and Feminist Criticism* (Manchester, 1996).

28 Phyllis Mack, *Visionary Women: Ecstatic Prophecy in Seventeenth-Century England* (Berkeley and Los Angeles, CA, 1992), p. 9.

9

The twentieth century:
local and regional studies

One of the basic problems throughout the Great Rebellion was the
unresolved tension between the provincial's loyalty to his local world
and his loyalty to the state. (Alan Everitt, *Change in the Provinces:
The Seventeenth Century* (Leicester, Occasional Papers in Local
History, 2nd series, 1, 1969), p. 47)

Rather than a simple dichotomy, many historians have perceived a
more complex, subtle interrelationship between local and national
concerns. A local gentleman sought powerful friends at court in order
to obtain office and privileges while the standing of a government
official was enhanced if he had local influence. Particularist disputes
within counties inevitably took on a more than local dimension as
the participants appealed to the centre for help. (Ann Hughes, *Politics, Society and Civil War in Warwickshire 1620–1660* (Cambridge,
1987), p. 87)

Local history today has become one of the chief laboratories for
the study of social history; its small scale and the relative manageability of its source materials have encouraged kinds of experimentation and analysis that would have been less feasible or impossible
at the national level. Local and regional studies of seventeenth-century England have certainly become one of the most thriving
branches of the recent historiography of the English Revolution,
and most of this chapter will be concerned with analysing first the
reasons for this development and second the main trends in this kind
of research. Such studies, however, have a long and fascinating
ancestry and we should begin by briefly recalling it.

Civil War local histories, in fact, date back to the seventeenth
century. The puritan divine John Corbet, for instance, produced *An*

Historical Relation of the Military Government of Gloucester . . . in 1645, and in it stressed the peculiar value of the close-up portrait of a particular area.

> Authors more universal could never gain to be styled the writers of unquestionable verities, for they see at a greater distance, and by a more obscure and dusky light. Certainly a nearer approach, and some kind of interest is required of him that desires to show not only some track and footsteps but the express image of things.

Corbet was an acute observer of the local scene and his comments on the social composition of the parliamentary side in the Civil War put future historians in his debt.[1] Royalist local history of the same period is represented by such works as *The Most True and Exact Relation of that as Honourable as Unfortunate Expedition of Kent, Essex and Colchester* (1650) by Matthew Carter.

But it was in the nineteenth century, with a receptive audience of gentry, clergymen, and others from the swelling ranks of the professions, that the local history of the English Revolution took on a new lease of life. Robert Halley's valuable study of *Lancashire: its Puritanism and Nonconformity* (1869) dealt at some length with the Civil War in that county. J. R. Phillips's *Memoirs of the Civil War in Wales and the Marches 1642–46* appeared in 1874. Alfred Kingston's two books on *Hertfordshire During the Great Civil War* and *East Anglia and the Civil War* came out in 1894 and 1897 respectively. These works, some of them very thorough indeed, took their place among a growing collection of county histories of the Civil War period. But the main achievement of Victorian local historians in this field, it could be argued, lay in making available a vast number of seventeenth-century texts. In Lancashire, for example, the newly founded Chetham Society brought out as one of its earliest volumes a collection of *Tracts Relating to Military Proceedings in Lancashire During the Great Civil War . . .* (1844). This was shortly followed by an edition of the lives of two puritan clergymen of this period, *The Life of Adam Martindale* (1845) and *The Autobiography of Henry Newcome* (1852), an edition of a seventeenth-century *Discourse of the War in Lancashire* (1864) and, later, *Tracts Relating to the Civil War in Cheshire* (1909). The Lancashire and Cheshire Record Society produced an edition of *The Commonwealth Church Surveys of Lancashire and Cheshire*

1649–1655 as its first volume in 1879. The same society's *Memorials of the Civil Wars in Cheshire* appeared ten years later. The publishing activities of these two societies were representative of others of the period. The Surtees Society, the Yorkshire Archaeological Society, the Somerset Record Society, to name but three, all contributed in a similar way by printing valuable source materials relating to the local history of the English Revolution.

In the early years of the twentieth century, with Gardiner and Firth's outline of national events to guide them, local historians offered a new crop of county studies. J. W. Willis-Bund's *The Civil War in Worcestershire 1642–1646 and the Scottish Invasion of 1651* (1905) made use of Gardiner's volumes on the Commonwealth and of Firth's *Cromwell's Army*. No fewer than three other new, and very good, county studies appeared in 1910. Ernest Broxap's *The Great Civil War in Lancashire 1642–51* and A. R. Bayley's *The Great Civil War in Dorset 1642–1660* were both written at Firth's suggestion.[2] Firth also gave an encouraging hand to Sir Charles Thomas-Stanford, whose *Sussex in the Great Civil War and the Interregnum 1642–1660* appeared in the same year. W. J. Farrow's book on *The Great Civil War in Shropshire 1642–49* (1926), like Broxap's study of Lancashire, originated as a University of Manchester MA thesis. Unlike Broxap and the other local historians of his vintage, however, Farrow did not restrict himself only to an account of the war itself, but said something about the growth of parties and of neutralism, and devoted a whole chapter to 'some social aspects of the struggle'.

Farrow's book, published at a time when the searing experience of the First World War was still fresh in the national mind, heralded a changing trend in the writing of county histories of the Civil War period. It was expressed more fully in two works published in the 1930s in the midst of a regionally diverse depression. The first was *Cornwall in the Great Civil War and Interregnum 1642–1660* (Oxford, 1933) by the Oxford historian Mary Coate (1886–1972), and her book placed the Civil War firmly in the context of the intense localism and isolation of Cornish society.

> The history of Cornwall is that of a county with a strong personality, priding itself on its peculiarities and alive with a local patriotism rooted in racial differences and fed by geographical isolation. . . .

Again and again this local patriotism . . . knit together in a common unity men of differing political and religious opinions.

Similarly in the economic life of the people, the custom of the manor, the petty life of the borough, and the traditional relation of landlord to tenant survived the changes and chances of Civil War, for they were the very fibre of which society was constituted, and beside them the political conflict appeared transient and superficial.[3]

The second of these two books to break new ground in the 1930s in offering a social, rather than a political and military, history of the Civil War in a particular county was *Nottinghamshire in the Civil War* (Oxford, 1937) by A. C. Wood (1896–1968).

The war in Nottinghamshire was predominantly local in character and it can be isolated for separate treatment without distortion or omission of the facts. I have endeavoured throughout to keep the parish pump linked up to the main stream, but my primary object has been to narrate the fortunes of this county during the twenty most febrile and dramatic years of its history.[4]

The social and economic characteristics of Nottinghamshire were clearly delineated at the outset, a separate chapter was devoted to Royalist and Roundhead organization, and, like Mary Coate, Wood covered the religious history of the county in his period in a final chapter. The device suggests that in neither case did the authors succeed in integrating this aspect properly into their county studies.

County studies of a fairly traditional kind have continued to be written. *Norfolk and the Civil War* (London, 1969) by the gentleman scholar R. W. Ketton-Cremer and *Devon and Exeter During the Civil War* (Newton Abbot, 1972) by the American historian E. A. Andriette are examples.[5] Some parts of the country – the Midlands especially – have been well served by such narrative histories focusing chiefly on the fighting and its impact. Books by Roy Sherwood and Philip Tennant on *The Civil War in the Midlands 1642–51* and *Edgehill and Beyond: The War in the South Midlands 1642–45* appeared in 1992. Malcolm Atkin – a county archaeologist – brought out his study of the history (and archaeology) of *The Civil War in Worcestershire* in 1995. David Eddershaw's volume on *The Civil War in Oxfordshire* was issued in the same year. Most recently, in 1996, the same publisher responsible for all of these Midlands studies brought out Philip Tennant's *The Civil War in Stratford upon Avon: Conflict and Community in South Warwickshire 1642–1646*. Other local and regional historians of the Civil War, however, have moved out in a number of new directions. This has been made possible by the opening of county record offices since 1945 and, going with this, the increased availability of private collections of family papers. Almost invariably, as well as being natives of the counties whose history they have explored, the local historians in question have been professionals; local history has become firmly established in higher education.

The 'gentry controversy' provided the stimulus to the exploration of one new direction in local and regional studies, since as its original participants, especially Tawney, came to realize, it was futile to continue the debate at the level of generalization. More research, more case studies of particular counties and particular families were preferable to further wild hypotheses. The American historian Alan Simpson made the point very clearly in one such case study of the gentry's fortunes which appeared in the early 1960s. In *The Wealth of the Gentry 1540–1660: East Anglian Studies* (Cambridge, 1961), Simpson argued that the 'gentry controversy', stimulating though it had been while it lasted, was no more than a 'cleansing operation' in which 'anyone with a good general knowledge of the century, and a clear head can have his say'.

> [But] the simple fact remains that the economic history which the whole controversy presupposes has still to be determined. It is an argument about incomes and expenditures, and the number of economic biographies which exist can be counted on two hands, with a few fingers to spare. It is an argument about land management, and there are even fewer studies of that, which clearly demonstrate its methods and its profits. It is an argument about movement upwards and downwards among the ruling classes, and there is not a county in England for which the attempt has been made to compare the leading families of 1640 with those of 1540 and to explain the differences.[6]

Honestly describing his own work as 'more limited than the range of the controversy which stimulated it', Simpson processed some difficult evidence from a part of the country (East Anglia) which had been surprisingly absent from the generalized treatments of Tawney, Stone and Trevor-Roper. Without offering any dogmatic conclusions, Simpson none the less, in a way which lent support to Tawney's thesis, was able to identify:

> the patterns which the demographic factor could produce – the possibilities of subdivision where there were too many children, of consolidation when some lines failed, and of extinction if there was no male heir. We learn something of the expenses as well as the profits of office; if the founder of the family owed everything to a career at court, the children of the second marriage knew all about its hazards. Finally, we discover the capacity of landed estates to weather the inflation.[7]

Overall, it was Simpson's impression that:

> Apart from a few Bacons that rose, a few Heydons that crashed, and rather more who disappeared through lack of male heirs, it is an interesting possibility, after all the talk of rise and fall, that the rest may just have endured. If so, it would be something of an anti-climax; but to one student, at least, the agrarian history of this century has turned out to be far more prosaic than he ever expected.[8]

A cautious and judicious case-study approach to the gentry of another county had characterized one of the first studies of this kind produced under the stimulus of the Tawney/Trevor-Roper debate. Mary Finch's careful and well-documented monograph of *The Wealth of Five Northamptonshire Families 1540–1640* (Northants Record Society, XIX, 1956) acknowledged Tawney and Stone in its preface. Dr Finch (1923–), like Simpson later, argued that steady if unspectacular profits could be gained from landowning in this period, provided that the gentry selected, consolidated, and improved their estates carefully and firmly grasped the realities of credit and investment.[9] But complicating any theory of the rise and decline of sections of the gentry was an erratic, unquantifiable aspect. 'Personality of the individual landowner', she concluded, 'is always the decisive factor.'

This conclusion was echoed in another case study of the gentry:

> Although general economic factors could be important, the financial success or failure of a landed family depended in the last resort on individual character. Whatever the prevailing conditions an estate could be seriously, even disastrously, impaired if the owner was an incompetent or negligent landlord, a lunatic or a spendthrift.[10]

This was J. T. Cliffe's observation in his weighty volume on *The Yorkshire Gentry From the Reformation to the Civil War* (London, 1969) which looked at the economic fortunes, religious affiliations and political attitudes of the social elite in that county. Dr Cliffe (1931–) drew a distinction between the economic opportunities open to the minor gentry and to those further up the scale in the social hierarchy.

> Although the theory that the 'mere landowner' rarely prospered cannot be sustained as a general proposition, it undoubtedly has some validity when applied to the small landed families with no other form of income. For them there was little prospect of economic advancement.[11]

Bad management, extravagance, lavish hospitality, litigation, demographic crises, could all help to put gentry families in a difficult position.

H. A. Lloyd's study of *The Gentry of South-West Wales 1540–1640* (Cardiff, 1968) grew out of an Oxford D.Phil. thesis supervised by Professor Trevor-Roper. Lloyd's work was less quantitative in approach than some of the other studies of this genre; 'statistical contrivances', he wrote, 'do not offset fundamental deficiencies of evidence'.

> The only general observation to be admitted is that the characteristics of the gentry as here portrayed are not consistent either with the aspirations or with the impact attributed to rising or declining 'generalized gentry' in England as a whole. This is a comment not upon the likely characteristics of gentry elsewhere, studied in accordance with the terms of this analysis, but upon the doubtful admissibility, for purposes other than that of academic stimulus, of broad hypotheses taking insufficient account of the variations within that agglomeration of localities which in this period made up the kingdom of England.

For south-west Wales, Lloyd (1937–) concluded that the gentry suffered from an economic and political lassitude.

> That community [of Wales] was conditioned by a heritage of disharmony and conflicting forces. Its leaders were able neither sufficiently to abandon old ways for new opportunities, nor effectively to seek development and adjustment of native forms to meet new circum-

stances. With the old order crumbling and the new world unexplored, south-west Wales lingered in limbo.[12]

For regional studies of this kind, the 'gentry controversy' provided a stimulus rather than a constraining framework and one, moreover, that has been very long-lasting. Two complementary volumes on the north-west have appeared within the last generation – B. G. Blackwood, *The Lancashire Gentry and the Great Rebellion 1640–1660* (Manchester, 1978) and B. Coward, *The Stanleys: Lords Stanley and Earls of Derby 1385–1672* (Manchester, 1983). The first of them was heavily statistical in its approach to different aspects of the gentry's fortunes and allegiances and the second provided a detailed individual case study. Both systematic and perceptive in their different ways the two books demonstrated the continuing validity of this kind of approach to the fortunes of the elite.

Work on the economic history of the gentry easily, and naturally, led on to reassessments of their role in county society and politics. Following the lead taken by W. B. Willcox in *Gloucestershire: A Study in Local Government 1590–1640* (New Haven, 1940), T. G. Barnes produced his study of *Somerset 1625–1640: A County's Government During the 'Personal Rule'* (Oxford, 1961). More recently S. K. Roberts has published his findings on *Recovery and Restoration in an English County: Devon Local Administration 1646–1670* (Exeter, 1985) – one of the few local studies of the English Revolution to give due weight to the changes of the Interregnum and to go beyond the Restoration. Anthony Fletcher has boldly written a synthesis which covers the administrative role of the gentry in the whole period 1603–1714. *Reform in the Provinces: The Government of Stuart England* (New Haven, 1986) dealt with the changing context of magistracy and the conduct of business, and illustrated the JPs' enforcement of policy in the regulation of the poor, social and personal behaviour, and the militia, and set forth claims about 'the triumph of the gentry' as the principal residual outcome of the mid-century Revolution. Earlier, D. H. Pennington and Ivan Roots had published *The Committee at Stafford 1643–1645: The Order Book of the Staffordshire County Committee* (Manchester, 1957). Another county committee was one of the subjects documented in Alan Everitt's *Suffolk and the Great Rebellion 1640–1660* (Ipswich, 1961).

Primarily a collection of source material, Everitt's book on Suffolk hardly gave its author scope to produce a rounded interpretation of provincial society in the 1640s and 1650s. Such an opportunity, however, was offered and was firmly grasped in his study of *The Community of Kent and the Great Rebellion 1640–1660* (Leicester, 1966), a landmark in this branch of the recent historiography of the Revolution. The book's title accurately indicated where its main emphasis lay; the county community came first in Everitt's interpretation. Even the chapter headings proclaimed this fact.[13] Himself a native of Kent, Everitt (1926–), formerly Hatton Professor of English Local History at the University of Leicester, offered a refreshingly different and stimulating approach to the regional history of the English Revolution.

> In many respects, despite its ancient centralized government, the England of 1640 resembled a union of partially independent county-states of communities, each with its own distinct ethos and loyalty. . . . One important aspect of the history of the Great Rebellion is certainly the gradual merging or submerging of these communities, under the stress of revolution, in the national community of the New Model Army and the Protectorate.[14]

Rejecting the limited, imitative model of local history accepted by an earlier generation of local historians who had set out simply to illustrate the familiar pattern of national events, Everitt emphasized the need to penetrate the internal intricacies of the local world itself and to appreciate the true significance of the local determinants of local issues. In the crisis years of the Civil War the community divided, though at first the two 'parties' in Kent were minorities of extremists with the majority preferring to remain neutral for as long as possible; 'the most striking political feature of Kent during 1640–1660 was precisely its insularity'.[15] Local resistance, however, to the centralizing efforts of Parliament during the Interregnum was as strong as any opposition which had confronted Charles I, and sprang from the same origins. In this way the county community reunited, and the 'natural rulers', the old gentry families, by 1660 were back in the saddle. 'The local power of the gentry had not been diminished but rather increased by the

Great Rebellion' even though 'the community of 1660 was not identical in character with that of 1640'.[16] The community of Kent, as Everitt defined it, was essentially that of the gentry, almost three-quarters of whom (an unusually high proportion) were indigenous to the county. Intermarriage reinforced their insularity and separateness and helped define their notion of an integrated county community. From men like these arose the distinctive ideals and ethos of provincial society.[17]

Everitt has returned to these themes repeatedly in his later work. For instance, in 1969 he brought out two complementary essays on *Change in the Provinces: The Seventeenth Century* and *The Local Community and the Great Rebellion*.[18] Despite its title, the first of these essays devoted rather more attention to the conservatism and continuity of provincial life than it did to changing patterns of social relations associated with the arrival of the 'new gentry', the growth of the wayfaring community, the professions, and the pseudo-gentry.[19] None the less, Everitt argued that the growth in provincial self-awareness was one of the most important developments of the seventeenth century.

> It emerged with the growing power of the county commonwealths of England. It emerged with the rise of the county capitals, focusing as they did so many aspects of the shire communities around them. It developed, too, with the rise of the professional classes, called into being to serve the new needs of both town and countryside. It arose with the expansion of trade and wealth generally, for this expansion greatly increased the wealth of provincial townsmen and yeomen. Indeed, it was one of the ironies of provincial life that even the revolutionary developments of the time, such as the rise of the new gentry and the emergence of the wayfaring community, in the end came to be accepted and neutralized within it and to buttress its independence. The new developments were grafted into the old tree, so to speak, rejuvenating and invigorating its productive powers without fundamentally altering its identity. In a real sense the events of 1660 were a compromise between the power of this provincial world and the power of the nation-state. Or rather they were an agreement to differ, an *entente*, a recognition that each world needed the other in order to survive.[20]

It was the continuities of everyday social and economic life rather than the dramatic, but short-lived, impact of the Civil War that Everitt dwelt on in the second of these essays, on *The Local Community and the Great Rebellion*. Following the suggestion made more tentatively by Mary Coate thirty years earlier, Everitt pleaded at the end of his essay that, above all, the Civil War ought to be placed firmly in a wider local perspective. It should be seen

> as one of a succession of problems to which society at the time was peculiarly vulnerable. The recurrent problems of harvest failure, and the malnutrition and disease that often followed in its wake, were, for most English people, more serious and more persistent than the tragic but temporary upheaval of the Civil War. . . . The stubbornness and the resilience of country people, over the generations, in the face of this alternating harshness and generosity of nature were equally remarkable. Their experiences certainly go some way to explain that latent intransigence of the provincial world which, in the last resort, was one of the principal factors in the failure of both Charles I and Cromwell. For if you have been engaged for centuries in hand-to-hand warfare with the forces of nature, you naturally develop a certain dumb obstinacy towards the world at large – and not least towards the strange doings of princes and protectors.[21]

Professor Everitt's 'gentry community' perspective on the English Revolution has been an important influence on subsequent county studies of this period. It was discernible, for instance, in Anthony Fletcher's substantial work *A County Community in Peace and War: Sussex 1600–1660* (London, 1975). The chronological coverage of Fletcher's study was longer than Everitt's, although his definition of the 'county community' was the same. The gentry held the centre of the stage throughout; their wealth, social standing, political experience, administrative service, religious allegiance, and kinship and friendship networks all received due attention. Little was offered on the aristocracy, who by the 1620s had lost control in the county, and even less, except through the eyes of their betters, on the great mass of the rural and urban population. Popular agitation, such as the Sussex episodes in the Clubmen movement in 1645, got only perfunctory treatment. The tensions between gentry and an urban oligarchy – as at Chichester – had more interest for this historian.[22]

Everitt's work also clearly influenced David Underdown's *Somerset in the Civil War and Interregnum* (Newton Abbot, 1973), although in line with this historian's previous work the main emphasis here was political;[23] his local study drew both its many strengths and occasional weaknesses from being written in tandem with his work on parliamentary politics, *Pride's Purge* (see pp. 211–12). But Professor Underdown's dual interest in politics at the centre and in the counties enabled him to explore the relationship between the two, the way, for instance, in which MPs' attitudes were based on local conditions.

A similar concern with the constant interaction between regional and national politics underlay Clive Holmes's study of *The Eastern Association in the English Civil War* (Cambridge, 1974). Everitt had broached this subject earlier in his book on Suffolk, and there had offered a regional explanation of the Association. Circumstances in East Anglia, he argued, were especially conducive; there was 'a considerable body of Suffolk people who were capable of thinking in terms not only of their native village and county, but of East Anglia as a whole'.[24] Holmes (1943–), however, showed convincingly that the rise and fall of the Eastern Association in the 1640s could not be explained primarily in local and regional terms. 'The Association was formed in spite of, rather than because of, the socio-economic substructure of the region.' Nor could the Association be explained as another dimension of the puritanism of the eastern counties, a factor emphasized since Gardiner's day; 'the supposed religious homogeneity of the region', he contended, 'has been over-emphasized'. In a political sense, too, it was necessity rather than choice which brought the eastern counties together. 'The initial pressure for the formation of the Eastern Association came from those counties which were least enthusiastic in their support for the Parliamentary cause.'[25] Local and regional forces, then, were not in themselves strong enough either to justify the Association in the first instance or to hold it together subsequently. The impressive and practically unique success of the Eastern Association was made possible by the 'complex and tension-ridden dialogue' between local and national politics, and in the last analysis it was the politicians at Westminster who first created and then dismantled this instrument of aggression.

While Holmes challenged Everitt's emphasis on purely local explanations, John Morrill (1946–) in his *Cheshire 1630–1660: County Government and Society During the 'English Revolution'*

(Oxford, 1974) took a critical look at Everitt's definitions of 'county community' and 'crisis'. He drew distinctions between the parochial gentry and county gentry and contrasted the different socio-political worlds in which they moved. 'My aim', the author went on, 'has been to convey an impression of a whole community [not just the gentry] under stress'.[26] The kind of crisis facing society in the 1640s, Morrill argued, went much deeper than Everitt had allowed. (The latter's preference for the term 'Great Rebellion' was significant.) A new self-consciousness was developing at *village* level, and the stirrings of this grassroots social revolution induced a fear in the county elite which was translated into political action.

Other county case studies have also called into question particular aspects of Everitt's county-community model – never intended, it should be stressed, to fit every case. Arguably it said too little about ideology and religion. Its preoccupation with the gentry necessarily made it an elitist view rather than a total picture. Vigorous election contests in the early 1640s told another story and showed that the gentry did not have it all their own way; much more, it has now been realized, has to be said about those below the ranks of the county elite and about the importance of popular politics. Moreover, historians have had more to say about the divisions within county communities – over religion, for example – and pointed to the ways in which allegiance and a sense of identity could be shaped by factors other than the mere geography of English counties. 'Local' and 'national' were not mutually exclusive categories, and overlapping loyalties were more common than allowed for in Everitt's model. Moreover, even at the level of the gentry, the notion of the independence and introversion of the county community can easily be exaggerated. There is the danger, for example, on the one hand of underestimating the melting-pot experience of university education – which more and more of the sons of gentlemen were receiving – and the impact of London. On the other hand, even within counties, much of the work of JPs was divided and decentralized, thus reducing the significance of the county unit as a single entity. 'There is a danger', Christopher Hill has written, 'of sentimentalizing the "county community" of the gentry'.[27]

John Morrill's important study of *The Revolt of the Provinces: Conservatives and Radicals in the English Civil War 1630–1650*

(London, 1976, 2nd edn, 1980) encapsulated many of the changing tendencies of post-Everitt writing on the local history of the English Revolution. The 'Revolt' in Morrill's title referred both to local resistance to the policies of Charles I and to local reactions to the experience of Civil War. Like Everitt, Morrill was concerned here with the ways in which localism actually shaped the events of the English Revolution. But Morrill placed greater weight than Everitt on the measurable impact of the Civil War on local communities – through plundering, the physical destruction of men, buildings, and crops, the loss of livestock and horses, the quartering of troops, and the increased, apparently unending, burden of taxation. '*On top of* the destructive forces of nature came widespread destruction by men.'[28] Morrill, too, made much more than Everitt of the perceived *local consequences* of national events, policies, and alignments, and emphasized the importance of radical conservatism and neutralism in the range of provincial responses to the events of the decades after 1630.

Two other county studies illustrated in different ways later historians' modifications to, or abandonment of, Everitt's model of the county community. The first of them, appropriately, related to Kent, Everitt's own starting point. This was Peter Clark's *English Provincial Society from the Reformation to the Revolution: Religion, Politics and Society in Kent 1500–1640* (Brighton, 1977). Tracing Kentish society back to the early years of the sixteenth century enabled Clark to show that, as a political phenomenon at any rate, Everitt's county community of the Civil War period was a recent creation, and had emerged in the wake of the final collapse of the old clique of court-orientated county governors in the 1620s. For Clark, however, the gentry community provided only one of many themes, and was less prominent than that of the changing relations between Westminster and Kent. Like Holmes before him, Clark had much to say about the interaction between local and national affairs in this period. The gentry were not allowed to monopolize the reader's attention in Clark's book. There was a full discussion of the place of the professions in Kentish society and of other social and occupational strata down to the poorest.

Ten years on from Clark's book, Ann Hughes brought out her important and challenging study of *Politics, Society and Civil War in Warwickshire, 1620–1660* (Cambridge, 1987). In virtually every respect it rejected the Everitt county community model in the light of Warwickshire evidence. The geography and economy of Warwickshire, it is true, were hardly conducive to community-building in the Everitt sense. Diverse and disparate economically, with no major urban centre, Warwickshire's county boundaries were quite irrelevant to many of its inhabitants. Trade, industry, agriculture, and landholding all had more complex, extended patterns. Lawyers in the county had a professional range which reached beyond the boundaries of the shire. The gentry, too, lacked social cohesion. They were as likely to marry outside the county as within it, and their friendship networks were not confined to Warwickshire. It was exceedingly rare to find operational county-wide ties among the gentry. Though in Warwickshire, as elsewhere, the gentry indulged in county antiquarianism – Dugdale's connections were with Warwickshire – heraldic interests were as important as county loyalty. Above all, Everitt's notion of the gentry's conflicting national and local loyalties was called into question by Hughes's investigations. No such simple dichotomy fitted the Warwickshire facts. Civil War, when it came, emerged from *within* as well as from outside the county. Hughes found little evidence to support Everitt's thesis that the Civil War line-up involved a division between 'county-minded' moderates and nationally minded extremists. There was much neutralism in Warwickshire, as elsewhere, but it took different, disunited forms. There was no neutrality pact in the county in 1642, and no moderate, neutral appeal to preserve the stability and independence of the shire. It was the lack of 'county-mindedness' not the strength of it, Hughes concluded, that provides the key to Warwickshire's Civil War history.[29]

A recent case study of a single gentry family of Hertfordshire by Jacqueline Eales, *Puritans and Roundheads: The Harleys of Brampton Bryan and the Outbreak of the English Civil War* (Cambridge, 1990), aligned itself in a number of respects with Hughes's departure from the Everitt model. Although in one sense a county study, Eales's book demonstrated beyond all doubt that for the puritan Harleys the community of the godly elect was of more importance that their county community. Links with co-religionists elsewhere counted for more than mere geographical and social proximity, and it was their deep-rooted religion that did most to determine their choice of marriage partners, friends, servants, tenants, education and political allegiance, and that consoled them in the face of isolation and hostility. The Harleys believed that 'they were involved in a war to secure true religion in England and that Parliament was the bulwark that would protect the Church from its enemies'. For this gentry family the mid-seventeenth-century upheavals were indeed a 'Puritan Revolution'.[30] Eales's book was also distinctive in that it was a woman – Lady Brilliana Harley – who emerged from this monograph in a more direct and rounded way than any other member of the Harley family. The siege of Brampton Bryan and Lady Brilliana's death in the course of it provided the most dramatic and poignant moments in the whole book.

Everitt's stress on county communities of gentry has been countered also by the development of specifically urban case studies of the English Revolution. Not surprisingly London has been much studied. The antiquarian Norman Brett-James long ago led the way with his book *The Growth of Stuart London* (London, 1935). Devoted chiefly to a study of the building process Brett-James provided vivid depictions of the rapidly growing city before, during and after the Civil Wars. By contrast Valerie Pearl (1926–), a former student of Hill and Trevor-Roper at Oxford, focused on the city's politics. *London and the Outbreak of the Puritan Revolution* (Oxford, 1961) took a long and critical look at the notion, repeated so frequently by historians that it had become an accepted cliché, that London's active support for Parliament pre-dated the onset of Civil War. Her conclusion, in fact, was very different and was that parliamentary puritans captured control of the city government and trained bands only on the very eve of Civil War in 1642. They enlarged the role of the Common Council and in due course formally diminished that of the Lord Mayor and aldermen. New, middle-rank men took power from the monopolists, customs farmers and elites of the chartered trading companies and modified, rather than destroyed, the oligarchical structure which they had entered.[31]

Pearl's work on London was challenged in some respects by Robert Ashton's *The City and the Court 1603–43* (Cambridge, 1979) which re-assessed the 'municipal revolution' of 1642 which had been the centrepiece of his predecessor's book.[32] Keith Lindley has extended the investigation of the shifting composition of London's elite and, more particularly, its exposure to the insistent pressures of popular radicalism.[33] Tai Liu in a book-length study examined the complexities of the impact of Presbyterians and Independents alongside the survival of Anglicanism in the city parishes.[34] Stephen Porter's book on *London and the Civil War* (London, 1996), on the other hand, was chiefly devoted to military, economic and social aspects. In one of his own contributions to this collection of essays Porter attempted to construct a rough balance sheet of the city's gains and losses during the crisis years of Civil War. The capital clearly gained from the continuous presence within it of Parliament, the Parliamentarian administration, and the Westminster Assembly. London tradesmen profited from the bulk orders they received for clothing and equipment. London suffered, however, from the absence of the royal court and noble households, from shortages of labour, fuel, other raw materials and food as inland trade routes and the coastal trade were disrupted by the fighting and by blockades. The city's legal profession experienced a dramatic downturn in business. Retailing was sluggish. Many houses were empty and rents had to be reduced. Poverty increased while charitable giving declined. The burdens of wartime taxation became heavier. In the last analysis Porter's balance sheet showed losses outweighing gains. Keith Roberts in another chapter surveyed both the actual military manoeuvres of the city's eighteen infantry and cavalry regiments as well as London's longer lasting financial contribution to the war effort. Ian Gentles drew out the propaganda surrounding four very different political funerals in 1640s London.

London's economic links with the provincial capitals formed part of the subject matter of studies of Newcastle, Norwich and Exeter. *Newcastle upon Tyne and the Puritan Revolution* (Oxford, 1967) by the American historian Roger Howell (1936–89) reinforced Everitt's stress on the importance of local determinants of Civil War politics. The main significance of the upheavals of the 1640s for Newcastle was that they provided new opportunities to attempt to prise open the grip of the ruling oligarchy on the corporation and the coal trade. The political elite also formed the subject of John T. Evans's book on *Seventeenth-Century Norwich:*

Politics, Religion and Government, 1620–1690 (Oxford, 1981). The long time span surveyed enabled him to try to take in Whigs and Tories as well as Parliamentarians, Royalists, Presbyterians and Independents. The Parliamentarian/puritan victory in the 1640s, he argued, did not lead to profound social change and revolution in the city. None the less Evans provided significant insights into the geography of politics and puritanism in Norwich and into Bishop/Corporation and city/county relations. Mark Stoyle's study of Exeter – *From Deliverance to Destruction: Rebellion and Civil War in an English City* (Exeter, 1996) – was chiefly a study of the military impact of the first Civil War in the city and of the political and religious ramifications of the troubled times. Archaeological evidence as well as written sources was utilized to study the three major sieges which the unfortunate city endured between 1642 and 1646. The local dynamics of the Civil War were insisted upon here. Stoyle's central argument in fact was that 'the inhabitants of early Stuart Exeter were not mere witnesses to the political shifts of the 1640s – uncomprehending victims of an imported conflict – but were rather committed players in a politico-religious game which possessed local, as well as national, dimensions'.[35]

All of these urban studies gave some attention to religion; other historians have concentrated specifically on the local and regional history of this important subject. R. A. Marchant looked at *The Puritans and the Church Courts in the Diocese of York 1560–1642* (London, 1960). R. C. Richardson's *Puritanism in North West England* (Manchester, 1972), though it did not deal with the Civil War period itself, covered part of the preconditions to it by analysing the structure and organization of the puritanism of that area and of the different forces at work within it. Another study, this time of Essex by the American historian William Hunt, was more focused on the dynamics of the situation which led to *The Puritan Moment: The Coming of Revolution in an English County* (Cambridge, Mass., 1983). Cornwall's puritanism, like that of the North West, flourished in the 1630s under the benign influence of a local bishop, and its adherents were able to seize new opportunities after 1640. These and other aspects of the religious and political landscapes of the county formed the substance of Anne Duffin's *Faction and Faith: Politics and Religion of the Cornish Gentry before the Civil War* (Exeter, 1996). The puritan takeover in Dorchester in the decades after 1613, bringing an unrivalled reputation for religious radicalism and unsurpassed levels of charitable giving, was examined in David Underdown's *Fire from Heaven: Life in an English Town in the Seventeenth Century* (London, 1992). The Roman Catholic recusant community of the English counties (and of London) has been explored in the works of John Bossy, Keith Lindley, M. J. Havran, Hugh Aveling, and P. R. Newman.[36]

Local and regional studies continue to proliferate and enhance the current importance of this branch of the recent historiography of the English Revolution. Redefined in the twentieth century as an integral part of a professionalized discipline and moulded under the stern experience of total war, depression, economic change, and by intrusive and often insensitive revisions to the geography of the country's political units, local history has come to be at the cutting edge of research and is vigorous and innovative in its methodologies. The dismissive strictures of Jonathan Clark, a Thatcherite Tory now transplanted to Kansas, on these local historians that 'they have been most effective in showing what did not happen' were unjust. Nor was Clark convincing when he argued (from his own distinctive political stance) that their work is 'an historiographical echo of the value nexus of the S. D. P.', and as such little more than a back projection to the seventeenth century of current preoccupations with conservation, environment, community and nuclear-free zones.[37] It is now widely recognized that no single county or town in the seventeenth century was typical of the whole country, and local historians would no longer see their function in terms either of simply illustrating the national picture or of displaying the absolute uniqueness or autonomy of a particular area. The relationship between local and national events in the seventeenth century, it has been demonstrated beyond all doubt, was much more diverse than either of these polar opposites would suggest. Part of the essence of local studies, as currently defined, involves resisting sweeping generalizations. That was the insistent message of the second stage of the 'Gentry Controversy'. Increasingly historians have come to recognize the complex, dialectical inter-relationships between the centre and the provinces and between town and countryside. Bolder by far than they used to be, today's local and regional historians are playing a fundamental and indispensable role in reassessing the English Revolution and its destructive and reorienting impact.[38] They have raised uncomfortably fundamental questions about the nature and distribution of allegiance and neutralism in the Civil Wars, about religious tension and disagreement, the seriousness of the impact of the military contests, and about the extent and speed of recovery. They have helped to lead an enquiry into how far the English Revolution, like its counterpart in France in the following century, was urban led, and have shown a willingness to treat losers no less seriously than winners in the mid-century upheavals.[39]

Notes

1 J. Washbourn (ed.), *Bibliotecha Gloucestrensis* (Gloucester, 1825), pp. 4, 9.
2 Broxap's book was reissued with a new introduction by R. N. Dore (Manchester, 1974).
3 Mary Coate, *Cornwall*, pp. 1, 351–2. Mary Coate taught history at Oxford from 1918 to 1947 and was subsequently connected with the Extra-Mural Department at the University of Exeter.
4 A. C. Wood, *Nottinghamshire*, p. ix. Wood – an Oxford-trained historian – spent his entire academic career at the University College (later University) of Nottingham, eventually becoming Professor in 1951.
5 All the volumes on Civil War history in the Midlands were published by Sutton (Stroud).
6 Simpson, *Wealth of the Gentry*, p. 2. Simpson also wrote *Puritanism in Old and New England* (Chicago, 1955).
7 Simpson, *Wealth of the Gentry*, pp. 20, 107–8.
8 *Ibid.*, p. 216.
9 Finch, *Five Northamptonshire Families*, pp. 165–70.
10 Cliffe, *Yorkshire Gentry*, p. 162.
11 *Ibid.*, p. 118.
12 Lloyd, *Gentry of South-West Wales*, pp. 211, 213.
13 The chapter headings are 'The community of Kent in 1640', 'The community in opposition, 1640', 'The community divides, 1640–42', 'The community at War, 1642–47', 'The community in revolt, 1647–48', 'The community in eclipse, 1649–59', 'The community of Kent and the Restoration, 1659–60'.
14 Everitt, *Community of Kent*, p. 13.
15 *Ibid.*, p. 23.
16 *Ibid.*, pp. 327, 326.
17 *Ibid.*, pp. 36, 44, 45–55.
18 The first was published as the opening number of the second series of Occasional Papers by the Department of English Local History at the University of Leicester; the second was a Historical Association pamphlet (now reprinted with an afterword in R. C. Richardson (ed.), *The English Civil Wars: Local Aspects* (Stroud, 1997)). See also Everitt's chapter on 'The county community',

in E. W. Ives (ed.), *The English Revolution* (London, 1968), and his essay 'Country, county and town: patterns of regional evolution in England', *TRHS*, 5th ser., 29 (1979), reprinted in Everitt, *Landscape and Community in England* (London, 1985), pp. 11–40.

19 Everitt, *Landscape and Community* brings together eleven of his essays. See also Everitt's essay on 'Social mobility in early modern England', *PP*, 33 (1966).

20 Everitt, *Change in the Provinces*, p. 48.

21 Everitt, *Local Community and the Great Rebellion*, pp. 26–7.

22 Fletcher also pursued his interest in the gentry in his later book *Reform in the Provinces* (New Haven, 1986).

23 See also Underdown's essays on 'Settlement in the counties', in G. E. Aylmer (ed.), *The Interregnum: The Quest for Settlement* (London, 1972), and 'Community and class: theories of local politics in the English Revolution', in Barbara C. Malament (ed.), *After the Reformation: Essays in Honour of J. H. Hexter* (Manchester, 1980). Other works by Underdown are discussed below, pp. 191–3, 211–12.

24 Everitt, *Suffolk*, p. 21.

25 Holmes, *Eastern Association*, pp. 15, 20, 34.

26 Morrill, *Cheshire*, p. 330.

27 For a fuller discussion of these points see A. Fletcher, 'National and local awareness in the county communities', in H. Tomlinson (ed.), *Before the Civil War* (London, 1983); C. Holmes, 'The county community in early Stuart historiography', *JBS*, xix (1980), reprinted in R. Cust and Ann Hughes (eds), *The English Civil War* (London, 1997), pp. 212–32; Cynthia Herrup, 'The counties and the country: some thoughts on seventeenth-century historiography', *Soc. Hist.*, viii (1983); C. Hill, 'Parliament and people in seventeenth-century England', *PP*, 92 (1981), p. 103.

28 Morrill, *Revolt of the Provinces*, p. 87.

29 Hughes, *Warwickshire*, pp. 20, 39–41, 43, 87, 167–8, 220, 163–5, 336.

30 Eales, *Puritans and Roundheads*, p. 200. This is also the conclusion emphasized by Eales in another, more general, book on puritanism: C. Durston and Jacqueline Eales (eds), *The Culture of English Puritanism, 1560–1700* (London, 1996).

31 See also Pearl's essays on 'London puritans and Scotch fifth columnists: a mid seventeenth-century phenomenon', in A. E. J. Hollaender and W. Kellaway (eds), *Studies in London History presented to Philip Edmund Jones* (London, 1969); 'London's counter-revolution', in G. E. Aylmer (ed.), *The Interregnum: The Quest for Settlement* (London, 1972).

32 Ashton's point was that the aldermanic Royalism of 1642 (which was overcome by the 'municipal revolution') had its origins most conspicuously in the short term. See also A. L. Beier and R. Finlay (eds), *London 1500–1700: The Making of the Metropolis* (London, 1986).

33 Lindley, 'London and popular freedom', in R. C. Richardson and G. M. Ridden (eds), *Freedom and the English Revolution: Essays in History and Literature* (Manchester, 1986); 'London's citizenry in the English Revolution', in R. C. Richardson (ed.), *Town and Countryside in the English Revolution*

(Manchester, 1992), and *Popular Politics and Religion in Civil War London* (Aldershot, 1997).

34 Liu, *Puritan London: A Study of Religion and Society in the City Parishes* (Newark, Delaware, 1986).

35 Stoyle, *From Deliverance to Destruction*, p. 141.

36 J. Bossy, *The English Catholic Community* (London, 1976); K. J. Lindley, 'The lay Catholics of England in the reign of Charles I', *J. Ecc. H.*, xxii (1971); Lindley 'The part played by the Catholics', in B. S. Manning (ed.), *Politics, Religion and the English Civil War* (London, 1973); M. J. Havran, *The Catholics in Caroline England* (London, 1962); H. Aveling, *Post Reformation Catholicism in East Yorkshire 1558–1790* (York, 1960); Aveling, 'The Catholic recusants of the West Riding of Yorkshire 1558–1790', *Proc. Leeds Lit. and Phil. Soc.*, X, pt vi (1963); Aveling, *Northern Catholics: The Catholic Recusants of the North Riding of Yorkshire 1558–1790* (London, 1966); P. R. Newman, 'Catholic royalist activists in the North', *Recusant Hist.*, xiv (1977).

37 J. C. D. Clark, *Revolution and Rebellion: State and Society in England in the Seventeenth and Eighteenth Centuries* (Cambridge, 1986), pp. 166, 57.

38 See R. C. Richardson (ed.), *The English Civil Wars: Local Aspects* (Stroud, 1997); S. Porter, *Destruction in the English Civil War* (Stroud, 1994).

39 See Richardson, *Town and Countryside*.

10

The twentieth century: 'history from below'

Why are you interested in those bandits? (Sir Lewis Namier to a prospective researcher on the Parisian *sans culottes* – recalled by Richard Cobb, *TLS*, 21 May 1971, p. 578)

Historians always, by the nature of the surviving evidence, tend to find ruling class views the easiest to recapture in any society; the viewpoint of the underdog has to be reconstructed painfully and piecemeal. (C. Hill, *Change and Continuity in Seventeenth-Century England* (London, 1975), p. 283)

The centre of [Hill's *The Experience of Defeat*] remains the cranks, crackpots, screwballs and fanatics, the nutters and kooks who appear in the wake of every genuine movement for social reform and who become the principal barrier to lasting change. . . . Nothing has done more to diminish the centrality of the English Revolution that did occur than obsessive concentration upon the English Revolution that didn't occur. (Mark Kishlansky, *THES*, 7 September 1984)

For all students of human society, sympathy with the victims of historical processes and scepticism about the victor's claims provide essential safeguards against being taken in by the dominant mythology. A scholar who tries to be objective needs these feelings as part of his ordinary working equipment. (B. Moore, *Social Origins of Dictatorship and Democracy* (Harmondsworth, 1973), p. 523)

The growth of democracy, socialism, and feminism since the late nineteenth century, the shift from the age of the elite to that of the masses, the levelling effects of two World Wars, the 1930s depression and the social protests of 1968 and after, have all contributed to a redistribution of emphasis in historical studies. 'History from below' or 'from the bottom up' has now joined the traditional top-level perspective which has always characterized the study of the past. This approach to history has a complicated ancestry which owes something to the Fabian paternalism of the Webbs and the Hammonds. French historians such as Lefebvre, Soboul, and the *Annales* school also made important contributions; this is no idiosyncratically insular English development.[1] But the leading Marxist historians in England – Hilton, Hill, Hobsbawm, Saville, and E. P. Thompson – have been particularly active in the development of this historical perspective, and works like Thompson's *The Making of the English Working Class* (London, 1963) have established themselves as classics of their genre. Such is the progress that it has made that 'history from below' is now seen – by all but the most diehard conservatives – as no less valid and necessary than the history of kings and parliaments. Not surprisingly, the seventeenth-century crisis – 'the greatest upheaval that has yet occurred in Britain'[2] – has figured prominently in this historical revolution.

Christopher Hill's *The World Turned Upside Down* (London, 1972) may be considered the major landmark, and in its exploration of radical ideas during the English Revolution dealt with groups such as the Levellers and Diggers, Ranters and Quakers, Muggletonians, and many more. Here in this book, Hill left the 'bourgeois revolution' on one side and concentrated on the unsuccessful 'revolt within the Revolution' which in its various forms came from the lower sections of society. This was a

> revolution which never happened, though from time to time it threatened. This might have established communal property, a far wider democracy in political and legal institutions, might have disestablished the state church and rejected the Protestant ethic.

The English Revolution was a period of incredible flux and excitement, and with the barriers of censorship down, 'teeming freedom' gushed out everywhere.

> Literally anything seemed possible; not only were the values of the old hierarchical society called into question but also the new values, the Protestant ethic itself. . . . [There had been challenges to order before but] what was new in the seventeenth century was the idea that the world might be *permanently* turned upside down.

(The dramatic qualities of this subject are self-evident and it is not surprising that they have been translated into plays and film by Keith Dewhurst, Caryl Churchill, and Kevin Brownlow.) In a way very reminiscent of Thompson's attempt to rescue the displaced workers and minor millenarian sects of the late eighteenth and early nineteenth centuries from 'the enormous condescension of posterity', Hill did the same for the lower class 'freedom fighters' of the English Revolution.[3]

Part of the strength of Hill's book lay in its genuinely comparative treatment of the different radical groups and his perception of the clear underlying links between them.[4] What the book also advertised in a more general, methodological sense was that 'history from below' was more than just another horizontal layer added to the bottom of the historian's picture. Hill made clear that his 'worm's eye view', appearances notwithstanding, could give 'a deeper insight into English society' than would otherwise have been possible if the neglected and forgotten groups and individuals recalled in his study had been allowed to remain in limbo. As R. H. Hilton has written of another period of English history: 'By looking from the bottom upwards we might get a more accurate picture of the whole of society, and of the state, than if we look at society from on high.'[5]

Hill, prolific as ever, has returned to, and extended, these themes in his later writings, most recently in *Liberty against the Law: Some Seventeenth-Century Controversies* (London, 1996). Hill's subject in this book was the self-reinforcing interconnections between law, liberty, property and Parliament, and the alternative perceptions of the majority of the population whose lot was to be kept outside the charmed circle. For a great many, he claimed, 'the law was the enemy', and 'opposed to their freedom' and customary rights. For others 'their religious duty was to break the law' so as to allow them to conform with their understanding of the higher code of heaven. In the light of these divergences of perception and experience provocative questions were pressed in this book about the making and enforcement of law and about the pronounced social variations encountered in accessing it and benefiting from its protection.

Hill stressed in this book, as in the many others he has written, the central importance of the seventeenth century to the processes and attitudes he was describing. The polarization of wealth increased during these decades, wage earners became a proportionately larger segment of society, enclosure had many casualties, and Civil Wars raised and dashed the hopes which some had entertained for radical change. Hostility to the law, as Hill made abundantly clear, was rampant, and lawyers, the operators of the detested system, attracted a crescendo of abuse in the overheated decade of the 1640s. The shrill and insistent cry for law reform went up in these years. The legal system, it was passionately argued, should be streamlined, delays and costs in litigation should be reduced, and the learned obscurities of Latin court transactions abandoned. Hill was not the first to write about this groundswell of opinion and about the agitation for law reform, but his treatment was undoubtedly more wide-ranging than that of historians who went before him. The seventeenth-century use of the Robin Hood legends, the ramifications of the Norman Yoke myth, smugglers, outlaws, pirates, gypsies, beggars and vagrants, imperial oppressions, marriage practices, and the appeal of antinomianism all found a place in these crowded pages. Gerrard Winstanley, the Digger leader and spokesman, got a longish chapter of his own in which the religious foundations of his audacious secular programme were rehearsed. Levellers, Ranters and Quakers were given a platform. But Hill's coverage of his subject – and fund of quotations – extended far beyond the seventeenth century. Eighteenth-century poets like Pope, Goldsmith, Blake and Burns were integrated into the discussion of key points. So were the early nineteenth-century voices of George Crabbe and the tragic figure of John Clare whose incarceration for madness formed a kind of epitaph in Hill's study.[6]

Besides Hill there have been others – and the number keeps growing – some of them his former students, who have shared his interests in the ways in which social groups below the ranks of the elite were becoming politicized in the early seventeenth century. (The spread of news was one obvious factor in this complex process as Richard Cust, for one, has underlined.) Research on popular politics, popular culture and popular religion has notably increased, and so have the controversies surrounding their interpretation. In popular politics the Levellers have continued to arouse the interest of historians, though to a lesser extent than was once the case. No longer seen as quite so far-sighted and 'democratic' as they appeared to an earlier generation of historians, the centre of interest has often tended to shift elsewhere. Winstanley and the Diggers apparently have more to say than Levellers like Lilburne to the late twentieth century. Besides Hill historians as diverse as G. E. Aylmer, T. W. Hayes, C. H. George and Oliver Lutaud are some of those who have answered the call.[7] Popular pressures and popular involvement in politics have been the subject of recent studies by Derek Hirst, Brian Manning, and David Underdown.

The Representative of the People? Voters and Voting in England under the Early Stuarts (London, 1975) by Derek Hirst (1948–), dealt with a theme which his own mentor, J. H. Plumb, had first begun to open up.[8] Based on a formidably large research effort in the archives using parliamentary journals, private correspondence, corporation records, and surviving voting lists, Dr Hirst argued that popular participation in politics was much greater than historians had allowed. Politics under the early Stuarts, Dr Hirst found, as E. P. Thompson and others have established for the eighteenth and early nineteenth centuries, was not simply elite politics.[9] Both the number of elections and the number of election contests were increasing in this period. Constituency pressures were exerted on MPs after their election. There were more voters than previously. In the countryside the simple process of inflation brought more men into the fold of the forty-shilling freeholders at a time when in any case the electoral definition of 'freehold' was becoming more flexible. A number of borough franchises were formally widened by the House of Commons, often for tactical reasons, in the 1620s. Enlarged electorates, it was widely felt, were less amenable to royal, and later Royalist, pressures and intimidation. Moreover, in Dr Hirst's words, 'a state of franchisal innocence' existed in the early seventeenth century which meant that the commons could take advantage of uncertainties about franchise qualifications and election management and exercise the vote whether or not they were so entitled. (Polling was unpopular with candidates and electors alike because of the time it took.) Both in town and countryside, then, voters were no longer a small, respectable minority; York's freemen franchise, for example, meant in practice that 75 per cent of the adult male population had the vote. By 1640, in Hirst's estimate, over the country as a whole, the electorate must have consisted of 27–40 per cent of adult males.[10]

An enlarged electorate, of course, brought more people into direct contact with the political process and, certainly by 1640, with national issues, and it meant increasingly that votes had to be won and could not be automatically relied upon. Partly due to the pressure of the commons themselves, and partly due to gentry willingness to use that pressure against the King, the popular presence was one of the most crucial elements in the political situation of 1640–1.[11]

Although quite accidentally, in a real sense Brian Manning's *The English People and the English Revolution 1640–1649* (London, 1976) followed on from where Hirst's book left off. His starting point was the elections of 1640 in which the political consequences of an enlarged electorate were unmistakably revealed.

> This enlarged electorate was less easy for the gentry to control and more capable of asserting its own opinions. . . . Political and religious questions became issues in the contests partly because of the intervention of the lower classes.

Manning (1927–), a radical himself, a former student of Christopher Hill, whose academic career was spent at Manchester University and at the University of Ulster, concentrated on 'the middle sort of people' and set out 'to discover the role of popular grievances, popular movements and popular aspirations in the revolutionary struggles of the decade 1640 to 1649'. Initially popular discontent focused on the trial of Strafford, and the death of the King's hated minister was viewed and exploited as a popular triumph. The aftermath, Manning continued, was a growing split in Parliament between those who reacted against the popular presence and those who responded and accommodated themselves to it. On the one hand the Royalist party 'arose from dislike of popular tumults: it was less the party of episcopalians or Straffordians than the party of order'. On the other hand, the Parliamentarian party in 1641 was a popular party whose members saw that popular support was essential if moderate reform was to be grasped from an obdurate King. The popular party, however, 'would ally with the people with the aim of drawing the teeth of popular movements, so as to ensure the safety of the ruling class'.[12]

Popular attitudes and intervention, Manning argued, were one of the principal determinants of the course of the English Revolution. It was the intervention of 'the mass of the ordinary people of London', a political move although it was fuelled by economic distress, which saved Parliament in the dark December days of 1641. 'The City was now the Parliament's – or rather the Parliament was now the City's'. 'The Royalists were right in thinking that their most formidable opponent was the ordinary citizen of London'. The grievances of the urban craftsmen against restrictive practices and monopolies forcefully penetrated the Parliament's cause. In the countryside there was agitation over tenures and enclosures directed against landlords, of whom the Crown was the largest. With puritanism as their ideology the middle ranks were a force to be reckoned with. As all restraints broke down the English Revolution came to express basic social conflicts which were articulated most clearly by the Levellers in their assault on the combination of wealth, power, and privilege and in their demands for decentralization.[13]

Manning's book dealt with urban and rural demonstrations, riots, and disturbances in the 1630s and early 1640s and with the taking of sides in the first Civil War. Its sequel – his book *1649: The Crisis of the English Revolution* (London, 1992) – examined the ways in which 'people from outside the governing class – private soldiers, apprentices, women, and numbers of the middle ranks of society – intervened in the great affairs of politics and religion'. He showed how 1649, the year in which the King was tried and executed, witnessed both the climax and the end of the popular revolution and the attempt to turn the world upside down. 'Military force triumphed over the more radical and populist wing of the revolution'. London and the Levellers both figured prominently in his account.[14] London and its popular movements have also been the focus of books by Keith Lindley and Tim Harris.[15] In the first of them Lindley, a former student of Brian Manning, examined the rise of mass politics in the capital at the beginning of the troubled decade of the 1640s, the outburst of anti-popery, the popular campaign for religious reformation by parish zealots, and the rise of the Levellers. Tim Harris took the same kind of investigation forward into the years after 1660 and in his book *London Crowds in the Reign of Charles II* (Cambridge, 1987) painstakingly examined the links between popular politics and the divided society and culture of late seventeenth-century London.

The fact that our own society in the late twentieth century has been confronting major problems relating to social order and disorder (with riots and violence in inner city areas and at football games a conspicuous phenomenon) has given added significance to further work on the social pathology of the seventeenth century. The American historian Buchanan Sharp examined food and enclosure riots, and the more widespread western risings. His book *In Contempt of All Authority: Rural Artisans and Riot in the West of England 1586–1660* (Berkeley and Los Angeles, 1980) expressed the view that these disorders were 'the result of social and economic grievances of such intensity that they took expression in violent outbreaks of what can only be called class hatred for the wealthy'.[16] Sharp's views on the politics of popular disturbances and their relationship to the Civil Wars found echoes in a parallel study of East Anglia. Keith Lindley explored the subject of *Fenland Riots and the English Revolution* (London, 1982) and found that the 'politics' of the commoners of that region had more to do with drainage, enclosure, and the loss of common rights than with the more distant doings of King, Parliament, and later Protector. The political consequences and significance of the fenmen's actions far outdistanced any political motives that may have helped to inspire them.

This has proved highly debatable territory. The politicization of the masses as seen by David Underdown, one of Hill's former students, was of a different and more deep-seated kind. The discernible patterns of popular allegiance in the Civil War, he argued in *Revel, Riot and Rebellion* (Oxford, 1985), were in a real sense 'ecological'. Popular Parliamentarianism and popular Royalism were the outcrops 'of the earlier emergence of two quite different constellations of social, political and cultural forces, involving diametrically opposite responses to the problems of the time . . . Contrasts in popular allegiance', he continued, 'had a regional basis and were related to local differences in social structure, economic development and culture'. Like Buchanan Sharp, Underdown focused on the western counties, provided a full-scale treatment of their social, economic, and cultural diversity, and attempted to make sense not only of the politicizing effects of the Civil War but of the long-term trends – population growth, inflation, enclosure, social regrouping, puritanism – which lay behind them. Of all the possible determinants of allegiance – social deference and class antagonisms included – it was the formative contribution of contrasting regional cultures that he found most important.[17]

The case he advanced for the extent and nature of popular involvement in the Civil War was a convincing one, though subsequent local studies, such as Mark Stoyle's excellent book on Devon, have scarcely eliminated the criticism of the 'ecological' dimension of Underdown's thesis which it initially encountered. His book presented a full survey of economic and social structures and relations, cultural tendencies, and patterns of parochial and manorial government. *Revel, Riot and Rebellion* usefully combined the characteristics of a detailed monograph with those of a general history. It displayed a good eye for illuminating details as well as the capacity to range widely and seek out patterns and trends. Problems remain in Underdown's analysis, however, on account of the sources, despite some valiant attempts at quantification. Due to the unequal survival of documentation Underdown could write with greater knowledge about rank and file Royalists than about the Parliamentarians. The widespread contemporary practice of conscription, in any case, self-evidently complicated any account he could provide of freely given popular allegiance.[18]

Underdown's most recent book, *A Freeborn People: Politics and the Nation in Seventeenth-Century England* (Oxford, 1996), was a continuation of its author's preoccupations with 'history from below' and his concern to bridge gaps separating the study of elite and popular culture and seventeenth-century social and political history. Polite and plebeian culture, Underdown argued persuasively in this book, substantially overlapped in early seventeenth-century England. The high temperature of politics in the 1620s, for example, was generated by disgruntlement at all levels of society and with the Duke of Buckingham as a prominent target. Religion intertwined with gentry politics no less than with the politics of the middling sort of people. In this as in other respects the Civil War period was a watershed and had the effect of driving a wedge between the Parliamentarian leaders and army grandees and those radicals beneath them in the social scale. Underdown recognized no less than others before him, that the popular revolution of the 1640s failed and both the Interregnum and the

Restoration reinforced this eclipse. Popular conservatism, in any case, in Underdown's view – and here he tended to part company with Christopher Hill – was more characteristic than popular radicalism. In his scenario Monmouth's Rebellion of 1685 was the last, doomed attempt to bring popular activism into play as a deciding force. The successful Glorious Revolution of 1688/9, by contrast, was enacted only by the elite. Its consequences, once safely decided, were then handed down to an acquiescing 'people'. Underdown looked carefully at the patterns and imagery of popular protests and here, as in *Revel, Riot and Rebellion*, he had much to say about popular rituals and sports and about popular appeals to mythical leaders. He also drew attention to the gendered rhetoric of both elite and popular politics and about the involvement, both actual and perceived, of women. Here Underdown lined up with historians such as Phyllis Mack and Susan Amussen in insisting on the necessity of recognizing such gender-related instabilities in the period. It is this which explains why a volume which was originally announced under the title *Freeborn Englishmen* came out more accurately entitled *A Freeborn People*.[19]

With or without active allegiance to one side or the other in the 1640s the military impact of Civil War was registered in the lives of ordinary men and women. *Going to the Wars: The Experience of the British Civil Wars 1638–1651* (London, 1992) by Charles Carlton presented the painful chronicle. He had much to say, for example, about conditions of service – pay, quarters, weaponry, food and clothing – and on the hardships of combat and sieges, and on the horrors of imprisonment. He pointed out an often overlooked consequence of the loss of royal control of London, that the parliamentary armies had more medical men at their disposal. Carlton made comparisons between the levels of violence in Scotland, Ireland and England, and between the First Civil War in England and its two successors. Women were noted both as activists and as victims. Attention was drawn to the high desertion rates from the armies of the time. The introduction of army uniforms was remarked on and much was made of the soaring price of horses in the 1640s. Observations were made about the relative scarcity of war poetry inspired by the Civil Wars. On the other hand, as Carlton pointed out, the English language was expanded by the wartime arrival of the word 'plunder' and such novel expressions as 'prisoners of war' and 'sending to Coventry', a favourite receptacle for the former.[20] Though his account was full of personal details, statistics provided a framework for, and reinforced, Carlton's many examples of the effects of war, though it is not always clear how they have been arrived at. Unlike others who have written on the subject Carlton played down the strength of ideological commitment in the First Civil War.

Carlton stopped short of assessing the rival armies as cultural and not just military forces. Others, however, have placed popular culture in its widest sense firmly on the agenda in ways that would have been considered inconceivable thirty years ago. Keith Thomas has undertaken a wide study of *Man and the Natural World: Changing Attitudes in England 1500–1800* (London, 1983). Crime, popular education, reading habits – all of which had a bearing on the developments of the Civil War period – have now found their historians.[21] Alehouses – which functioned amongst other things as popular meeting places or local 'parliaments' – and their place in the alternative society of the time have been surveyed by Peter Clark.[22] Steven R. Smith and Ilana Ben Amos have looked at apprenticeship as a social institution and the first of them went on to assess the connections between adolescence and protest.[23] Two important collections of essays on early modern popular culture in England were published in 1985 and 1995 respectively, the wider chronological limits of the second of them allowing a more satisfactory discussion of long-term trends. (Much popular literature, as Bernard Capp showed in one of the contributions, seemingly possessed an endless shelf life.[24]) The 'middling sort of people' figured prominently in both volumes. Regional differences, horizontal cultural variations, and divergences of perception were emphasized. It was the overlap rather than the rigid separation of elite and popular culture which came across more insistently. Like most revisionism the second volume discredited comfortable generalizations. Peter Burke's definition of popular culture as 'a system of shared meanings, attitudes and values and the symbolic forms in which they are expressed or embodied' no longer seemed adequate to describe plural forms and perceptions in constant flux. Popular cultures were bound up with the power relationships – some of them to do with gender – of this period. Problematizing the subject, as this volume did, still left many problems unresolved but the flow of questions, once the floodgate is opened, has become exhilaratingly unstoppable.[25]

In *Wallington's World: A Puritan Artisan in Seventeenth-Century London* (London, 1985) Paul Seaver focused microscopically on the life, habits, and values of a single individual – an unusual feat made possible by the substantial series of surviving notebooks which this prolific artisan left behind. For Nehemiah Wallington (1598–1658), a puritan turner of St Leonard's, Eastcheap, as for the well-documented clergyman Ralph Josselin,[26] God and religion were what mattered most, and it was from spiritual motives that he wrote so regularly and at such length. (A psychohistorian, however, would no doubt argue that Wallington retreated to his study because he was so ineffectual and crippled by shyness in his social dealings with others; it was only when he was writing that he could find the right words. Prone to depression, he was over fifty before he was unshakeably assured of his place among the puritan elect.) Wallington had no doubt that the world he inhabited was divinely made and dominated and that all that happened at the political, economic, and personal levels expressed the unfolding of God's mercies and judgements on a perverse generation. The Bible was his constant companion and sermons and prayers the staple of his life; he once attended nineteen sermons in a single week. That the longed-for Reformation never came out of the ample God-given opportunities of the 1640s and 1650s was for Wallington, as for others of his kind, a perplexing and mortifying experience.

Wallington's occupation or 'calling' was not for him an overriding priority and he deplored the business ethic of those who aimed at success at any price. We have much in this book about family life, domestic economy, mortality, kinship, and friendship networks stretching out as far as Connecticut and Massachusetts, and about disease, fire, and other hazards of London life. We learn much about the impact of the Civil War.

It was the morality rather than the mechanisms of the market place which concerned Wallington. He left behind no account book – a deficiency in the sources which prevented Seaver from pressing his economic analysis very far. None the less, we get some sense of the context of industrial organization in which Wallington worked as a member of the Turners' Company, about apprenticeship, and about Wallington's buying, selling, borrowing, and cash-flow problems. What is clear is that Wallington was not a successful businessman. His personality and social awkwardness hindered his commercial dealings. Though he jealously guarded his reputation as a godly tradesman his priorities in life clearly lay elsewhere. In any case the profit margin in his trade was very low. So Wallington's world – skilfully opened up by Seaver in this volume – displayed some of the tensions and paradoxes in the connections between religion and capitalism in the early modern period.[27]

In the nature of things the rediscovery of popular politics and culture – categories which clearly did not exist in self-contained isolation – has led to increased awareness of the complex dimensions of popular religion. Tessa Watt's *Cheap Print and Popular Piety 1550–1640* (Cambridge, 1991) was a good example. Principally concerned with different aspects of the production, distribution and reception of broadside ballads, broadside pictures, and chapbooks, her book was a case study in 'typographical acculturation'. Watt demonstrated that there was no clear-cut dividing line between the visual attributes of the pre-Reformation church and its Protestant successor. The iconic, she insisted, did not suddenly give place to the iconoclastic and logo-centric. Though there were indeed some changes, Watt argued, the persistence of a visual element in religion – evidenced in woodcuts, tables, frontispieces, and so on – was plain to see. Post-Reformation printed text and picture were not mutually exclusive categories. Watt was no less opposed to the confrontational model of popular and elite culture which some historians have insisted upon. While re-emphasizing the cultural importance of both Protestantism and the printed word, Watt was disinclined to see either as a coherent and unchanging force. 'The evidence of cheap print questions the rigidity of this "polarization" of experience between godly and ungodly, elite and poor. In these cheapest of printed wares, Protestant doctrine and conservative piety were integrated, and "religion" continued to have a place in the world of popular songs and alehouses, which were supposedly the preserve of the irreligious multitude'. Thus she argued that the habit of compartmentalizing religion, especially in the decades prior to the outbreak of Civil War, must be rejected. Historians of popular piety in this period, Watt insisted, cannot get far if they look only at churches.[28]

The religious extremes and irreligion are also finding their historians. The noisy, wild and often blasphemous confusion of religious unorthodoxies which burst out in the uncensored mid-seventeenth-century decades had been documented with fascinated loathing in *Gangraena* by the contemporary heresiographer Thomas Edwards.[29] Much of Hill's *The World Turned Upside Down* was devoted to the study of the forms and attitudes expressed in popular religious radicalism, as was Hill's later collection of essays on *Religion and Politics in the Seventeenth Century* (Brighton, 1986). A. L. Morton and Nigel Smith have written on the Ranters.[30] Robin Clifton has investigated the popular fear of Catholics during the English Revolution,[31] while other historians – some of them former students of the Master of Balliol College, Oxford – have explored additional aspects of radical religion. The collection of essays edited by J. F. McGregor and Barry Reay on *Radical Religion in the English Revolution* (Oxford, 1984) was a good indicator of current trends. Baptists, Seekers, Ranters, Quakers, Fifth Monarchists, Levellers, and Diggers came under discussion in this lively, argumentative symposium which not only moved into new territory and took issue with what had been written before by others, but also kept an eye firmly on the present. Ordinary people in the English Revolution, the editors stated in their preface, 'campaigned for notions that have yet to be realised: there is much that we can learn from them'. Tony Benn was quoted; an analogy was made with present-day Iran.

Other writers have brought the Muggletonians into sharper focus and readdressed the Quakers. *The World of the Muggletonians* by Christopher Hill, Barry Reay, and William Lamont (London, 1983) was responsible for the first achievement. Muggletonians were neither the most numerous, noisy, nor extreme of the mid-seventeenth-century religious groups, but studying them undoubtedly has revealed something of 'the potential of popular ideology and activity' and offered 'a glimpse at the English Revolution from below'.

> The fact that radical ideas could break through and flourish in what before 1640 and after 1660 appears a stable, hierarchical and deferential society [wrote Christopher Hill] may help us to understand that society better, to be less superficial in our acceptance of its self-

estimate. . . . The Muggletonians belong to the cultural underworld of the middling and lower classes rather than to the intellectual history of their time. As such they form part of the evidence that has to be incorporated into any study of the common people in seventeenth-century England.[32]

The chance discovery of their archive in the 1970s – probably the last survivor of the sect died in 1979 – has made modern historians better equipped to address their extraordinary theology, their informal, self-effacing organization, their peculiar brand of 'intellectual anti-intellectualism', the relations between Reeve and Muggleton, and the importance (social as well as religious) of the leaders' predilection for cursing.

Twenty years ago few outside the narrow ranks of the specialists would even have heard of the Muggletonians. By contrast everyone knew about the Quakers (or thought they did), but they, too, have been reassessed in ways which have brought us closer to the 'real' history and significance of this strikingly radical, resilient, and changing group. Barry Reay's *The Quakers and the English Revolution* (London, 1985) insisted that Quaker history had dimensions other than those normally commented upon by historians and that it provided distinctive vantage points for re-evaluating the lives and beliefs of ordinary people in the seventeenth century as well as the attitudes of the elite and the course of the English Revolution. Reay made clear that the early history of the Quakers had quite different characteristics from those displayed in its later development after 1660. The social composition of the movement was less solidly bourgeois. Ex-Levellers and Diggers joined its ranks; some came from the New Model Army. Women were attracted by the spiritual equality which the Quakers offered. In the 1650s, in short, Quakers were far from being sedate, accommodating, silent, and pacifist. Instead they did strange, bold, symbolic things and incurred not only the hostility of judges, justices, and clergy but also popular opposition as well. That the original Quakers met in remote rural locations and came from the strange and alien North no doubt fuelled popular misapprehensions, distrust, and fear. Hostility to Quakerism and the disorders attributed to it helped to make possible the Restoration of 1660. In this instance, therefore, as in others, 'history from below' helps to explain 'history from above'.[33]

Not all historians, however, have welcomed the development of these proletarian perspectives on the past and there have been critics – all stridently anti-Marxist – of its practice. G. R. Elton, who personified the traditional values, unsurprisingly held aloof from 'the present outburst of social history'.[34] John Miller denounced Brian Manning's book on *The English People and the English Revolution* as 'a museum piece' and criticized the author for his 'determination to fit his material, however uncomfortably, into a basically Marxist model of class conflict between 'the middle sort of people' and 'the ruling class'.[35] Hirst's book on early seventeenth-century voters and voting (see p. 188) was the subject of attack from Mark Kishlansky. Reacting against the prevailing tide that Englishmen in the seventeenth century were an 'ungovernable people' Anthony Fletcher and John Stevenson produced a volume of essays that was chiefly a celebration of stability. *Order and Disorder in Early Modern England* (Cambridge, 1985) vigorously rejected a class-conflict interpretation of this period and left-wing historians like Christopher Hill and E. P. Thompson were suitably admonished for getting it wrong. An essay dealing specifically with the English Revolution argued that the commonly invoked image of disorder in the Civil War was to a large extent an illusion, caused either by the politically inspired exaggerations of Royalists and Parliamentarians (the idea of a 'popular presence', for different reasons, suited both) or by the distortions of old people's imprecise recollections. Re-exploring adjacent territory, J. C. Davis in *Fear, Myth and History: The Ranters and the Historians* (Cambridge, 1986) concluded that the Ranters had no real existence as a movement or even as a coherent core of individuals. They were instead the mythical embodiment of the fears, prejudices, and uncertainties of seventeenth-century conservatives and have been confirmed in their place in the mythology of the English Revolution by modern Marxist historians like Morton and Hill for whom their existence was no less vital.

Criticisms and denunciations such as these arguably tell us as much about their respective authors as about the seventeenth-century past; present political attitudes and preferences – as the long debate on the English Revolution has eloquently testified – undoubtedly have helped to shape historical interpretations. The same Gerrard Winstanley can be for Hill 'a gentle communist' and for J. C. Davis a rigid, harsh totalitarian, 'a model for Joseph Stalin'.[36] Residual opposition to 'history from below' notwithstanding, however, the losers of history, the wrongly categorized 'lunatic fringes', are belatedly, and rightly, finding their historians in recent writing about the English Revolution.[37]

Notes

1 G. Lefebvre, *Les Paysans du Nord* (Paris, 1924) and *The Great Fear of 1789* (Paris, 1932; English trans., New York, 1973); A. Soboul, *The Parisian Sans Culottes and the French Revolution* (Oxford, 1964). See also F. Krantz (ed.), *History from Below: Studies in Popular Protest and Ideology* (Oxford, 1988). For the Annales historians see T. Stoianovich, *French Historical Method: The Annales Paradigm* (Ithaca, New York, 1976).

2 C. Hill, *The World Turned Upside Down: Radical Ideas during the English Revolution* (London, 1972), p. 11.

3 Hill, *World Turned Upside Down*, pp. 12, 14. Hill has written elsewhere on the breakdown of censorship: 'Censorship and English literature', in Hill, *Writing and Revolution in Seventeenth-Century England* (Brighton, 1985), pp. 32–71, and 'Political discourse in early seventeenth-century England', in C. Jones *et al.* (eds), *Politics and People in Revolutionary England* (Oxford, 1986), pp. 41–64. See also R. C. Richardson and G. M. Ridden (eds), *Freedom and the English Revolution: Essays in History and Literature* (Manchester, 1986), and Annabel Patterson, *Censorship and Interpretation: The Conditions of Writing and Reading in Early Modern England* (Madison, Wis., 1984).

4 Critics have argued that in so doing he gave too little weight to the millenarian aspects of popular religion and to the backward-looking features of popular radicalism. The *TLS* reviewer (18 August 1972) felt that Hill's treatment 'may be a little too orderly and over-categorized with too little of the kaleidoscope, too little account taken of apathy, misunderstanding, confusion, and the sheer randomness of things' (p. 970).

5 R. H. Hilton, *A Medieval Society: The West Midlands at the end of the Thirteenth Century* (1966, Cambridge 1983), p. 4.

6 Hill, *Liberty Against the Law, passim*. He quotes from Clare

> O England! boasted land of liberty
> Thy poor slaves the alteration see
> Like emigrating bird thy freedom's flown
> And every parish owns its tyrants now
> And parish slaves must live as parish kings allow.

> (*Ibid.*, p. 313.)

7 R. Cust, 'News and politics in early seventeenth-century England', *PP*, 112 (1980). See also D. Freist, *Governed by Opinion. Politics, Religion and the Dynamics of Communication in Stuart London, 1637–45* (London, 1996). On the Levellers see G. E. Aylmer (ed.), *The Levellers in the English Revolution*

(London, 1975); H. N. Brailsford, *The Levellers and the English Revolution* (London, 1961); B. Manning, 'The Levellers and religion', in J. McGregor and B. Reay (eds), *Radical Religion in the English Revolution* (Oxford, 1984), pp. 65–90. On Winstanley and the Diggers see, for example, G. E. Aylmer, 'The religion of Gerrard Winstanley', in McGregor and Reay, *Radical Religion*, pp. 91–120, T. W. Hayes, *Winstanley the Digger: A Literary Analysis of Radical Ideas in the English Revolution* (Cambridge, Mass., 1979); C. H. George, 'Gerrard Winstanley: a critical retrospect', in C. R. Cole and M. E. Moody (eds), *The Dissenting Tradition* (Athens, Ohio, 1975); O. Lutaud, *Winstanley: Socialisme et Christianisme sous Cromwell* (Paris, 1976); C. Hill, 'The religion of Gerrard Winstanley', in Hill, *Religion and Politics in Seventeenth-Century England*, pp. 185–252; and C. Hill, 'Winstanley and freedom', in Richardson and Ridden, *Freedom and the English Revolution*, pp. 151–68.

8 J. H. Plumb, 'The growth of the electorate in England from 1600 to 1715', *PP*, 45 (1969).

9 See E. P. Thompson, *Whigs and Hunters* (London, 1975).

10 Hirst, *The Representative of the People? Voters and Voting in England under the Early Stuarts* (London, 1975), pp. 31, 44–64, 95, 105.

11 *Ibid.*, pp. 148, 149, 152, 176.

12 B. Manning, *The English People and the English Revolution 1640–1649* (London, 1976), pp. v, 2, 20, 70. Joyce Lee Malcolm has examined commoners' attitudes to the Royalist cause in *Caesar's Due: Loyalty and King Charles, 1642–1646* (London, 1983).

13 Manning, *The English People*, pp. 96, 98, 197, 148, 137, 184. The small farmers and craftsmen, however, were not mutually exclusive categories. The proto-industrialization of parts of the countryside meant that large numbers with dual occupations shared the grievances of both groups; *ibid.*, pp. 102, 234, 162.

14 Manning, *The English People*, pp. 19, 215.

15 Lindley, *Popular Politics and Religion in Civil War London* (Aldershot, 1997).

16 Sharp, *In Contempt of All Authority*, p. 264.

17 Underdown, *Revel, Riot and Rebellion*, pp. 40, 4.

18 J. Morrill, 'The ecology of allegiance in the English Civil Wars', in Morrill, *The Nature of the English Revolution* (London, 1993); Underdown, *Revel, Riot and Rebellion*, esp. pp. 179–81, 200–7, 187–9.

19 Underdown, *Freeborn People*, pp. v–vi, 67, 92, 125–8.

20 Carlton, *Going to the Wars*, pp. 226–7, 196, 132, 238.

21 J. S. Cockburn (ed.), *Crime in England 1550–1800* (London, 1977), J. A. Sharpe, *Crime in Seventeenth-Century England: A County Study* (Cambridge, 1983), and J. A. Sharpe, *Crime in Early Modern England 1550–1750* (London, 1984). On popular education and reading habits see D. Cressy, *Literacy and the Social Order: Reading and Writing in Tudor and Stuart England* (Cambridge, 1980), Margaret Spufford, *Contrasting Communities: English Villagers in the Sixteenth and Seventeenth Centuries* (Cambridge, 1974), Margaret Spufford, *Small Books and Pleasant Histories: Popular Fiction and its Readership in Seventeenth-Century England* (London, 1981), B. Capp, *Astrology and the Popular Press: English Almanacs 1500–1800* (London, 1979).

22 P. Clark, *The English Alehouse: A Social History 1200–1830* (London, 1983), esp. pp. 145–65.
23 S. R. Smith, 'The London apprentices as seventeenth-century adolescents', in P. Slack (ed.), *Rebellion, Popular Protest and the Social Order in Early Modern England* (Cambridge, 1984), pp. 162–211, Ilana Krausman Ben Amos, *Adolescence and Youth in Early Modern England* (New Haven, 1994).
24 B. Reay (ed.), *Popular Culture in Seventeenth-Century England* (London, 1985), T. Harris (ed.), *Popular Culture in England c. 1500–1850* (London, 1995). Capp's essay is in Reay's volume, pp. 198–243.
25 Harris, *Popular Culture*, p. 1. See, especially, in this volume the essays by Harris ('Problematising popular culture', pp. 1–27), and by Amussen ('The gendering of popular culture in early modern England', pp. 48–68).
26 See A. Macfarlane, *The Family Life of Ralph Josselin, a seventeenth-century Clergyman* (Cambridge, 1970) and A. Macfarlane (ed.), *The Diary of Ralph Josselin 1616–83* (London, Records of Social and Economic History, n. s., III, British Academy, 1976).
27 Seaver, *Wallington's World*, esp. chs 4 and 5 which deal with Wallington's networks of family, friends, and business connections.
28 Watt, *Cheap Print and Popular Piety*, pp. 2, 322, 326, 328.
29 See C. Hill, 'Irreligion in the Puritan revolution', in McGregor and Reay, *Radical Religion*, pp. 191–212, G. E. Aylmer, 'Unbelief in seventeenth-century England', in D. H. Pennington and K. Thomas (eds), *Puritans and Revolutionaries* (Oxford, 1978), pp. 22–46, and M. Hunter, 'The problem of "atheism" in early modern England', *TRHS*, 5th ser., xxxv (1985), pp. 135–58.
30 A. L. Morton, *The World of the Ranters* (London, 1970), N. Smith (ed.), *A Collection of Ranter Writings from the Seventeenth Century* (London, 1983).
31 *PP*, 52 (1971), reprinted in Slack (ed.), *Rebellion, Popular Protest*, pp. 129–61.
32 Hill, Reay and Lamont (eds), *World of the Muggletonians*, pp. 11, 14.
33 See also R. Bauman, *Let your Words be Few: Symbolism of Speaking and Silence among Seventeenth-century Quakers* (Cambridge, 1983).
34 In Cockburn, *Crime in England*, p. 1.
35 Miller, *THES*, 28 May 1976, p. 16. The second edition of Manning's book has a long, new introduction which takes on his critics.
36 See Hill, 'The religion of Gerrard Winstanley', in Hill, *Religion and Politics in Seventeenth-Century England*, pp. 185–252, J. C. Davis, 'Gerrard Winstanley and the restoration of true magistracy', *PP*, 70 (1976), pp. 75–93. See also C. Hill, 'The Lost Ranters? A critique of J. C. Davis', *Hist. Workshop J.* (Autumn 1987), pp. 134–40: 'Why is it so important for Davis to prove that they did not exist? What is he frightened of?'
37 A. L. Rowse, arch snob and opponent of the despised 'idiot people' in his own day and in the past, attacked Hill for wasting his time writing a history of seventeenth-century nonsense! It was all so pointless and boring, he insisted (A. L. Rowse, *Historians I Have Known* (London, 1995), pp. 105–10).

11

The twentieth century:
politics, political culture, revisionism

The authoritative account, now almost 100 years old, remains that of S. R. Gardiner. His was a staggering achievement. His narrative only needs correction on a few points of detail. (Anthony Fletcher, *The Outbreak of the English Civil War* (London, 1981), p. viii)

It is rare, in laying down a book on a subject at first sight as trite as the parliamentary history of the England of the early Stuarts, to be stirred by feelings of mingled gratitude and surprise at the new vistas opened by it. (R. H. Tawney, introduction to D. Brunton and D. H. Pennington, *Members of the Long Parliament* (London, 1954), p. xxii)

However ancient and well established the writing of political history may be, it is at present under something of a cloud. At least some professional historians incline to treat it as a rather old fashioned and manifestly inadequate – even an uninteresting form. Some think it too 'easy'. (G. R. Elton, *Political History: Principles and Practice* (London, 1970), p. 57)

We must regret that the term 'revisionism' has entered our language since it clouds much and explains little. (Kevin Sharpe, *Faction and Parliament: Essays on Early Stuart History* (2nd edn, London, 1985), p. xvi)

Political history and intellectual history should not be divorced . . . Revisionist history of early Stuart England need not be a history with the ideas left out, indeed a better understanding of the seventeenth century requires a fuller study of the relationship of ideas, values and styles to politics and the exercise of power. (Kevin Sharpe, *Politics and Ideas in Early Stuart England* (London, 1989), p. xi)

The Civil War is not an enclosed English subject. It cannot be understood in any purely English context, which is perhaps why it has caused so much bewilderment to the English, both then and now . . . We have been trying to deduce the whole of the explanation from one part of the problem. (Conrad Russell, *The Fall of the British Monarchies 1637–1642* (Oxford, 1991), p. 525)

Much of the emphasis in historical writing on the English Revolution in recent decades, as previous chapters have demonstrated, has been on its social, economic, regional and local aspects, and on 'history from below'. Reacting against relics of Victorian liberalism and the prominence given to political explanations and high politics by Gardiner and Firth and their 'school', historians moved out into those areas of the period which still appeared to be most open and in which the need for research seemed most urgent. It was often felt that the political history of the Revolution (at least at the top and the centre) had already been established and mapped out in laborious detail. For a time, therefore, this branch of the historiography of the English Revolution seemed threatened with eclipse. Labelled as Whig history, it became unfashionable. Political history and detailed narrative of events – increasingly out of favour – seemed inseparably bound up with each other. The early seventeenth-century monarchy – biographies of James I and Charles I notwithstanding – attracted hardly any serious study.[1] Even the once proclaimed central institution of Parliament was relatively neglected. Firth's study of the House of Lords published in 1910 was not followed up by a comparable study for over seventy years (Elizabeth R. Foster, *The House of Lords 1603–49: Structure, Procedure and the Nature of its Business* (Chapel Hill, NC, 1983)). Foreign policy and war came to engage the attention of fewer and fewer historians. In short, although political histories of the Revolutionary period continued to be written they were done, until relatively recently at least, under the long shadow cast by S. R. Gardiner.

Amongst the traditionalists C. V. Wedgwood (1910–97) justly acquired the reputation of being the most accomplished of the nineteenth-century narrative historians' successors. Although she wrote extensively on European history, she became best known for her work on seventeenth-century England.[2] Veronica Wedgwood's greatest skill as a historian was in telling a story, in making clear how and in what order political events occurred. Apparently after graduating at Oxford, she had been about to embark on research under Tawney. Instead she settled for Trevelyan and identified with his preference for descriptive, narrative history. Both the achievements and limitations of this kind of historical approach were displayed in her volumes on *The King's Peace 1637–1641* (London, 1955), *The King's War 1641–1647* (London, 1958), and on *The Trial of Charles I* (London, 1964). 'She is a shortbread historian', it has been asserted. 'She tells stories simply and entertainingly in the manner of Somerset Maugham'.[3] Reviewing *The King's War*, Christopher Hill opined:

> Miss Wedgwood's book as a whole is a narrative, not an explanation. It tells us all about the war except what they fought each other for . . . Many of her pages are full of one rather breathless incident after another . . . Two hundred facts do not make an interpretation . . . Too often Miss Wedgwood leaves us bewildered in a flux of events. . . . [Her] refusal to analyse makes it impossible to see below the surface of mere events.[4]

C. V. Wedgwood freely admitted as much herself. She never made false claims for her kind of history and was obviously content to follow in the footsteps of illustrious predecessors like Macaulay and Trevelyan. More than once she defended the reputation of the former and her book *The King's Peace 1637–1641* was dedicated to Trevelyan, her mentor, and was written in a manner which the master himself would have been proud of.[5] In the introduction she justified her decision to produce what was first and foremost 'a straightforward and chronological narrative'. Her aim in writing the book, she declared, had been above all to restore 'the immediacy of experience', 'the admitted motives and the illusions of the men of the seventeenth century'. Historians themselves had intruded too frequently in their efforts to reconstruct the seventeenth-century past. 'It is equally legitimate', Wedgwood insisted, 'to accept the motives and explanations which satisfied contemporaries'. 'The behaviour of men as individuals', she went on, 'is more interesting to me than their behaviour as groups or classes'. Her book, therefore, was 'not an economic analysis, not a social study; it is an attempt to understand how these men felt and why, in their own estimation, they acted as they did'.[6] Given these preferences the writing of biography had obvious attractions. Her study of *Strafford* (London, 1935) was, in fact, her first book, and it was revised and reissued in the light of subsequent research nearly thirty years later as *Thomas Wentworth, First Earl of Strafford 1593–1641: A Revaluation* (London, 1961).[7]

Another traditionalist, this time from the other side of the Atlantic, was Wedgwood's almost exact contemporary J. H. Hexter (1910–96), who developed during his tenure at those universities the Yale Center for Parliamentary History and Washington University's Center for the History of Freedom. His first major publication – only recently coming in for a full-frontal attack – was *The Reign of King Pym* (Cambridge, Mass., 1941).[8] C. V. Wedgwood was acknowledged in the introduction to a book whose prime concern was with the emergence and management of a middle group in the House of Commons in the 1640s. Pym shone through Hexter's pages – and the image is only now being dismantled – as a political artist of consummate skill. He was no idealist. Above all 'he was a political tactician, a political engineer'. Of the three men in the middle group – Essex and Hampden were the others – holding the balance between the extremes of the war party and the peace party, it was Pym whose role was in a real sense most crucial, particularly after the outbreak of war when Parliament had no effective organization, no military or administrative machine of its own. '[Pym] had the dull but useful knack of squeezing the maximum political energy out of the most unpromising raw materials, and of applying that energy at the time and in the place where it would be most effective; somehow or other he kept things going'.[9]

Always at home in historical controversy – his savage encounter with Hill (see pp. 137–8) should have left the reader in no doubt on that score – Hexter fired the first shots in what has since proved a lively debate with his article on 'The Problems of the Presbyterian Independents' in 1938.[10] Most recently, as a counter to what he considered a growing tendency to treat the politics of the seventeenth century as mere epiphenomena, he edited and contributed to *Parliament and Liberty from the Reign of Elizabeth to the English Civil War* (Stanford, CA, 1992). Its title advertised its central concern: the ways in which an English institution and the notion of freedom came to be closely bound up with each other in this period. 'The privileges of Parliament', it was contended, were viewed 'simultaneously as a principal right of Englishmen and as an essential bulwark to protect all their rights and freedoms'. The importance of free elections was emphasized and the well-known linkages between the common law and political thinking were rehearsed. Not surprisingly, most contributors to this volume came back repeatedly to the Petition of Right as a key document, as they did to the Commons Apology of 1604. Politics loomed much larger here than religion. Magna Carta got three times as many mentions as the Bible. It is clear then that there was much in this rather old-fashioned book that was thoroughly Whiggish or neo-Whiggish, not least in its designation of landmarks, its simplistically linear reading of history, and in its unabashed admiration for early seventeenth-century England as the beacon light of the modern world. The distinctions in this period between 'liberty' and 'freedom', though recognized, were not fully worked through, and too often the rhetoric and self-estimates of Parliament men were accepted at face value. Curiously the Civil War period was passed over almost as an irrelevance. 'The Civil Wars', Hexter asserted, 'like religion, stood apart from the growth of freedom, except insofar as men caught up in battle rode roughshod over the liberties of their opponents and those of many innocent bystanders'. The concept of an 'English Revolution' in these years evidently was denied. 'The authors of this volume have not forgotten the decades of the 1640s and 1650s but neither, given the present purpose, do they need to dwell on them'. That the Petition of Right had a mixed legacy and that Parliament at times conducted itself in a far from high-minded way were unthinkable ingredients in Hexter's noble and inspiring story. Lord Acton's ghost still stalked these and other pages penned by this writer and the editor of his Festschrift struggled hard and ultimately unconvincingly to claim for Hexter the label 'humanist' rather than Whig.[11]

American historians have figured prominently in the twentieth-century historiography of Stuart parliaments. Chief among them, undoubtedly, was Professor Wallace Notestein (1878–1969), whose teaching career was spent in the universities of Kansas, Minnesota, Cornell, and Yale. Part of Notestein's contribution to the re-examination of parliamentary history in the early seventeenth century was in editing source material. In 1921 he brought out an edition of the *Commons Debates for 1629* and the seven volumes of *Commons Debates 1621* followed in 1935. In addition, in 1923, Notestein began the publication of *The Journal of Sir Simonds D'Ewes*.[12] Notestein, however, is best remembered for his famous essay on Jacobean parliaments, 'The winning of the initiative by the House of Commons', one of the most prominent and influential of all signposts pointing out the highroad to Civil War. His narrative history of *The House of Commons 1604–1610* (New Haven, 1971) was published posthumously.[13]

Some of Notestein's former students joined him in the work on English parliaments that he had begun. D. H. Willson's *The Privy Councillors in the House of Commons 1604–1629* came out in 1940. The appearance of T. L. Moir's *The Addled Parliament of 1614* (Oxford, 1958) was widely welcomed. Robert Zaller acknowledged Notestein's guidance (and that of J. H. Hexter) in his study of *The Parliament of 1621: A Study in Constitutional Conflict* (Berkeley, CA, 1971). A further contribution to the parliamentary history of the reign of James I arrived in the form of R. E. Ruigh's reassessment of *The Parliament of 1624: Politics and Foreign Policy* (Cambridge, Mass., 1971). Other parliamentary studies of this period by American authors have included the ambitious but less than successful effort by W. M. Mitchell to trace *The Rise of the Revolutionary Party in the English House of Commons 1603–1629* (New York, 1957). Esther S. Cope of the University of Nebraska-Lincoln brought out a kind of chronological follow-up in her book on *Politics without Parliaments 1629–1640* (London, 1987). J. R. MacCormack's *Revolutionary Politics in the Long Parliament* (Cambridge, Mass., 1973) also belonged to this same transatlantic gallery of scholarship.

The parliamentary studies by Notestein and his disciples rested, partly at least, on a biographical analysis of MPs. Indeed Notestein, though he never held an appointment in England, was associated with the official History of Parliament Trust in this country which had been created in 1928 with the object of compiling a biographical register of all MPs who had sat in the House of Commons between 1264 and 1901.[14] Its leading light for many years was Sir Lewis Namier (1885–1960), Professor of History at Manchester University from 1931 to 1953 and author of *The Structure of*

Politics at the Accession of George III (London, 1929). But the 'atomizing' or 'Namierization' of parliamentary history by means of collective biography extended outside the eighteenth century, Namier's own chosen research field, and was applied, for example, to the Long Parliament.

Members of the Long Parliament by Douglas Brunton (1917–52) and D. H. Pennington (1919–) came out in 1954. The research for it was begun at Namier's suggestion in 1947 when both authors were junior members of his History Department at Manchester, and although Namierite methods were not uncritically adopted in a wholesale fashion, none the less the book was clearly written under his influence.[15] *Members of the Long Parliament* dealt with the composition and organization of that body in the period 1640–53, with chapters on the original members, the recruiters who came in after 1645, and on the Rump. Case studies of the members from the eastern counties and from the south-west were included as well as a separate chapter on the merchant body in the House of Commons. Statistical tables of the numbers of Parliamentarian and Royalist members, their experience in earlier parliaments, and their family links with other MPs were appended, as were lists of county and borough members with their political affiliations. Although in essence, like Namier's work, an analysis of collective biography, *Members of the Long Parliament* did not, in fact, include individual biographies of each MP. These were deliberately omitted in view of the impending publication of another work on the same subject, *The Long Parliament 1640–1641: A Biographical Study of its Members* by the American historian Mary F. Keeler. In the event this, too, came out in 1954, the same year as Brunton and Pennington's own volume and its preface paid a fulsome acknowledgement to Wallace Notestein. Mary Keeler contented herself with a study of the original members in the firm belief that:

> To attempt a composite portrait of the membership for the whole period of the Parliament . . . would be useless. A series of group portraits would be better. The picture of the Commons of 1640 and 1641 would not be the same as the picture for 1646 or 1649 or 1653. Changes in personnel developed a body quite different from the one which made its bold attack on the structure of absolutism in the early period.[16]

Accordingly, although the introduction dealt with such matters as elections and returns, attendance, management, factions, MPs' religious and political allegiances, their previous financial experience, age, wealth, and social, occupational, and educational backgrounds, the body of the book consisted of a detailed biographical dictionary of the 547 members in question.

Because of its wider scope and no doubt also because of the ways in which its findings relating to the similarities between the two sides provided potential anti-Marxist ammunition, Brunton and Pennington's work attracted particular attention and criticism. In 1986 the Thatcherite Tory Jonathan Clark confidently insisted that Brunton and Pennington had conclusively disposed of the Marxist myth of the English bourgeois revolution. The historians of a generation earlier would have regarded this as little more than wishful thinking. Brian Manning accused the two authors of asking the wrong questions and looking in the wrong places for answers, of failing to examine the relations between the MPs and their constituents, and above all of omitting the House of Lords (the chief stronghold of Royalism) from their study.[17] Christopher Hill was similarly unconvinced by Brunton and Pennington's findings and by their methodology. Namier himself had been accused of taking the mind out of history by concentrating exclusively on the minutiae of the structure and organization of politics at the expense of its ideas and practice. If this was true of Namier's own work on the eighteenth century, ostensibly a period of calm and stability, how much more true would this be of the work of his two disciples writing on Parliament in a period when civil war was fought over irreconcilable differences and principles? Hill, like Manning, felt that *Members of the Long Parliament* obscured the differences between Royalists and Parliamentarians.[18]

Criticism of this kind, however, ran the risk of distorting what Brunton and Pennington themselves, as opposed to their defenders and opponents, actually said. The claims which the authors made for their work were in fact extremely modest, and it was certainly not launched as a kind of anti-communist manifesto. They claimed for their work – and this contrasts starkly with the strident boasts of Jonathan Clark – 'only a limited and largely negative value', and admitted that their evidence did not 'go far enough to enable us to make any confident generalizations on the relation of the Civil War to the great economic changes of the age'. 'There is no such thing as a typical county. Each county and each borough has its own history' and until very much more research has been done on politics, society, and economic change in the seventeenth century 'it is very well to be guarded in explanations of the causes and consequences of the Revolution'.[19] Nor was it part of Brunton and Pennington's brief to explain why and how the Long Parliament acted in the way it did, how its multiple groupings actually operated and how allegiances shifted.

The dynamics of parliamentary politics in these years have been explored by other historians, most notably by David Underdown and Blair Worden. David Underdown's magisterial re-examination of *Pride's Purge: Politics in the Puritan Revolution* (Oxford, 1971) which, as its title made clear, provided not just an elucidation of one major event in 1648, when the army ruthlessly intervened in parliamentary politics, but threw light on a whole area of the English Revolution. Following the lead taken by Hexter and others, Underdown's analysis of the complexity of political groupings in this period demonstrated beyond all doubt that historians' old notions of two-party conflict were false and misleading.

> Parties, it is clear, were at best vague, ephemeral and transitory, loose associations of individuals or groups who might temporarily co-operate on some of the major issues of the day, but might equally well be divided quite differently on others.

National politics, in any case, had a local dimension:

> Pride's Purge was not the straightforward outcome of the familiar party division of Presbyterians and Independents. Nor can the revolution be understood exclusively, or even mainly, in terms of parliamentary politics. To grasp its meaning it is necessary to explore the relationship between politics at the national and grass-roots levels, between the revolution at Westminster and the revolution in the counties and boroughs, and between the State and the local communities.

Pride's Purge, like the other major events of the Interregnum, had wider social implications and highlighted different conceptions of political rights; Oliver Cromwell was 'impaled between the dictates of Providence and gentry constitutionalism'.

Pride's Purge was both a symptom and a cause of the failure of the Puritan Revolution. The circumstances which produced it, and the way in which it was conducted, demonstrate the revolutionaries' fatal divisions, their inability to agree on a common programme. The real pressure for revolution came from the Army, the Levellers, and the sects, but the leaders who made policy both then and in the weeks that followed, shared only a few of the desires of their supporters.[20]

The Rump Parliament 1648–1653 (Cambridge, 1974) by Blair Worden (1945–), ably complemented Underdown's earlier work and triumphantly demonstrated the value of re-exploring the politics of the English Revolution.

> The study of politics, which are both a reflection and a determinant of men's thoughts, beliefs, economic activities and social attitudes, can tell us as much about a past age as can research into its other aspects. . . . The problem of the political historian is not that he is working in a vacuum, but, on the contrary, that in seeking to understand political events he is seeking to understand the society which gave rise to them.

Worden's main concern was with the politics of Parliament – its factions and internal mechanics – rather than with the Rump's efforts at government, although he did examine the problem of why the Rump, supposedly a revolutionary body, achieved so little in the way of reform. The reason, according to Worden, was that the Rump was in fact far less revolutionary than historians, including Underdown, had supposed. Its members were largely moderates who had stayed on after the Purge simply to prevent direct military rule. The reforming impulse came from the army not from Parliament. But the Rump's 'failure' to carry through a programme of social reform ought to be placed in a longer perspective. Worden reminded his readers that:

> Seventeenth-century parliaments were never the most eager of reforming institutions. The great reformers of the early seventeenth century, Cranfield, Bacon, Strafford, were all broken by parliaments. Cromwell, as Lord Protector, came – like Strafford before him – to rely on administrative rather than legislative reform, and achieved it only when parliament was in abeyance. . . . Seventeenth-century politicians, unlike their twentieth-century counterparts, did not normally look to state legislation as the obvious instrument of social

amelioration. . . . Most MPs, whether Cavaliers or Roundheads, were apolitical in outlook, regarding political differences as of secondary importance to the preservation of the ordered world they knew, and sharing conventional and non-partisan assumptions about the ends of government.[21]

The books by Underdown and Worden were symptomatic of an upsurge of interest in the neglected period of the Interregnum. Ivan Roots (1921–), then Professor of History at the University of Exeter, devoted a substantial part of his useful survey of *The Great Rebellion 1642–1660* (London, 1966, 3rd edn, 1995) to the 1650s, in the belief that 'this decade is too readily brushed aside as a mere tottering obstacle to the inevitable Restoration of 1660'; he has gone on in other studies to devote himself to this period.[22] Ronald Hutton, now Professor of History at the University of Bristol, offered a linked pair of vigorously argued books on *The Restoration: A Political and Religious History of England 1658–1667* (Oxford, 1985) and *The British Republic 1649–1660* (London, 1990).[23] Roger Hainsworth's readable narrative history of *The Swordsmen in Power: War and Politics under the English Republic 1649–1660* (Stroud, 1997) followed on, chronologically and methodologically, from where Veronica Wedgwood's account had left off at the King's execution. A book of a quite different kind was *Commonwealth to Protectorate* (Oxford, 1982) by Austin Woolrych (1918–), then Professor of History at Lancaster University. Originally conceived as a study of the Barebones Parliament of 1653 the study opened out into a wider investigation of the changing political conditions of the 1650s in which the quasi-monarchy of Oliver Cromwell emerged. Biographies and studies of Cromwell – a publishing industry in their own right – have continued to proliferate. Peter Gaunt's *Oliver Cromwell* (Oxford, 1996) and R. C. Richardson's collection of historiographical essays (*Images of Oliver Cromwell*, Manchester, 1993) are two of the most recent. T. C. Barnard's magisterial reassessment of *Cromwellian Ireland* (Oxford, 1975) dislodged all the myths attaching to this subject. Cromwellian Scotland and Cromwell's Navy also found their historians.[24] Research and writing on the 1650s has clearly been burgeoning in ways which were still less than clear when G. E. Aylmer brought out a collection of new essays on *The Interregnum: The Quest for Settlement 1646–1660* (London, 1972).

Gerald Aylmer (1928–), a former student of Christopher Hill and sometime Professor of History at the University of York and then Master of St Peter's College, Oxford, has become best known for his detailed studies of seventeenth-century administration. *The King's Servants: The Civil Service of Charles I 1625–1642* (London, 1961) was a pioneering and experimental study of the institutions and personnel of the central government. Impressive though it was in its own right, however, it was designed to be a prologue to, or framework of reference for, a study of the administration of the Interregnum. *The State's Servants: The Civil Service of the English Republic 1649–1660* (London, 1973) used the same analytical techniques employed in its predecesor. Its quantitative method, however, was more sophisticated and its conclusions were even more cautious and guarded. Aylmer's second book, none the less, was more wide-ranging than *The King's Servants* and raised a number of general questions about the development of bureaucracy and its place in society. 'Institutional pressures and practices can operate causally upon the economy of a country as well as upon people's ideas about government and about society'. So Aylmer contended on his first page, and his book, among other things, was an illustration of that claim. The author looked at the economic cost of government to seventeenth-century society as well as examining the financial benefits of office-holding for the administrators themselves. Aylmer's approach and method, although not an exact replica of either of them, clearly owed much to the combined influence of Namier and Tawney. 'This is a study of the interaction between administration and politics, and of the relationship between bureaucracy and social structure', Aylmer wrote in his introduction.[25] The book began with a largely chronological account of the institutions of republican government which looked at the successive regimes in relation to each other, to the army, and to the general quest in these years for political settlement. It moved on to deal with the terms of administrative service and, most interesting of all, with the social biography of the republican administrators themselves. It was this section, full of statistical tables, which revealed Namier's influence most clearly. What the tables showed was that the social complexion of the administration was changing under the republic and, as in the counties, men of lower rank were becoming increasingly conspicuous in the machine of government. The notion of 'revolutionary bureaucrats' was not a contradiction in terms. A new kind of public service, Aylmer argued, with salaries going up and illicit fringe benefits being reduced, was taking shape in those years and only the Restoration in 1660 halted its development.

Aylmer's work was done with meticulous thoroughness and still holds the ground. Other historians, however, by and large, have continued to be drawn to politicians and the politics of this period rather than to administrators. Allegiances, party groupings, factions, institutions and the personnel of politics have been prominent in the work of modern historians of the English Revolution. The American historian Perez Zagorin (1920–) of the University of Rochester, New York, moved away from the kind of microscope used by historians such as Brunton and Pennington, Keeler and Aylmer in favour of the wide-angled lens. His wide-ranging *The Court and the Country: The Beginning of the English Revolution* (London, 1969) was deliberately intended to serve as a rejoinder to the Marxists. The Civil War, he insisted, was not a class war. Marxist historians had committed a grave error in accepting contemporary Royalist propaganda about the social inferiority of their opponents at face value and in presenting the events in seventeenth-century England as a prototype of the French bourgeois revolution. Nor, Zagorin argued, did men in the seventeenth century have a political conception of revolution.

> It is the total absence of this highly charged idea of revolution born in France and elevated to a theoretical principle by Marx that we have to notice as we look back across the abyss of time to the 1640s. 'Revolution' had then another, mainly non-political meaning.

The English Revolution was, in fact, the result of a division within the political elite itself, a division which contemporaries recognized as a cleavage between 'Court' and 'Country'.

> Around this widening split, all the various conflicts in the kingdom gradually became polarized. The antagonism was thus not a lateral one between the orders of socety; it was vertical, by degrees dividing the peerage, the gentry and the merchant oligarchies of the towns. At last it drew in also the unprivileged and normally inarticulate mass of men.[26]

'The Country', Zagorin continued, 'was the first opposition movement in English history whose character transcended that of a feudal following or a faction'. But it was a conservative opposition and, although there were political and religious differences, socially speaking, according to Zagorin, it was drawn from the same ranks as the Court group it opposed.

> The outstanding characteristic of the Country from a social-structural standpoint was its uniformity with the governing class. To imagine the Country as 'progressive' in the sense of incarnating, even unwittingly, a new ordering of society, is completely erroneous. Equally so is the supposition that its relation to the Court was the antipathy of 'Outs' to 'Ins' – the social resentment of men denied admission to influence and favour. What made the Country so formidable was that its adherents were pillars of society.[27]

Later events, of course, Zagorin recognized, changed the course and character of the Revolution. There was a substantial realignment of political forces in the years 1640–42, in which a new Royalism was born, and Charles I built up, almost out of nothing, a party and an army with which to fight the first Civil War. The labels 'Parliamentarian' and 'Royalist' replaced those of 'Country' and 'Court', the religious issue in the struggle became more central, and political arguments which a conservative opposition had first used against the King came in time to be directed against Parliament itself by groups like the Levellers.[28]

Though in itself a full-scale treatment of the revolutionary events in England, *The Court and the Country* has been dwarfed by Zagorin's later two-volume epic on *Rebels and Rulers 1500–1660* (Cambridge, 1982). Many of the themes, most of the same assumptions, and the same stridently anti-Marxist stance were still there but the English Revolution was now firmly placed within a wider context which embraced not simply Scotland and Ireland but also France, Spain, Italy, the Netherlands, and Germany. The various disturbances, rebellions, and revolutions of this period were then accommodated within a fourfold classification.

As general surveys of political developments Zagorin's books were bold and informative but more than one reviewer underlined the weak points in this author's methodology and argument. The theoretical framework has been seen as inadequate, the notion of comparative history too restricted, the attitudes too negative and hostile. Zagorin's attack on simplistic social explanations of the seventeenth-century crisis, although in some respects salutary, none the less ended in an unwillingness to see any social patterns in the evidence concerning puritanism and the political struggle.[29] His denial that there was any recognizably modern concept of revolution in the seventeenth century undervalued the role of popular movements and of millenarianism. (Results as well as conscious motives and strategies, in any case, should surely be taken into account in any assessment or definition of revolution.) Zagorin's claim that the peers and the gentry never lost the initiative in their own well-managed revolt did not convince other historians such as Brian Manning who emphasized the decisiveness of the popular contribution (see pp. 189–90). Moreover the labels 'Court' and 'Country', to which Zagorin attached such great significance, were not in fact the political novelty of the 1620s which he claimed, nor were these the only party tags then current.

Attacks on Marxist interpretations of the seventeenth-century crisis, of course, have not been restricted to the United States. *The English Civil War* (London, 1978, 2nd edn, 1989) by Robert Ashton (1924–), then Professor of English History at the University of East Anglia, accurately proclaimed its own preferences in its subtitle *Conservatism and Revolution 1603–49*. To Ashton the Marxist interpretation of seventeenth-century politics was no more convincing than the earlier, different version of historical inevitability advanced by the Whig historians. Rather than giving pride of place to revolutionary ambitions and achievements in these years Ashton made more of the backward-looking nature of Parliamentarian political and social thinking, of the conservatism of the mainstream of English puritanism, and of the long-maintained moderation of most of the King's opponents. Even former radicals, he noted, moved to the right in the 1640s and early 1650s leaving convinced republicans as a small, unrepresentative group of cranks, even in 1648–49. In so far as he dealt with popular movements at all – this was very much top-level history – he emphasized popular conservatism.[30] A very different kind of book from Ashton – this time a densely detailed and impeccably researched monograph on *Counter Revolution: The Second Civil War and its Origins*

1646–48 (New Haven, 1995) – focused the microscope, however, in ways reminiscent of the earlier general survey. Again Ashton's book was to do with top-level history. Conservatism and its expression in attempted counter revolution (Royalists, Parliamentary Presbyterians, and Scots) occupied centre stage. Radicalism and the road to revolution received short shrift. There was not much here to suggest that Ashton had been one of Tawney's students!

The rejection of sweeping Marxist generalizations also characterized Anthony Fletcher's very different study of *The Outbreak of the English Civil War* (London, 1981). Fletcher's book – returning, apparently, to the narrative tradition of S. R. Gardiner – offered a densely detailed chronological account of the years 1640–42, insisting as he proceeded that there was no 'highroad to Civil War' in the early seventeenth century and no deeply ingrained antithesis between Court and Country. Far from being in any way an inevitable conflict, the Civil War, said Fletcher (1941–), now Professor of History at the University of Essex, was 'a war that nobody wanted, a war that left men bewildered and that they marvelled at as it broke out by fits and starts all over England in the summer of 1642'.[31] The untidy outbreak of Civil War was as noticeable as the slow, reluctant, confused build-up to it. He made much of the competing delusions which increasingly enmeshed the King and the leading members of the House of Commons, and he underlined the potency of anti-Catholicism as Caroline Hibbard was to do even more strongly in a book published two years later.[32] He emphasized the importance of localism and the varying degrees of commitment and of neutralism.

Fletcher's emphasis on very detailed political narrative is one of the very few shared characteristics of that exceedingly heterogeneous group known as the 'Revisionists'. (Another is that politically all are anchored elsewhere than the extreme Left and share a common antipathy to Marxist interpretations of history.) The term itself is hopelessly inadequate, not least because it seems to imply firstly that these historians somehow have come to monopolize what is in fact a general characteristic of historical writing, and secondly that this particular group is a united band of brothers. Clearly they are no such thing. Commentators cannot even agree on 'membership lists'. Conrad Russell, John Morrill, Thomas Cogswell, Richard Cust, Mark Kishlansky, and Kevin Sharpe, though connected by some common denominators, in other respects have gone their separate ways. Some Revisionists have considered Russell's emphasis on the 'British dimension' of the Civil Wars to be overstated and to reflect his fixation with elite politics.[33] Some of the revisionists have at times been locked in bitter conflict with each other.[34] Individual interpretations and emphases have varied enormously, especially over the role of religion. John Morrill, though he has contributed variously to the reinterpretation of the mid-seventeenth century, has been drawn chiefly to its religious dimensions and is inclined to describe the Civil Wars as the last of the European wars of religion. Part One of his collected essays – *The Nature of the English Revolution* (London, 1993) – is devoted to these aspects of the period and takes up nearly 200 pages of text. Religion also bulks large in his edited collections of essays on *The Impact of the English Civil War* (London, 1991) and on *Revolution and Restoration: England in the 1650s* (London, 1992). And puritanism in both its personal and social dimensions is made to figure no less prominently in his edited volume on *Oliver Cromwell and the English Revolution* (London, 1990). In contrast Conrad Russell and Kevin Sharpe have been at odds over the weight to place on religious 'factors'. And John Adamson has argued that the Civil War is best seen as a baronial revolt.[35] Perhaps Glen Burgess is right when he suggests that Revisionism is 'not a school but an amorphous generational trend' – though even that seems not quite elastic enough.[36]

Conceptually and methodologically however, it can be said that the Revisionists have rediscovered the historian's microscope. They have gone back to detailed week by week, day by day investigations of what happened. Generally they have been most interested in high politics, in short-term factors, in the shifting basis of politics, in factions, bureaucratic failings, and in the ramifications of patronage. For the Revisionists there was no swelling crescendo of constitutional issues between 1604 and 1642. Consensus politics not adversary politics were the order of the day; the House of Commons was not ambitiously power seeking.

> There is no sign during the 1620s of any change in the idea that parliaments were occasional and short-term assemblies [Conrad Russell has written]. Without a change in this point, parliaments could not enjoy much more status than they already did. Charles I's

continental wars offered the prospect of very frequent parliaments, but the reaction of members was not to cry out for annual parliaments; it was to cry out against annual subsidies.[37]

An integral part of the Revisionists' work, therefore, has been an assault on what are seen to be the patently plain inadequacies of both Marxist and Whig interpretations. Social change/crisis interpretations, they have argued, are conceptual dead ends. So are the scenarios depicting the steady growth of parliamentary opposition and a floodlit, multi-round intensifying contest between King and Commons. Such negative reactions from Revisionists, however, have been accompanied by major advances – the productive revisiting of both cliché-ridden and bypassed aspects and sub-periods (Parliament itself and the personal rule of Charles I, for example), the opening up of court politics and court culture, and the exploration of the British context of the English Civil Wars.

Conrad Russell (1937–), now Professor of British History at King's College, London (and thus one of S. R. Gardiner's successors!), a member of a patrician family whose ancestors were actively involved in Civil War politics, a Liberal Democrat peer, and a passionate believer in the parliamentary system, has had added reasons to reinvestigate parliaments of the early Stuart period.[38] *Parliaments and English Politics 1621–1629* (Oxford, 1979) saw Russell rejecting the view that these years could be seen as a mere curtain raiser to the English Civil Wars. Parliament in the early seventeenth century, he insisted, was an event not an institution. Studying it, therefore, could not provide a comprehensive history of English politics. Even within the limits of his own field, however, the parliamentary historian could only tell half a story since it was so difficult to penetrate the hidden activities of the intervals between parliamentary sessions. Russell found seventeenth-century MPs much less preoccupied with political theory than had often been supposed. They 'lacked the opportunity to study Montesquieu'. 'They did not come to Westminster to move the pieces on a constitutional chessboard. They were not in training for the Civil War or for the Bill of Rights'. Until 1628, at any rate, most parliamentary diarists omitted reference to political ideas in their accounts of day-to-day parliamentary proceedings. 'It is remarkable', Russell opined, 'how little ideological division developed during these years'. He found – like Kevin Sharpe (see pp. 224–7) – that the political consequences of puritanism had been much exaggerated by previous writers on the subject. The parliaments of this decade, in Russell's view, were fearful rather than ambitious, and for the most part they proceeded with immense caution. 'Most members were not struggling to achieve increased national responsibilities; they were struggling to avoid them'.[39]

Three further books have followed. The first of them, *Unrevolutionary England 1603–1642* (London, 1990) was a collection of seventeen of his essays written over a twenty-seven year period. They were reprinted unchanged and therefore charted Russell's progress as a Revisionist over these years. An early essay (1965) on the trial of Strafford tentatively exposed a disjunction between the ideas actually held at the time and those which later Whig historians attributed to the period. Other essays showed Russell more confidently and boldly rejecting 'struggle for sovereignty', 'two side' models of the course of early seventeenth-century history which presented the reign of James I and the early part of Charles I's as no more than preliminaries to an inevitable Civil War. 'Straight line' theories such as this, he has insisted, tell us more about the historians who make them than about history. Gardiner's identification of the 'English nation' with puritans was a case in point, as was his conviction that 'the Parliament of England is the noblest monument ever reared by mortal man'. Parliament before 1640 was neither powerful nor power seeking, and it did not contain an identifiable opposition. Nor, moving on, was the outcome of the Civil Wars much more than a pyrrhic victory for Parliament. 'The survival of Parliament and of Protestantism', Russell declares, 'was still an open question in 1688'. This was, indeed, an *Unrevolutionary England*, a quite different country from that made familiar by both Whig and Marxist historians.[40]

The other two volumes – *The Causes of the English Civil War* (Oxford, 1990) and *The Fall of the British Monarchies 1637–1642* (Oxford, 1991) – stand together. The project began in a very anglo-centric way in 1977 but since then, following work on Europe by Koenigsberger and Elliott, Russell has become increasingly convinced that the English Civil Wars only make sense when fitted into the context of the inter-relations of the multiple kingdom over which Charles I ruled. England, Russell has emphasized, was the most docile of Charles I's three realms and the last to confront him with armed resistance.

> The *primum mobile* of the British crisis . . . was the conflict between Charles and the Scottish Covenanters. . . . It enshrined visions of the Church, and of authority, so far apart that no real compromise was ever likely to be possible between them. It was this conflict which was the vortex into which the other kingdoms were drawn.[41]

It did more than anything else to polarize politics in England and helped to make religion the principal dividing line which separated the two sides in the Civil War. The military and financial repercussions of rebellion in Scotland brought the English Parliament back after an eleven-year interval. Rebellion in Ireland ensured that the reinstated English Parliament could not be dissolved. 'England, as always, was cast in the unhappy position of pig in the middle between Ireland and Scotland'. Irreconcilable traditions made real unity between the three kingdoms an impossibility. Charles I's and Laud's Arminian strategy for uniformity failed most blatantly in Scotland. Conversely, it was the 'Scottish imperial' vision of British unity which did most to drive Ireland into rebellion.

While the integration of the English Civil War into a broader framework of British history has unquestionably become the main thrust of Russell's Revisionism it has clearly not been the only component. Many cherished interpretations withered under his exacting scrutiny. The notion, familiar enough, that resistance to ship money was an expression of a Court/Country divide was obviously weakened by Russell's disclosure that some of those refusing to pay lived in Windsor Castle! Russell's account of the King's departure from London made much of the implications this had for the House of Lords, 'both by drawing away much needed votes and by leaving the Lords to face the hostility of London crowds alone'. The many declarations issued by the King and Parliament in the paper war of 1642 which preceded open hostilities, Russell argued, were 'intended for recrimination more than persuasion', and were not evidence of 'parties already psychologically prepared for war'. Time and again Russell directed new shafts of light on to familiar events. Individuals, too, were re-examined. Clarendon's significance was trimmed down somewhat. Pym and Charles I were reassessed. The

King emerged from Russell's account as an active participant in politics, less duplicitous and more of a statesman than has often been recognized. That said, however, Russell showed that Charles often enjoyed most success when he did least, that he was often inconsistent, and that he was apparently unable to differentiate between the possible and the impossible.[42]

But in the last analysis Russell's conviction has remained that Civil War was not the inevitable outcome of deep-seated problems in England itself. 'England in 1637 was a country in working order and was not on the edge of revolution'. That was still the case, in his view, in 1640, and 'the depth of social tolerance which held local communities together combined with a devotion to consensus politics' kept Civil War at bay for another two years. Even in the early part of 1642 Civil War was impossible since Charles I was too weak to start one and Parliament 'was still hoping for a walkover'. The deep-seated ingredients in Russell's interpretation were not within England itself but in the fraught relations between the component parts of Charles I's multiple kingdom.[43]

Mark Kishlansky (1948–), former research student of David Underdown and now Professor of English History at Harvard University, has contributed both to the reinvestigation of peacetime political conditions in England and (unusually among the Revisionists) to the study of the war effort itself.[44] *Parliamentary Selection: Social and Political Choice in Early Modern England* (Cambridge, 1986) was an assault on Whig platitudes about the nature of the political nation in the early seventeenth century and a scaling down of the claims made about electoral behaviour in Derek Hirst's book *The Representative of the People* (see pp. 188–9). Kishlansky's provocative argument – and Revisionists as a group are no friends to 'history from below' – was that Hirst overestimated the strength of popular consciousness and the role of popular activism and saw electoral contests where they did not exist. MPs arrived at Westminster, he argued, chiefly by selection within the small circles of the elite; the real political business had already been done before the freeholders came together on election days.[45]

The Rise of the New Model Army (Cambridge, 1979), Kishlansky's first book, was a reworking of his doctoral thesis and likewise trimmed the popular contribution down to size, this time that of the Levellers. The first major study of its subject since Firth's at the beginning of the century, Kishlansky's set out to delineate the ways in which, and the reasons why, the New Model Army underwent a basic political transformation in the course of 1647. His thesis was that the New Model Army was not politically radical at its inception. Indeed it was not primarily political in any sense at all. Called into being for strictly military reasons, the New Model in the first fifteen months of its life was an army, no less and no more, without political aspirations or influence of its own. It was not at first more 'professional' or 'national' than Parliament's earlier armies. Its religious complexion initially also seems to have been less clear cut than usually supposed. The radicalization of the army in 1647, however, was a response to the harsh economic pressures of increasingly irregular pay, to the attempted disbandment and part-transfer to Ireland, to fears of judicial retribution, and to a vigorously defended sense of honour. The process coincided with a noticeable shift at Westminster from consensus to adversary politics which weakened the status and authority of Parliament.[46]

Of all the Revisionists Kevin Sharpe (1949–), now Professor of History at Southampton University, has made the most varied and prolific contribution to the reinvestigation of early seventeenth-century politics, not least in its cultural ramifications and resonances. Though the editor or co-editor of three stimulating collections of essays, two of them interdisciplinary, Sharpe stands out principally for other obvious landmarks.[47] The award-winning *Criticism and Compliment: The Politics of Literature in the England of Charles I* (Cambridge, 1987) called into question the 'often anachronistic assumptions' and untested preconceptions which previously held the field about the nature of the Court in the early seventeenth century, about puritanism, and about the supposed polarity between Court and Country, and offered provocative and challenging reassessments of Sir William Davenant, Thomas Carew, Aurelian Townsend, and the Caroline court masques. Criticism as well as praise (which could itself be an active exhortation) came from within the Court as well as from outside it. The Court which Sharpe depicted was a loose, plural phenomenon, not a tightly organized and uniform party. Seen in this way the court masques need to be understood above all as political occasions, varied in their nature, form, purpose and methods of engaging the larger issues of the age. The freedoms permitted in the theatre were exploited to the full at a time when official censorship of drama was neither habitual, harsh nor effective. 'The study of culture', declared Sharpe, 'takes us to the centre of politics'. Indeed, in Sharpe's view, courtly literature did more than express the politics of the period; it contributed to its making.[48]

Politics and Ideas in Early Stuart England (London, 1989) offered Sharpe's collected essays together with retrospective glances at his own work and at 'Revisionism' in general. The title of this book in fact proclaimed not simply a conviction but a regret that the revisionists had frequently lost sight of the history of ideas.

> The passions and principles, ideas and values which creatively fermented in the cultural and political life of early Stuart decades find little or no place in some revisionist narratives of parliaments and high politics.[49]

It has been the ideas, beliefs and attitudes of the elite, however, not those of ordinary folk that have interested him. 'Whitehall, I think, may be the key to intellectual as to political history'. (Sharpe has little time for those historians – Christopher Hill again! – who spend their time studying 'minor sects and crackpots'.) He has envisioned a conjunction of political history and the history of ideas which should not restrict itself to established canonical texts but be willing to embrace, in a way that would once have been considered inconceivable, 'acting and being, everyday behaviour and existence'. He again spoke out for the importance of literature as historical evidence and paraded his deep regret that by and large historians have not joined literary critics in the interdisciplinary enterprise.[50]

Sharpe's magnum opus, undoubtedly, has been *The Personal Rule of Charles I* (New Haven, 1992). 1000 pages long and with a total of almost 7000 footnotes it must undoubtedly be considered the weightiest Revisionist contribution to early Stuart history. Not since Lawrence Stone's *Crisis of the Aristocracy* in 1965 has a theme in early modern English history been dealt with on such a lavish scale. Impressively researched – making abundant use of local sources as well as the central records – well written and deftly orchestrated, Sharpe's book in many ways complemented Russell's *Fall of the British Monarchies*. But the two writers were at odds over the importance to be attached to religion as a cause of discontent and over the implications of the multiple nature of Charles I's kingdom. Part of the value of Sharpe's book indeed was its capacity to distance itself somewhat from earlier Revisionism – including his own! – which 'has gone too far'.

> The 1630s offer us the rich opportunity to study Charles I as a King at peace, to understand his values and ideology of kingship and his priorities for the church. And they open a new perspective on the importance of parliaments in early Stuart England by enabling us to investigate the process of government during the only decade without them.[51]

Sharpe in this book certainly has made a telling case for Charles I and has attempted to see the unfolding events and crises of the period through his eyes and not through those of his contemporary and later detractors. He firmly repudiated the notion of reading history backwards. He emphasized the real financial problems which the King faced and his determination to come to terms with them, his preoccupation with order and with the dignity of king-ship, his dedication to duty, and his capacity for the routine busi-ness of administration and government. He played down the political influence of Queen Henrietta Maria over her husband, and rescued Archbishop Laud and Thomas Wentworth from the con-temporary charges made against them. Since, in Sharpe's view, there was no royal tyranny in these years, Laud and Wentworth could hardly have been the instruments responsible for its creation. The courts of Star Chamber and High Commission administered justice and did not buttress royal absolutism. Ship money was presented here as a royal success story: the money came rolling in, with Hampden's resistance merely delaying its collection. He denied that there was widespread constitutional opposition to Charles I's poli-cies. Sharpe went on to contend that both the numerical strength and religious and political significance of puritanism have been greatly exaggerated. Parliaments seem not to have been sorely missed in the 1630s. There was remarkable stability in the country even in 1639 and the 'normal political procedures' were seen as perfectly capable of resolving such discontents as there were. While conceding that Charles I was 'no politician', Sharpe insisted in this spirited defence that the King was a man spurred on by conscience, duty, and an unswerving sense of honour, one who saw himself as 'the good physician of the Commonweal'. In this interpretation external circumstances, not Charles I's character, wrought his downfall. For Sharpe Charles I – the personal rule notwithstanding – remained 'an exponent of anti-absolutist theories', even a 'wet', committed 'to the traditions and norms of English government'. Sharpe identified no direct causal link between the personal rule of Charles I and the coming of Civil War in 1642.[52]

Part of Sharpe's reassessment of Charles I was to exonerate both the King and Archbishop Laud from charges made against the religious policy of the reign. The politics of early Stuart religion, however, now as then, are a battleground. To Patrick Collinson, then Regius Professor of History at Cambridge and hardly a lone and uninfluential voice, 'Archbishop Laud was indeed the greatest calamity ever visited on the English church'. Nicholas Tyacke, of University College London, by contrast, has argued that 'William Laud deserves to rank amongst the greatest archbishops of Canterbury since the Reformation'. Tyacke's views on Laud and on the politics of early Stuart religion were set out most fully in his book *Anti-Calvinists: The Rise of English Arminianism* (Oxford, 1987), though he had been defending them against attack from Peter White and others since the 1970s.[53] The most controversial parts of the book were those which surveyed the development of Arminianism during Charles I's personal rule and made clear how critical to the process was the absence of a Calvinist parliament in these years. It was Arminianism, Tyacke argued, which shattered the religious consensus of the English church, decisively changed the stance of the bishops, and forced the most unyielding and unrepentant of Calvinists into the mould of militant puritanism. It is easy to understand, therefore, how for contemporary opponents, the dividing line between Popery and Arminianism was unclear and how in these ways Arminianism made a decisive contribution to the causes of the English Civil War. Arminians and puritans became respectively Royalists and Parliamentarians.

Julian Davies's *The Caroline Captivity of the Church: Charles I and the Remoulding of Anglicanism* (Oxford, 1992) also set out to exonerate Laud, convinced that the Archbishop had been greatly misrepresented by historians too willingly accepting the hostility of contemporary opponents. Laud, in Davies's judgement, was no Arminian revolutionary, indeed no Arminian! For the Archbishop 'an Arminianization of the church was an evil equal only to its Calvinization'. Davies, in fact, has argued convincingly that the whole subject of Arminianism and its presentation as the religious pace-setter of the 1630s and the polar opposite of Calvinism have been fundamentally misunderstood by historians such as Nicholas Tyacke. 'The word "Arminian"', Davies has said, 'confuses more than it clarifies'. 'Arminian' and 'Calvinist', he has insisted, cannot be seen as closed categories, nor can 'Arminian' be equated with 'orthodox' in the 1630s. 'The Arminianization of the decade is a myth. . . . English Arminianism was less a cause of the anti-Calvinism of the Caroline church than one of its consequences'.[54]

Davies's book began and ended with *Carolinism*, and when discussing the contentious policies connected with the reissuing of the Book of Sports in 1633, the stress on the altar-wise placing (and railing off) of communion tables, the restraint on lecturers, and the promulgation of the canons of 1640 and the notorious *et cetera* oath, he found that the central figure in each case was the King and not his Archbishop. The title of Davies's book struck the keynote. It was, in Davies's view, Charles I's obsession with order, his paranoia about a puritan threat or plot, his 'attempt to subvert the Church for his own purposes', which shaped the religious policies of the personal rule. In the political crisis after 1640 Laud became the scapegoat – a fate to which his own personality defects, isolation from the court, the hostility of lawyers, and opposition from the nobility and gentry (whose privileges he had challenged) all conspired to condemn him. Davies, in a way which would have dumbfounded Macaulay, exonerated Laud, and like L. J. Reeve in *Charles I and the Road to Personal Rule* (Cambridge, 1989), blamed the King. 'If Charles I', he concluded, 'is a historical enigma it is because Laud has carried his mask for too long. . . . All the attributes which historians have traditionally awarded Laud: intransigence, intolerance, authoritarianism, paranoia, duplicity, suit the King better'.[55]

Sharpe's Revisionism, therefore, is surrounded by contention. Part of his brief, however, has been to re-explore the ideas of the early Stuart period set firmly in context. Political thought indeed has for decades been one of the trends in the historiography of the English Revolution and has attracted some notable exponents – J. N. Figgis, J. W. Allen, Margaret Judson, Perez Zagorin, J. G. A.

Pocock, C. B. Macpherson, W. H. Greenleaf, Robert Eccleshall, and Quentin Skinner. And there have been disagreements and controversies. J. P. Somerville, for example, in a well-known text, emphasized the deep-rooted, scarcely reconcilable ideological divisions which lay behind the outbreak of Civil War in 1642. Glen Burgess, in contrast, has argued that the early decades of the seventeenth century were chiefly remarkable for political consensus.[56] The reception into England of Machiavelli's ideas has been carefully investigated.[57] The political ideas of Thomas Hobbes have received a steady flow of studies.[58] The importance of James Harrington and his *Oceana* have been properly recognized.[59] The co-existence of continuities and new departures in classical humanism and republicanism in England's mid-century crisis were the subject of three books published in 1995. Milton necessarily received much attention but second rank, elusive and frenetically active pamphleteers like Henry Parker were brought into sharper focus.[60]

The political culture of the early Stuart period, as these and other studies have shown, has become firmly integrated into the agenda of many of today's historians. Festschriften for Patrick Collinson and David Underdown published in 1994 and 1995 respectively bore witness to the fact.[61] The language, imagery and spectacle of court culture – seen as a key to so much else by Kevin Sharpe – have received a growing amount of critical attention from Stephen Orgel, Graham Parry, Malcolm Smuts, and Roy Strong.[62] Sean Kelsey has written thoughtfully on the subject of *Inventing a Republic: The Political Culture of the English Commonwealth* (Manchester, 1997). Convinced republicans might have been few in 1649 but Kelsey made much of their political self-fashioning, the pride they took in launching and upholding the new regime. He depicted not only their actions but the institutions which they revised or created, the political vocabulary and iconography they adopted, the spectacle which was carefully designed, and the code of honour which underpinned the republican system. The appropriation of the former royal palace of Whitehall – scene of the King's execution in 1649 – was discussed at some length as a deliberate device 'to supplant and outshine the Stuarts'. So was the republic's cultivation of ceremonial and pageantry. Banquets, ship-launchings, military reviews, state funerals, honorary degree ceremonies at the universities, the reception of ambassadors, the public celebration of Cromwell's victories, were all systematically orches-trated to achieve the maximum effect. Kelsey also examined the new republican icons which replaced those of the defeated and abolished monarchy – its great seals, coinage, the Commonwealth coat of arms, the proliferation of Parliamentarian portraits and prints, and the maces of Parliament and of corporations through-out the country. Though, as other commentators have noted, some use was made in this achievement of the republican ideology of classical Greece and Rome, what emerged in England in the early 1650s in both language and forms, as Kelsey has shown, was an unmistakably 'vernacular republicanism' in which familiar domes-tic motifs were brandished with aggressive and telling effect.[63]

The interface between early seventeenth-century literature and history has been fruitfully explored, though as Hill and Sharpe have rightly pointed out, more by literary critics than by historians. Annabel Patterson's *Censorship and Interpretation: The Condi-tions of Writing and Reading in Early Modern England* (Madison, Wis., 1984) significantly filled a major gap. R. C. Richardson and G. M. Ridden edited an interdisciplinary volume of essays dealing with the diversity of concepts of freedom in the English Revolution and the rhetoric and forms used to express them.[64] Lois Potter explored *Secret Rites and Secret Writing: Royalist Literature 1641–1660* (Cambridge, 1989) while Joad Raymond provided the first full-length study of *The Invention of the Newspaper: English Newsbooks 1641–49* (London, 1996). Elizabeth Skerpan examined the interdependence of discourse and ideology in her book *The Rhetoric of Politics in the English Revolution 1642–1660* (Columbia, Missouri, 1992). *Literature and Revolution in England 1640–1660* (New Haven, 1994) by Nigel Smith was more wide-ranging in its scope. It assessed the impact of new kinds of author, forms of writing – pamphlets and newsbooks, for example – and the exploding phenomenon of journalism in the overheated mid-century decades. *Eikon Basilike*, 'the most popular book of the century', received extended treatment. Lilburne, Nedham and Cowley were reassessed; the analysis of Cowley's *The Civil War*, his unfinished, and unfinishable!, epic of 1643 was particularly inci-sive. Smith's insistence that 'discourse and genre are not separate categories but part of the same process' is well taken, as is his sub-stitution of the more active term 'political *writing*' for 'political

thought'. Smith's central argument – and though largely unac-
knowledged it is very closely in line with that previously advanced
by Christopher Hill – was that

> the literature of mid-seventeenth-century England underwent a series
> of revolutions in genre and form, and that this transformation was a
> response to the crises of the 1640s: the Civil War and the political revo-
> lution which followed. It is also part of my contention that literature
> was part of the crisis and the revolution, and was at its epicentre.

But Smith's interpretation was even bolder than Hill's and went
further. He was not content simply to stake a claim for literature
as an integral element of the revolutionary situation but presented
it in fact as the *central* component.

> Without literature to articulate these openings-up of the collective
> imagination, the 'English Revolution' as we know it could not have
> been. And since these 'discoveries' and 'new lights' emerged through
> a civil conflict, cultural polarisation was endemic; literature was one
> of the major ways in which the disease of division spread.

It was in the 'war of words', the author concluded, 'where
the impact of the crisis was most strongly registered. . . . By the
summer of 1660 the revolution was lost but literature had
triumphed'.[65]

Drama, also, not just as text but as performance, has been
receiving its due – though again chiefly from historically minded
literary critics. Margot Heinemann's *Puritanism and Theatre:
Thomas Middleton and Opposition Drama under the Early Stuarts*
(Cambridge, 1980) succeeded in showing that hostility to drama
was not a necessary ingredient of puritanism and that puritans
actually made use of drama in their opposition to the Stuart court.
Martin Butler's *Theatre and Crisis 1632–1642* (Cambridge, 1984)
came from the same stable, asked some of the same questions, and
formed a valuable companion piece to Heinemann's earlier study.
Behind both books lay the conviction that there was an integral
and active connection between the drama and politics of the period
before the outbreak of Civil War.

> The playwrights [Butler declared] were dramatizing the conflicts and
> tensions at work in their society, embodying men's dilemmas and
> voicing their grievances, anxieties and frustrations. . . . Their drama
> was not merely the product of its society but was itself part of the

historical process, an agent of change as much as the mirror of change, a participant engaged with its society's compromises and not merely an observer of them.

Resonant with politics and political purposes, the drama of these years has not only benefited from, but arguably has needed, a socio-political approach to draw out its highly charged agendas.[66] To end this chapter with expressions of the growing interest in political culture and in drama forcefully demonstrates some of the shifts in emphasis that have taken place in the twentieth-century political historiography of the English Revolution. For Gardiner and his disciples the only 'drama' to be considered was that contained within the development of the Puritan Revolution itself. Though the traditionalists have not been extinguished, the political history of this period has been redefined and re-animated as a result of its interactions with other historical approaches and methodologies. Namierization played its part. So most certainly has Revisionism. So also have the New Historicists in the field of literary studies. The political historiography of the English Revolution has become increasingly plural and is hyperactive in engendering publications. Monographs proliferate, introductory overviews and collections of new essays are legion. (John Morrill's *The Impact of the English Civil War* (London, 1991) and *Revolution and Restoration: England in the 1650s* (London, 1992) are but two examples.) There is no shortage of new, lively and comprehensive textbooks: Martyn Bennett's *The Civil Wars in Britain and Ireland 1638–1651* (Oxford, 1997) is one of the most recent examples. The 'British problem' and the interrelated trends and events of Charles I's multiple kingdom have been repeatedly underlined. The roles and interractions of the King, his chief ministers, the Court, Parliament and civil service have all been re-examined.

Unsurprisingly, the political histories of this period are as contentious as ever. Mark Kishlansky's concise introductory survey *A Monarchy Transformed: Britain 1603–1714* (London, 1996) was positively fought over in the first reviews. To Keith Thomas, Oxford social historian, the book was seen as reflecting the 'One Damn thing after Another' philosophy of history, 'even if it does occasionally rise above it'. Kishlansky's 'conception of political history is unilluminatingly narrow . . . an unbroken political nar-

rative which largely eschews interpretation or explanatory gener-
alisation'. Thomas found it impossible to agree that *A Monarchy
Transformed* was ' "the definitive history for our day and generation" which the new Penguin History claims to be. It should be
noted that, in his excellent bibliography, Kishlansky tells us that
Hill's *Century of Revolution* is "still worth reading" '.[67] In stark
contrast Kevin Sharpe – fellow revisionist – lavished high praise on
the book. The opening chapters were described as

> masterpieces in miniature, packed with informative detail that never
> obscures our vision of the whole. . . . Kishlansky is excellent on the
> histories of early Stuart parliaments, on the battles of civil war, on
> the politics of the Restoration. . . . The story after 1660 . . . is as
> confidently narrated as the events leading to civil war.

He is praised for dismissing the 'tired old' clichés of both Marxist
and Whig interpretations of the period. For Sharpe, Kishlansky's
rewriting of 'the narrative of high politics so as "to recreate the fascination" of the Stuart age for a new generation . . . succeeds
admirably'.[68]

Notes

1 See, for example, D. H. Willson, *King James VI and I* (London, 1956) and C.
Carlton, *Charles I: The Personal Monarch* (London, 1983).
2 C. V. Wedgwood's books on European history include *The Thirty Years War*
(London, 1938), *William the Silent* (London, 1964), and *Richelieu and the
French Monarchy* (London, 1949).
3 V. Mehta, *Fly and the Fly Bottle* (London, 1962), pp. 159, 155.
4 *Spectator*, 12 December 1958.
5 C. V. Wedgwood, *Velvet Studies* (London, 1946), p. 157.
6 Wedgwood, *The King's Peace*, pp. 16, 15, 17. See also *History and Hope: The
Collected Essays of C. V. Wedgwood* (London, 1987) and R. Ollard and
Pamela Tudor-Craig (eds), *For Veronica Wedgwood These: Studies in
Seventeenth-Century History* (London, 1986); Elizabeth Johnson, 'C. V. Wedgwood and her historiography', *Contemporary Rev.*, CCI (1962), pp. 208–14.
7 The appearance of H. F. Kearney's *Strafford in Ireland* (Manchester, 1957)
and J. P. Cooper, 'The fortunes of Thomas Wentworth, Earl of Strafford',
Ec. H. R., 2nd ser., xi (1958), made necessary a fundamental revision of
Wedgwood's original study.
8 J. Morrill, 'The unweariableness of Mr Pym: influence and eloquence in the
Long Parliament', in Susan Amussen and M. A. Kishlansky (eds), *Political
Culture and Cultural Politics in Early Modern England: Essays presented to
David Underdown* (Manchester, 1995), pp. 19–54. For a general perspective

on Hexter as a historian see W. H. Dray, 'J. H. Hexter, neo Whiggism and early Stuart historiography', *Hist. and Theory*, 26 (1987), pp. 133–49.

9 Hexter, *King Pym*, pp. 200, 115, 15, 14.

10 Hexter's article was first published in *AHR*, xliv (1938) and was reprinted with revisions in his *Reappraisals in History* (London, 1961).

11 Hexter, *Parliament and Liberty*, pp. 12, 19. Barbara C. Malament (ed.), *After the Reformation: Essays in Honour of J. H. Hexter* (Manchester, 1980), p. x.

12 Notestein's edition (New Haven, 1923) carried the diary to the trial of Strafford. It was continued in W. Coates (ed.), *The Journal of Sir Simonds D'Ewes from the First Recess of the Long Parliament to the Withdrawal of King Charles from London* (New Haven, 1942). Other American contributions to the editing of parliamentary papers of this period include Maija Jannson (ed.), *Proceedings in Parliament 1614 (House of Commons)*, (Memoirs of the American Philosophical Soc., 172, Philadelphia, 1988), Maija Jannson (ed.), *Two Diaries of the Long Parliament* (Gloucester, 1984), W. H. Coates, Anne Steele Young and V. F. Snow (eds), *The Private Journals of the Long Parliament 3 Jan – 5 March 1642* (New Haven, 1982).

13 'The winning of the initiative by the House of Commons' was originally published in the *Proceedings of the British Academy* (1924/5). It has been suggested that the political process which Notestein placed in the seventeenth century needs to be relocated to the late eighteenth and early nineteenth centuries. (Valerie Cromwell, 'The losing of the initiative by the House of Commons, 1780–1914', *TRHS*, 5th ser., 18 (1968).)

Notestein's other publications included *A History of Witchcraft in England* (New York, 1911, reprinted 1968), *The English People on the Eve of Colonisation* (New York, 1954). See also W. A. Aiken and B. D. Henning (eds), *Conflict in Stuart England: Essays in Honour of Wallace Notestein* (London, 1960), and T. K. Rabb, 'Parliament and society in early Stuart England: the legacy of Wallace Notestein', *AHR*, lxxvii (1972).

14 In 1932 Notestein collaborated with other members of the Committee in producing an *Interim Report of the Committee on House of Commons Personnel and Politics, 1264–1832*.

15 'To Sir Lewis Namier we owe even more gratitude than do most students of parliamentary history', Brunton and Pennington, *Members of the Long Parliament*, p. viii. R. H. Tawney, however, supplied the introduction.

16 Mary F. Keeler, *The Long Parliament 1640–1641: A Biographical Study of its Members* (Memoirs of the American Philosophical Society, 36 (Philadelphia, 1954), p. 5.

17 J. C. D. Clark, *Revolution and Rebellion: State and Society in England in the Seventeenth and Eighteenth Centuries* (Cambridge, 1986), p. 25. Manning, *PP*, 5 (1954), pp. 71–6.

18 See, for example, H. Butterfield, 'George III and the Namier School', in *George III and the Historians* (London, 1957). C. Hill, 'Recent interpretations of the Civil War', in his *Puritanism and Revolution* (London, 1958). See also S. D. Antler, 'Quantitative analysis of the Long Parliament', *PP*, 56 (1972) and the ensuing debate in *PP*, 68 (1975).

19 Brunton and Pennington, *Members of the Long Parliament*, pp. 184, 176–7, 10, 185.

20 Underdown, *Pride's Purge*, pp. 2–3, 354, 358, 337, 336. See also H. R. Trevor-Roper, 'Oliver Cromwell and his parliaments', in R. Pares and A. J. P. Taylor (eds), *Essays presented to Sir Lewis Namier* (London, 1956).

21 Worden, *The Rump Parliament*, pp. 17, 56, 58.

22 On the 1650s see W. Lamont, 'The left and its roots: revising the 1650s', *Hist. Workshop J.*, 23 (1987), pp. 141–53; R. C. Richardson, 'Changing perspectives on England in the 1650s'; *Festschrift for Professor Ju Hwan Oh* (Taegu, Korea, 1991), pp. 544–66. D. Hirst, 'Locating the 1650s in England's seventeenth century', *Hist.*, 81 (1996), pp. 359–83. Roots, *Great Rebellion*, p. vii. Roots has also written 'Cromwell's Ordinances: the early legislation of the Protectorate', in G. E. Aylmer (ed.), *The Interregnum: The Quest for Settlement* (London, 1972), 'Swordsmen and decimators: Cromwell's Major Generals', in R. H. Parry (ed.), *The English Civil War and After* (London, 1970), 'The tactics of the Commonwealthsmen in Richard Cromwell's Parliament', in D. H. Pennington and K. Thomas (eds), *Puritans and Revolutionaries* (Oxford, 1978), '*Into another Mould: Aspects of the Interregnum* (Exeter, 1981), and 'The debate on the "Other House" in Richard Cromwell's parliament', in Ollard and Tudor-Craig (eds), *For Veronica Wedgwood These*. See D. Pennington, 'Ivan Roots', in C. Jones *et al.* (eds), *Politics and People in Revolutionary England* (Oxford, 1986), pp. x–xiv.

23 Hutton also wrote a major biography of *Charles II King of England, Scotland and Ireland* (Oxford, 1991).

24 F. D. Dow, *Cromwellian Scotland 1651–1660* (Edinburgh, 1979), B. Capp, *Cromwell's Navy: The Fleet and the English Revolution 1648–1660* (Oxford, 1989).

25 Aylmer, *King's Servants*, p. 6; Aylmer, *State's Servants*, p. 3.

26 Zagorin, *Court and the Country*, pp. 22, 13, 16, 32.

27 *Ibid.*, pp. 74, 90.

28 *Ibid.*, pp. 329–51.

29 For example, Zagorin's comments on the basic similarities of Royalist and Parliamentarian peers (pp. 95, 333) are not borne out by G. F. Trevallyn-Jones, *Saw Pit Wharton: The Political Career from 1640 to 1691 of Philip, fourth Lord Wharton* (Sydney, 1967). The latter argues that not all Stuart-created peers became Royalists but only those who owed their titles to Charles I himself.

30 Ashton's 'history from above' approach is particularly illuminating on the politics of the London business community, a subject he subsequently explored at greater length in *The City and the Court 1603–1643* (Cambridge, 1979).

31 Fletcher, *Outbreak of the English Civil War*, p. xxx. Fletcher edited (with John Stevenson) *Order and Disorder in Early Modern England* (Cambridge, 1985) and is the author of *Reform in the Provinces: The Government of Stuart England* (New Haven, 1986). For Fletcher's most recent, and very different, work on gender see pp. 156–7.

32 Caroline Hibbard, *Charles I and the Popish Plot* (Chapel Hill, NC, 1983). Hibbard's book was effectively the first full-scale attempt to explain, not explain away, the grounds of anti-Catholicism and to confront the phenomenon of Catholic plotting at court.

33 T. E. Cogswell, *The Blessed Revolution: English Politics and the Coming of War 1621–1624* (Cambridge, 1989), R. P. Cust, *The Forced Loan and English Politics 1626–1628* (Cambridge, 1987). On Revisionism see T. K. Rabb and D. Hirst, 'Revisionism revised: two perspectives on early Stuart parliamentary history. I: The role of the Commons; II: The place of principle', *PP*, 92 (1981), pp. 55–99; J. H. Hexter, 'The early Stuarts and Parliament: Old Hat and Nouvelle Vague', *Parliamentary Hist.*, 1 (1981), pp. 181–216; C. Hill, 'Parliament and people in seventeenth-century England', in Hill, *People and Ideas in Seventeenth-Century England* (Brighton, 1986); Mary Fulbrook, 'The English Revolution and the Revisionist Revolt', *Soc. Hist.*, vii (1982), pp. 249–64; G. Burgess, 'On revisionism: an analysis of early Stuart historiography in the 1970s and 1980s', *HJ*, 33 (1990), pp. 609–27; G. Burgess, 'Revisionism, politics and political ideas in early Stuart England', *HJ*, 34 (1991), pp. 465–78; R. Cust and Ann Hughes (eds), *The English Civil War* (London, 1997), editor's introduction. A. Fletcher, 'Power, myths and realities', *HJ*, 36 (1993), p. 212.
34 The assault on John Adamson's interpretations and methodology in 1991–2 spearheaded by Mark Kishlansky is a vivid and unedifying example. The swordfight rattled through the pages of learned journals (*Historical Journal* and the *Journal of British Studies*) and spilled over into *The Times* (21 Feb. 1992), the *TLS*, and the *Independent on Sunday* (1 March 1992).
35 J. Morrill, 'The religious context of the English Civil War', in Morrill, *The Nature of the English Revolution* (London, 1993), p. 68. Other writings by Morrill on the religious ramifications of the English Civil Wars include 'The church in England, 1642–1649', in Morrill (ed.), *Reactions to the English Civil War* (London, 1982); *The Scottish National Covenant in its British Context 1638–1651* (Edinburgh, 1990); 'Sir William Brereton and England's Wars of Religion', *JBS*, 24 (1985). J. S. Adamson, 'Parliamentary management, men of business and the House of Lords, 1640–49', in C. Jones (ed.), *A Pillar of the Constitution: The House of Lords in British Politics 1640–1784* (London, 1989), pp. 21–50, Adamson, 'The *Vindiciae Veritatis* and the political creed of Viscount Saye and Sele', *Hist. Research*, 60 (1987), pp. 45–63, 'The English Nobility and the projected settlement of 1647', *HJ*, xxx (1987), pp. 567–602, Adamson, 'Politics and nobility in Civil War England', *HJ*, xxxiv (1991), pp. 231–55.
36 *HJ*, xxxiii (1990), p. 617.
37 Russell, 'The nature of a parliament in early Stuart England', in H. Tomlinson (ed.), *Before the English Civil War* (London, 1983), pp. 141–2.
38 See *THES* (11 April 1997) p. 15.
39 Russell, *Parliaments and English Politics*, pp. 3, 35, 23, 8.
40 Russell, *Unrevolutionary England*, pp. x, 89–110, xxvi.
41 Russell, *Fall of the British Monarchies*, pp. 27, 526. Russell has been criticized for seeming to assume that, political differences notwithstanding, the three kingdoms were alike socially and economically. (N. Canny, 'The attempted anglicization of Ireland in the seventeenth century', in J. F. Merritt (ed.), *The Political World of Thomas Wentworth, Earl of Strafford 1621–1641* (Cambridge, 1996), p. 158.)
42 Russell, *Fall of the British Monarchies*, pp. 531, 530, 9, 467, 486.
43 *Ibid.*, pp. 1, 497.

44 Appropriately, Kishlansky co-edited (with Susan Amussen) David Under-down's Festschrift – *Political Culture and Cultural Politics in Early Modern England.*

45 Kishlansky, *Parliamentary Selection,* pp. 22, 23, 31, 32.

46 Kishlansky, *Rise of the New Model Army,* esp. pp. 223–72, 273, Kishlansky's book on the New Model has since been followed up, and in some respects challenged and modified, by A. Woolrych, *Soldiers and Statesmen: The General Council of the Army and its Debates 1647–1648* (Oxford, 1987), and I. Gentles, *The New Model Army in England, Ireland and Scotland 1645–1653* (Oxford, 1992).

47 K. Sharpe (ed.), *Faction and Parliament: Essays on Early Stuart History* (Oxford, 1978; 2nd edn, London, 1985, containing a new introduction on 'Revisionism revisited'); (with Steven N. Zwicker) (eds), *Politics of Discourse: The Literature and History of Seventeenth-Century England* (Berkeley, Los Angeles, CA, 1987); (with P. Lake) (eds), *Culture and Politics in Early Stuart England* (London, 1994). See also by Sharpe, *Sir Robert Cotton 1586–1631: History and Politics in Early Modern England* (Oxford, 1979).

48 Sharpe, *Criticism and Compliment,* pp. 14, 291, 293, 22. Sharpe is unfairly dismissive of Christopher Hill's long-standing efforts to address literature as history.

49 Sharpe, *Politics and Ideas in Early Stuart England,* p. ix.

50 *Ibid.,* pp. 64, 306, 52.

51 Sharpe, *Personal Rule,* pp. 732, xvii.

52 *Ibid.,* pp. 954, 196. Reviewers could, perhaps, be forgiven for wondering why – if there was no fire – there was undoubtedly so much smoke!

53 P. Collinson, *The Religion of Protestants: The Church in English Society 1559–1625* (Oxford, 1982), p. 90; Tyacke, 'Archbishop Laud', in K. Fincham (ed.), *The Early Stuart Church* (London, 1993), p. 51. P. White, 'The rise of Arminianism reconsidered', *PP,* 101 (1983), took issue with Tyacke's interpretation ('Puritanism, Arminianism and Counter Revolution', in C. Russell (ed.), *The Origins of the English Civil War* (London, 1973)) at practically every point.

54 Davies, *Caroline Captivity,* pp. 117, 125.

55 *Ibid.,* pp. 304, 303.

56 Figgis, *The Divine Right of Kings* (Cambridge 1896, 2nd edn, 1914, reprinted, with an introduction by G. R. Elton, New York, 1965); Allen, *English Political Thought 1603–1660* (London, 1938); Judson, *The Crisis of the Constitution: An Essay in Constitutional and Political Thought* (New York, 1949); Pocock, *The Ancient Constitution and the Feudal Law: A Study of English Historical Thought in the Seventeenth Century* (Cambridge, 1957, 2nd edn, 1987); Pocock, *Politics, Language and Time. Essays on Political Thought and History* (London, 1971); Macpherson, *The Political Theory of Possessive Individualism* (London, 1962); Greenleaf, *Order, Empiricism and Politics: Two Traditions of English Political Thought 1500–1700* (London, 1964); Eccleshall, *Order and Reason in Politics: Theories of Absolute and Limited Monarchy in Early Modern England* (Oxford, 1978); Skinner, *The Foundations of Modern Political Thought* (2 vols, Cambridge, 1978); G. Burgess, *The Politics*

of the Ancient Constitution: An Introduction to English Political Thought 1603–1642 (London, 1992) and J. P. Somerville, *Politics and Ideology in England 1603–1640* (London, 1986).

57 F. Raab, *The English Face of Machiavelli: A Changing Interpretation 1500–1700* (London, 1964).

58 On Hobbes see the series of articles by Quentin Skinner: 'Hobbes' Leviathan', *HJ*, vii (1964), 'History and ideology in the English Revolution', *HJ*, viii (1965), 'The ideological context of Hobbes's political thought', *HJ*, ix (1966), 'Conquest and consent: Thomas Hobbes and the Engagement controversy', in Aylmer (ed.), *The Interregnum*; R. Ross *et al.* (eds), *Thomas Hobbes in his Time* (Minneapolis, Minn., 1974); F. S. McNeilly, *The Anatomy of Leviathan* (London, 1968); A. A. Rogow, *Thomas Hobbes, Radical in the Service of Reaction* (New York, 1986); J. P. Somerville, *Thomas Hobbes: Political Ideas in Historical Context* (London, 1992).

59 J. G. A. Pocock (ed.), *The Political Works of James Harrington* (Cambridge, 1977).

60 M. Peltonen, *Classical Humanism and Republicanism in English Political Thought 1570–1640* (Cambridge, 1995); D. Armitage *et al.* (eds), *Milton and Republicanism* (Cambridge, 1995); M. Mendle, *Henry Parker and the English Civil War: The Political Thought of the Public's 'Privado'* (Cambridge, 1995).

61 Even the titles of the books were eloquently expressive: A. Fletcher and P. Roberts (eds), *Religion, Culture and Society in Early Modern Britain: Essays in Honour of Patrick Collinson* (Cambridge, 1994); Amussen and Kishlansky, *Political Culture and Cultural Politics in Early Modern England*.

62 Orgel, *The Illusion of Power* (Berkeley, Los Angeles, CA, 1975); G. S. Lytle and S. Orgel (eds), *Patronage in the Renaissance* (Princeton, NJ, 1981); Parry, *The Golden Age Restor'd: The Culture of the Stuart Court 1603–42* (Manchester, 1981); R. M. Smuts, *Court Culture and the Origins of a Royalist Tradition in Early Stuart England* (Philadelphia, Pa., 1987); Strong, *Splendour at Court: Renaissance Spectacle and Illusion* (London, 1973), *Henry Prince of Wales and England's Lost Renaissance* (London, 1986).

63 Kelsey, *Inventing a Republic: The Political Culture of English Commonwealth, 1649–1653* (Manchester, 1997), pp. 40, 107.

64 R. C. Richardson and G. M. Ridden (eds), *Freedom and the English Revolution* (Manchester, 1986).

65 Smith, *Literature and Revolution*, pp. 112, 207–12, 9, 95, 1, 2, 19.

66 Butler, *Theatre and Crisis*, p. 281. See also J. Limon, *Dangerous Matter: English Drama and Politics in 1623/1624* (Cambridge, 1986); Jean F. Howard, *The Stage and Social Struggle in Early Modern England* (London, 1994); J. R. Mulryne and Margaret Shewring (eds), *Theatre and Government under the Early Stuarts* (Cambridge, 1993); D. L. Smith *et al.* (eds) *The Theatrical City: Culture, Theatre and Politics in London 1576–1649* (Cambridge, 1995); Lisa Hopkins, *John Ford's Political Theatre* (Manchester, 1994).

67 *Guardian*, 30 January 1997.

68 *Sunday Times*, 3 November 1996.

12

The twentieth century: reverberations

The very fact that there has not been a civil war in England since the mid seventeenth century probably causes that conflict to loom larger in our historical consciousness than would otherwise be the case. (G. E. Aylmer, *Rebellion or Revolution? England from Civil War to Restoration* (Oxford, 1987), p. 205)

Of all the centuries it is the seventeenth that still lives with us and shapes us. . . . The legacy of those battles . . . is still with us. We are all at heart either Royalists or Roundheads. (Kevin Sharpe, *Sunday Times, Books* (3 November 1996))

Though dictatorship of the soviet type has failed, the ideas of collectivism, of full employment and a right to work for all citizens and other similar ideals will survive. The victory of capitalism does not mean the end of history here, any more than the restoration of Stuarts and Bourbons meant the end of democracy, of republicanism and of religious liberty after 1660 and 1815. (Christopher Hill, *England's Turning Point: Essays on Seventeenth-Century English History* (London, 1998), p. 9)

The opposing verdicts delivered by Keith Thomas and Kevin Sharpe with which the previous chapter ended, and the countless others rehearsed in this book, show how forcefully the English Revolution has reverberated down the centuries. The intrinsically contentious issues embodied in the original events have been invested with renewed and varying significance in the successive backward glances of generations of historians. As C. V. Wedgwood observed, 'the final, dispassionate, authoritative history of the Civil Wars cannot be written until the problems have ceased to matter'.[1] G. R. Elton was quite wrong to describe the mid-seventeenth-century crisis as 'the *unexplained* revolution'.[2] In a historiographical sense, unquestionably, it has been the *variously explained* revolution. New questions have been asked as historians have critically assessed the answers and explanations of their predecessors and contemporary opponents. At no point since the 1640s has consensus characterized historical writing on this subject. The period remains almost as controversial today as it was over three centuries ago, though of course for different reasons. Since the study of the past is invariably and inseparably connected with changing social and political circumstances, accepted definitions of the scope and possibilities of history have themselves altered enormously over time. Clarendon in the seventeenth century saw history as a route to political and moral wisdom. Eighteenth-century Whigs and Tories deployed it as a weapon in their own contemporary political struggles. Macaulay used it as a Victorian celebration of the English nation. S. R. Gardiner tried (ultimately unsuccessfully) to take history out of the noise of current controversies into the secluded calm of academic detachment. Tawney proclaimed the need for a new present-mindedness and urged the relevance of the humane concerns of social history. Today's neo-Whigs, Marxists, feminists, conservatives, Revisionists, sociologists, political scientists and historically minded literary critics are bringing different perspectives to bear on the seventeenth-century past and shifting the emphasis of debate.

Those living through the three and a half decades after the accession of Charles I in 1625 had no concept of revolution in the sense in which it has later come to be understood.[3] Guizot was the first historian to employ the term 'English Revolution' as a description of the events of the mid-seventeenth century. Despite vigorous resistance in some quarters – the anti-Marxists particularly – it has become the most commonly applied label for England's crisis years. 'Those who use it', Barry Coward has written, 'are not necessarily waving an ideological banner, and it need not be a bar to well-rounded and objective historical reappraisals'.[4] But, like any term, its significance has varied according to its users. It has had no fixed and finite meaning – a fact made perfectly clear in the three different answers given by John Morrill, David Underdown and Brian Manning in 'a special issue of *History Today* in 1984 devoted to 'What was the English Revolution?' The terms 'English Revolution' and 'English Civil Wars' clearly cannot be used interchangeably. And the term 'English Revolution' itself in some obvious ways has come under some strain now that Conrad Russell and others have insisted on the need to conceive of a mid-seventeenth-century crisis involving the whole of the British Isles.[5]

Some historians have gone further than this and have attempted to connect and compare political and social developments in England in the seventeenth century with what was happening elsewhere in Europe at that time. The notion of a General Crisis of the seventeenth century, in fact, has been profitably examined to unravel the involvement in it of such countries as France, Spain, the Netherlands, Sweden and Russia. R. B. Merriman's *Six Contemporaneous Revolutions* (Oxford, 1938) pointed to what might be done in this field. A series of articles published in the journal *Past and Present* in the 1950s and 1960s took up the theme again with renewed energy. Eric Hobsbawm and H. R. Trevor-Roper, both historians with an indefatigable capacity for meaningful generalization, were the leading contributors, and they differed markedly from each other in offering economic and political explanations respectively. Hobsbawm, in his article published in 1954, suggested that

> The European economy passed through a 'General Crisis' during the seventeenth century, the last phase of the general transition from a feudal to a capitalist economy. . . . The seventeenth-century crisis . . . led to as fundamental a solution of the difficulties which had previously stood in the way of the triumph of capitalism as that system will permit.[6]

Trevor-Roper, on the other hand, argued that the General Crisis of the seventeenth century was a series of problems, aggravated by war, in the relations between society and the parasitically bureaucratized Renaissance state. The crisis in England was so much more serious than in other countries because England had the 'most brittle, most overgrown, most rigid court of all', a political system untouched by antecedent partial reforms and one made intolerable by 'a fatal lack of political skill' in the country's rulers. 'Instead of the genius of Richelieu, the suppleness of Mazarin, there was the irresponsibility of Buckingham, the violence of Strafford, the undeviating universal pedantry of Laud'.[7] The provocative nature of the original articles as well as the intrinsic importance of the subject combined to attract further contributions to the debate which continued its momentum for a considerable time.[8] Perez Zagorin's *Rebels and Rulers 1500–1660: Society, States and Early Modern Revolution* (Cambridge, 1982) has already been referred to in an earlier chapter (see p. 216).

For other historians the wider ramifications of the English Revolution were to be sought in the inter-relationships between England and its American colonies. The literature on that subject has become voluminous and has embraced the economic, social and political issues involved. David Cressy's *Coming Over: Migration and Communication between England and New England in the Seventeenth Century* (Cambridge, 1987) showed what a 'mixed multitude' the migrants were. There were few gentry, hardly any paupers, but many servants. Controversially, Cressy scaled down the significance of the specifically puritan migration. Myths notwithstanding, few New Englanders, in fact, had direct experience of religious persecution in the old country (though to their astonishment some felt it on the other side of the Atlantic), and for large numbers desire for economic betterment counted for more than religious scruples. Cressy looked at the survival, significance, and operation of transatlantic and colonial kinship networks. Correspondence, though abundant, was slow, and news, too, took a long time to move in both directions. Partly because it took place in winter (when there were far fewer sailings) it was six months before Charles I's execution in January 1649 became widely known in New England. D. G. Allen's *In English Ways* (Chapel Hill, NC, 1981) explored the ways in which the early settlers painstakingly reproduced in their colonial setting the same distinctive features of the local economies, social structures, law, customs, and local government they had left behind. The English Revolution of the 1640s and 1650s was, unavoidably, a shared experience in New England. *Revolution and Empire: English Politics and the American Colonies in the Seventeenth Century* (Manchester, 1990) by Robert Bliss made this absolutely clear. Bliss demonstrated that the politics of England and its American colonies were actively interconnected. The English Revolution had an ambiguous impact on the colonies, which responded in both revolutionary and conservative ways. A significant number of temporary exiles returned to the old country as the prospect of building a New Jerusalem opened there in the course of the 1640s. In the 1650s, the colonies complained about the attempted invasion of local government in much the same way as English communities did when faced with Oliver Cromwell's major generals. The Restoration in England in 1660 provoked divided reactions across the Atlantic Ocean. A few years later one of the impeachment charges against Clarendon was that he had 'introduced an arbitrary government in the plantations'. The Glorious Revolution of 1688 in England had clear implications for America. Insofar as it 'represented parliament's coming of age it was unlikely to enhance colonial autonomy'.[9] 1776, more painfully for England, was another revolution shared with the American colonies.[10]

At yet another level, the seventeenth-century crisis in England has figured in a number of comparative studies of the major revolutions of the western world. For example, the Harvard political scientist Crane Brinton (1898–1968) looked at seventeenth-century England, eighteenth-century America and France, and twentieth-century Russia, with a view to tracing some of the obvious uniformities in the development and structure of revolutionary crises. The series of common features he identified in his book *The Anatomy of Revolution* (New York, 1938, rev. edn 1965), were those of economic change, growing status, and class antagonisms, the presence of groups of alienated intellectuals, inept and insecure ruling elites, and failures in government finance.

Another American writer, the sociologist Barrington Moore Jnr. (1913–), surveyed the English Revolution in connection with his work on *The Social Origins of Dictatorship and Democracy: Lord and Peasant in the Making of the Modern World* (Harmondsworth, 1973). Looking at seventeenth- and eighteenth-century England, the French Revolution, the American Civil War, and twentieth-century Asia, Moore's aims were 'to understand the role of the landed upper classes and the peasants in the bourgeois revolutions leading to capitalist democracy, the abortive bourgeois revolutions leading to fascism, and the peasant revolutions leading to communism'. These were the three main routes to the modern world identified by the author and, at a methodological level, he vigorously defended the value of the broad generalizations which resulted from such a wide-ranging survey.

In the effort to understand the history of a specific country a comparative perspective can lead to asking some very useful and sometimes new questions. There are further advantages. Comparisons can serve as a rough negative check on accepted historical explanations. And a comparative approach may lead to new historical generaliztions. . . . Generalizations that are sound resemble a large-scale map of an extended terrain, such as an airplane pilot might use in crossing a continent. Such maps are essential for some purposes just as more detailed maps are necessary for others.

Although, unavoidably in a work conceived on such a massive scale, labels and blanket descriptions were frequently used, Moore himself was ready to admit the deficiencies of such terminology.

The central difficulty is that such expressions as 'bourgeois revolution' and 'peasant revolution' lump together indiscriminately those who make the revolution and its beneficiaries. Likewise these terms confuse the legal and political results of revolution with social groups active in them.[11]

Barrington Moore's book provided a challenging example of the application of sociological models to the study of the English Revolution. Another was advanced by the American political scientist Michael Walzer (1935–). Walzer's volume on *The Revolution of the Saints: A Study in the Origins of Radical Politics* (London, 1966) clearly owed much to the stimulus provided by the works of Max Weber. It attracted a great deal of attention on two fronts, first as a provocative reinterpretation of English puritanism, and second as a contribution to the sociology of revolution in general. Stressing the roles of the clergy (as intellectuals) and the gentry (as patrons) rather than Christopher Hill's and Brian Manning's 'middling sort of people', Walzer presented puritanism as a kind of politico-theological response to the neuroses of a sixteenth-century society bewildered by the consequences of population increase, inflation, the discovery of the New World, and by the Reformation break with the past.

Calvinism in its sixteenth- and seventeenth-century forms was not so much the cause of this or that modern economic, political, or administrative system as it was an agent of modernization, an ideology of the transition period. And as the conditions of crisis and upheaval in which Calvinism was conceived and developed did not persist, so

Calvinism as an integral and creative force did not endure ... The very existence and spread of Puritanism in the years before the revolution surely suggest the presence in English society of an acute fear of disorder and 'wickedness' – a fear ... attendant upon the transformation of the old political and social order. The (later) triumph of Lockeian ideas, on the other hand, suggests the overcoming of anxiety, the appearance of saints and citizens for whom sin is no longer a problem.

Walzer's conclusion was a model of radical politics that easily lent itself, so he believed, to comparison with the French and Russian Revolutions. Ideological equivalents of English puritanism – and by that (in the context of the Civil War itself) it is clear that he meant Independency – were thrust up by the logic of later revolutionary situations, similar in many respects to that in seventeenth-century England.

All forms of radical politics make their appearance at moments of rapid and decisive change, moments when customary status is in doubt and character (or 'identity') is itself a problem. Before Puritans, Jacobins, or Bolsheviks attempt the creation of a new order, they must create new men. ... There is a point in the modernization process when large numbers of men, suddenly masterless, seek a rigid self-control; when they discover new purposes, dream of a new order, organize their lives for disciplined and methodical activity. These men are prospective saints and citizens; for them Puritanism, Jacobinism, and Bolshevism are appropriate options. At this point in time they are likely options.[12]

The most recent work of this kind – again coming from the United States – was Jack Goldstone's *Revolution and Rebellion in the Early Modern World* (Berkeley and Los Angeles, CA, 1991). Goldstone, Professor of Sociology and Director of the Center for Comparative Research in History, Society, and Culture at the University of California, Davis, concentrated on two periods of general crisis to one of which the English Revolution belonged. What made his contribution distinctive was his insistence on a Eurasian frame of reference. The Ottoman Empire and Ming China, he argued, no less than the countries of Europe went through a period of upheaval and 'state breakdown'. (Interestingly China, too, had its seventeenth-century Levellers.) All these states and their political, economic and social systems had much in common, not least their shared characteristic of being ill-equipped to cope with population explosions. Goldstone indeed made much of the demographic factor in his construction of a quasi-mathematical conjunctural model 'whose basic principles may be useful in understanding even today's (and tomorrow's) crises'. He vigorously resisted the tendency of conventional social theory to raise empirical problems into theoretical disputes. He challenged the often assumed correlations between revolution and progress.[13]

Alongside macro interpretations conceived on this scale even Christopher Hill's bold generalizations begin to look quite modest! But Hill has remained the most active and determined champion of the idea of the English Revolution as the great turning point in English history, the effective end of the Middle Ages. This was the principal theme of his social and economic history textbook *Reformation to Industrial Revolution* (London, 1967) and it was restated and developed in a contribution to J. G. A. Pocock's symposium on *Three British Revolutions: 1641, 1688, 1776* (Princeton, NJ, 1980).

> The English Revolution, like all revolutions, was caused by the breakdown of the old society; it was brought about neither by the wishes of the bourgeoisie, nor by the leaders of the Long Parliament. But its outcome was the establishment of conditions far more favourable to the development of capitalism than those which prevailed before 1640.[14]

Hill accepted that useful analogies could be made between the English Revolution, the French Revolution, and the Russian Revolution of 1905, but such an exercise did not require them all to be forced into the same mould. Nor was it helpful or convincing to offer a purely economic interpretation of revolution. This point was underlined in his *Intellectual Consquences of the English Revolution* (London, 1980) which dealt not only with Locke and Newton but (amongst other things) with the Revolution's stimulus to the growth of a reading public, to its replacement of church courts by the individualized arbiter of conscience, and with its 'hypocrisies and lost causes'.

Hill's turning-point theory of the English Revolution has had its critics. Angus McInnes has contended that the real revolution in the seventeenth century was that at the end of it (under William

III) and not that of the Civil War and Interregnum, the significance of which he found exaggerated in Hill's account.[15] Lawrence Stone for his part insisted that the English Revolution was no 'bourgeois revolution'. 'There is little evidence to suggest that it did more than accelerate and consolidate trends that were already apparent long before the Revolution began'. No new class of landowners, he stated, emerged as a result of the Revolution. It was not the Revolution which explained England's special social configuration. 'The conclusion seems inescapable that the principal consequences of the Great Revolution of the mid-seventeenth century were negative'. In the long term the chief consequence of the English Revolution was its 'ideological legacy', 'an immensely rich reservoir of ideas that were to echo and re-echo down the ages, and would reappear again over a century later during the American and the French Revolutions'.[16]

Others were more extreme and intemperate in their criticisms. Peter Laslett (1915–), founder of the Cambridge Group for the History of Population and Social Structure, proclaimed that 'English Revolution' was a term best expunged from the historian's vocabulary altogether. England in the seventeenth century in his view was a 'one-class' society (in the sense that there was only one class which mattered). That being the case, though there was social mobility there was no – and could not have been – class struggle.[17] But this was relatively polite banter compared with the swingeing attack from Jonathan Clark (1951–), now of the University of Kansas, in his *Revolution and Rebellion: State and Society in England in the Seventeenth and Eighteenth Centuries* (Cambridge, 1986). 'Old Guard' Marxists, no less than 'Old Hat' Whigs and 'the class of 68' – so this swept up Hill, Stone, Hexter, and Trevor-Roper all in one scoop! – were all mercilessly rebuked. Lifting what he considered to be the curse of narrow specialization dividing seventeenth-century historians from those of the next century, Clark's new stock-taking of England's ancien regime discounted the importance of 'revolution' – whether political or industrial – in English history. 'Rebellion', 'reaction against innovation', 'resistance to undesired change', were in Clark's view expressions better calculated to describe what happened in England in the 1640s.[18]

Clark's book demonstrated beyond all doubt how the historian's writing about the English Revolution is embroiled in, and reverberates with, the present. For Clark, luxuriating in the late 1980s in the blessings of Conservative rule, mesmerized by high politics, dismissive of 'Attlee-esque social engineering', and for whom Mrs Thatcher was a second Gloriana, the English Revolution self-evidently could not have happened; 'historians have been chasing a shadow: a reified category'.[19] As a very different creature of his times Christopher Hill in 1990 declared

> Cynics say that when historians claim that they are describing the past they are really writing contemporary history or autobiography. . . . A kind reviewer even said that a book which I published in 1984 called *The Experience of Defeat* represented my reaction to Margaret Thatcher.[20]

True or untrue, Hill's deep-seated disillusionment with England in the 1980s was hard to hide.

> History is written by winners. . . . The memory of our national revolution has been suppressed. . . . When we ask ourselves what has gone wrong with England in the past three centuries, one part of the answer is that the arrogant self-confidence of a ruling class enjoying an unprecedented security and prosperity was for too long unchecked by any need to pay serious attention to the views of those beneath them.[21]

Claims for historical objectivity notwithstanding, some mingling of present and past is unavoidable in the work of historians. It can take extreme forms. In the 1940s the American historian W. C. Abbott claimed that his generation's painful experience of the inter-war dictators had *enabled* it to reach a proper assessment of Oliver Cromwell as a dictator.

> The events of the past twenty years [he wrote in 1947] were required to find an appropriate descriptive phrase to fit the position which Cromwell held. . . . The rise of an Austrian house painter to the headship of the German Reich, of a newspaper editor-agitator to the leadership of Italy, and of a Georgian bandit to the domination of Russia, have modified our concept of Cromwell's achievement, and perhaps our concept of his place in history.[22]

Lawrence Stone's 'enlightenment' as a historian of seventeenth-century England came with the troubles of 1968.

In subtle ways, of all of which I am probably not fully conscious, I have also been influenced by my experience of revolutionary outbreaks in the contemporary world. As a passive observer of 'les événements de mai' in Paris 1968, and as an active participant in the crisis triggered off at Princeton by the invasion of Cambodia in May 1970, I have learned much about the nature and process of revolutions. In particular I have been made aware of the electric atmosphere of a revolutionary occasion, the drunken sense of euphoria, the belief in the limitless possibilities of improvement in the human condition. I have also been persuaded of the critical importance of the response of those in authority in determining whether or not the revolutionary mood will lead to physical violence and destruction, or to peaceful accommodation and constructive adjustment'.[23]

In a less obvious, but no less real, kind of way present responses to the past and (self-evidently) to history as a subject are embodied in Niall Ferguson's *Virtual History: Alternatives and Counterfactuals* (London, 1997). Seen as a 'necessary response to determinism' in all its forms (Marxist and Whig among them), counterfactual history or 'chaostory' underlined the advantages to be gained by exploring what might have happened rather than submit to the prescriptive tyranny of what in the event actually did take place. Controversial revisionist John Adamson, recruited to Ferguson's contributors, extrapolated from the available mid-seventeenth-century evidence to consider an alternative 'trajectory of British (and Irish) history which would have looked very different: almost certainly no Civil War, no regicide, no Glorious Revolution, and Oliver Cromwell pursuing a career of blameless obscurity among the rustic countryfolk of Ely'.[24]

Less novel than it seems – it actually has a long ancestry – the counterfactual history of the English Revolution has underlined the ingrained tendency of historians to re-interpret and speculate in the light of the evidence and in the light of their own and their own society's beliefs and priorities. Revisionism – and here the term is used in a broader sense than that applied to Conrad Russell's particular cricket team in the previous chapter – is a constant and necessary feature of historical studies. Although this is a truism applicable to history in general, the subject matter of this book has amply demonstrated it by way of example. Historians' attempts to explain and make sense of the English Revolution – a long running debate already three and a half centuries old – show no sign whatever of losing momentum.

Notes

1 Wedgwood, *The King's Peace, 1637–1641* (London, 1955), p. 14.
2 Elton, 'The unexplained revolution', reprinted in Elton, *Studies in Tudor and Stuart Politics and Government*, II (Cambridge, 1974).
3 V. Snow, 'The concept of revolution in seventeenth-century England', *HJ*, v (1962); G. M. Straka, 'Revolutionary ideology in Stuart England', in P. J. Korshin (ed.), *Studies in Change and Revolution: Aspects of English Intellectual History 1640–1800* (London, 1972).
4 B. Coward, 'Was there an English Revolution in the middle of the seventeenth century?', in C. Jones *et al.* (eds), *Politics and People in Revolutionary England* (Oxford, 1986), p. 10.
5 On Russell's view of the 'British problem' see pp. 221–2. See also S. G. Ellis and S. Barber (eds), *Conquest and Union: Fashioning a British State 1485–1725* (London, 1995), A. J. Grant and K. J. Stringer (eds), *Uniting the Kingdom? The Making of British History* (London, 1995), and B. Bradshaw and J. Morrill (eds), *The British Problem c. 1534–1707* (London, 1996).
6 Hobsbawm, 'The crisis of the seventeenth century', reprinted in T. Aston (ed.), *Crisis in Europe 1560–1660* (Routledge, 1965), pp. 5–6.
7 Trevor-Roper, 'The general crisis of the seventeenth century', in Aston, *Crisis in Europe*, p. 95.
8 Later articles in *Past and Present* which explored aspects of this theme included: J. V. Polisensky, 'The Thirty Years War and the crises and revolutions of seventeenth-century Europe', and H. Kamen, 'The economic and social consequences of the Thirty Years War', *PP*, 39 (1968); J. H. Elliott, 'Revolution and continuity in early modern Europe', *PP*, 42 (1969); A. Clarke, 'Ireland and the general crisis', *PP*, 48 (1970); J. I. Israel, 'Mexico and the general crisis of the seventeenth century', *PP*, 63 (1974). See also A. D. Lublinskaya, *French Absolutism: The Crucial Phase 1620–1629* (Cambridge, 1968); N. Steensgaard, 'The economic and political crisis of the seventeenth century', *Thirteenth International Congress of Historical Sciences* (Moscow, 1970); J. H. Elliott, 'England and Europe: a common malady?', in C. Russell (ed.), *The Origins of the English Civil War* (London, 1973); D. Stevenson, *The Scottish Revolution 1637–1644* (Newton Abbot, 1973); R. Foster and J. P. Greene (eds), *Preconditions of Revolution in Early Modern Europe* (Baltimore, 1970); G. Parker and L. M. Smith (eds), *The General Crisis of the Seventeenth Century* (London, 1978); G. Parker, *Europe in Crisis 1598–1650* (Oxford, 1980); P. J. Coveney (ed.), *France in Crisis 1620–1675* (London, 1977); O. Ranum, *The Fronde: A French Revolution* (New York, 1993).
9 Bliss, *Revolution and Empire*, pp. 161, 222.
10 See J. Holstun, *A Rational Millenium: Puritan Utopias of Seventeenth-Century England and America* (New York, 1987); J. G. A. Pocock (ed.), *Three British Revolutions: 1641, 1688, 1776* (Princeton, 1980); Margaret J. Jacob and

J. Jacob (eds), *The Origins of Anglo-American Radicalism* (London, 1984); Alison G. Olson, *Anglo-American Politics 1660–1775* (New York, 1973); J. M. Sosin, *English America and the Restoration Monarchy of Charles II: Transatlantic Politics, Commerce, and Kinship* (Lincoln, Nebraska, 1980); D. S. Lovejoy, *The Glorious Revolution in America* (Middletown, CT, 1972); P. S. Haffenden, *New England in the English Nation* (Oxford, 1974).

11 Moore, *Social Origins*, pp. xiv, x, xi, 428.

12 Walzer, *Revolution of the Saints*, pp. 300, 303, 315. See also G. Lewey, *Religion and Revolution* (Oxford, 1974).

13 Goldstone, *Revolution and Rebellion*, pp. 7, 3, xxii, 39.

14 Hill, 'A bourgeois revolution?', in Pocock, *Three British Revolutions*, p. 111.

15 A. McInnes, 'When was the English Revolution?', *Hist.*, lxvii (1982), pp. 377–92.

16 Stone, 'The results of the English Revolution of the seventeenth century', in Pocock, *Three British Revolutions*, pp. 24, 40, 60, 94, 61.

17 Laslett, *The World We Have Lost*, 3rd edn (London, 1983), esp. pp. 22–52, 182–209.

18 Clark, *Revolution and Rebellion*, pp. 64, 66.

19 *The Times* (12 November 1987) (review of Jasper Ridley, *Elizabeth I*).

20 C. Hill, *A Nation of Change and Novelty: Radical Politics, Religion and Literature in Seventeenth-Century England* (London, 1990), p. 244.

21 C. Hill, *Some Intellectual Consequences of the English Revolution* (London, 1980), pp. 32–3, Hill, *Nation of Change and Novelty*, p. 251. This is not dissimilar from Tawney: 'The revolution, which brought constitutional liberty, brought no power to control the aristocracy, who for a century and a half alone knew how such liberty could be used – that blind, selfish, indomitable aristocracy of county families, which made the British empire and ruined a considerable proportion of the English nation', quoted by L. Stone, introduction to R. H. Tawney, *The Agrarian Problem in the Sixteenth Century* (New York, 1967), p. x.

22 Abbott (ed.), *Letters and Speeches of Oliver Cromwell*, IV (Cambridge, Mass., 1947), p. 898.

23 L. Stone, *Causes of the English Revolution* (London, 1986), p. ix.

24 Adamson, 'England without Cromwell: what if Charles I had avoided Civil War?', in Ferguson (ed.), *Virtual History*, pp. 91–124. Conrad Russell made a brief foray into counterfactual history in his 'The Catholic Wind' (a *virtual history* of the events of 1688 which had James II triumphing), reprinted in *Unrevolutionary England 1603–1642* (London, 1990), pp. 305–8.

FURTHER READING

The real bibliography of this book lies in its notes. What follows is simply a selection of some of the most important and easily accessible secondary sources, those that evaluate the histories and historians discussed in this survey.

General

H. Butterfield, *The Whig Interpretation of History* (London, 1931)

M. G. Finlayson, *Historians, Puritans and the English Revolution: The Religious Factor in English Politics before and after the Interregnum* (Toronto, 1983)

C. H. Firth, 'The development of the study of seventeenth-century history', *TRHS*, 3rd ser., 7 (1913)

P. Gay, *Style in History* (London, 1975)

J. R. Hale, *The Evolution of British Historiography* (London, 1967)

C. Hill, *Puritanism and Revolution* (London, 1958)

J. P. Kenyon, *The History Men: The Historical Profession in England since the Renaissance* (London, 1983)

Anne Pallister, *Magna Carta: The Heritage of Liberty* (Oxford, 1971)

R. C. Richardson (ed.), *Images of Oliver Cromwell: Essays for and by Roger Howell Jnr* (Manchester, 1993)

A. L. Rowse, *Historians I Have Known* (London, 1995)

L. Stone, *The Causes of the English Revolution 1529–1642* (London, 1972, 2nd edn, 1986)

The seventeenth century

R. Hutton, 'Clarendon's history of the rebellion', *EHR*, xcvii (1982)

D. Kelley and D. H. Sacks (eds), *The Historical Imagination in Early Modern Britain: Historical Rhetoric and Fiction 1500–1800* (Cambridge, 1997)

R. MacGillivray, *Restoration Historians and the English Civil War* (The Hague, 1974)

J. G. A. Pocock, *The Ancient Constitution and the Feudal Law: A Study of English Historical Thought in the Seventeenth Century* (Cambridge, 1957, 2nd edn, 1987)

R. H. Tawney, 'Harrington's interpretation of his age', in J. M. Winter (ed.), *History and Society: Essays by R. H. Tawney* (London, 1978)

D. R. Woolf, *The Idea of History in Early Stuart England: Erudition, Ideology and 'the light of truth' from the Accession of James I to the Civil War* (Toronto, 1990)

B. H. G. Wormald, *Clarendon, Politics, Historiography and Religion 1640–1660* (Cambridge, 1964)

P. Zagorin, 'Clarendon and Hobbes', *JMH*, lvii (1985)

The eighteenth century

J. B. Black, *The Art of History* (London, 1926)

A. Cobban (ed.), *The Debate on the French Revolution* (London, 1950)

H. T. Dickinson, *Liberty and Property: Political Ideology in Eighteenth-Century Britain* (London, 1977)

Bridget Hill, *The Republican Virago: The Life and Times of Catharine Macaulay* (Oxford, 1992)

L. Okie, *Augustan Historical Writing* (Lanham, Maryland, 1991)

T. P. Peardon, *The Transition in English Historical Writing 1760–1830* (New York, 1933)

H. R. Trevor-Roper, 'A Huguenot historian: Paul Rapin', in Irene Scouloudi (ed.), *Huguenots in Britain and their French Background* (London, 1987)

E. E. Wexler, *David Hume and the History of England* (Philadelphia, PA, 1979)

The nineteenth century

P. M. B. Blaas, *Continuity and Anachronism: Parliamentary and Constitutional Development in Whig Historiography and in the Anti-Whig Reaction between 1890 and 1930* (The Hague, 1978)

J. W. Burrow, *A Liberal Descent: Victorian Historians and the English Past* (Cambridge, 1981)

C. H. Firth, *A Commentary on Macaulay's History of England* (London, 1938)

G. P. Gooch, *History and Historians in the Nineteenth Century* (2nd edn, London, 1952)

J. Hamburger, *Macaulay and the Whig Tradition* (Chicago, 1978)

D. Johnson, *Guizot: Aspects of French History* (London, 1963)

T. Lang, *The Victorians and the Stuart Heritage: Interpretations of a Discordant Past* (Cambridge, 1995)

C. E. McClelland, *The German Historians and England* (Cambridge, 1971)

J. Morrow, 'Republicanism and public virtue: William Godwin's *History of the Commonwealth of England*', *HJ*, xxxiv (1991)

P. R. H. Slee, *Learning and a Liberal Education: The Study of Modern History in the Universities of Oxford, Cambridge and Manchester* (Manchester, 1986)

The twentieth century

The Gardiner tradition

D. Cannadine, *G. M. Trevelyan: A Life in History* (London, 1992)

D. M. Fahey, 'Gardiner and Usher in perspective', *J. Hist. Studs.*, i (1968)

C. H. Firth, *Essays Historical and Literary* (Oxford, 1938)

J. P. Kenyon, 'Sir Charles Firth and the Oxford School of Modern History 1892–1925', in A. C. Duke and C. A. Tamse (eds), *Clio's Mirror: Historiography in Britain and the Netherlands* (Zutphen, 1985)

Social interpretations

G. Eley and W. Hunt (eds), *Reviving the English Revolution* (London, 1988)

J. H. Hexter, *On Historians* (London, 1979)

C. Hill, *A Nation of Change and Novelty: Radical Politics, Religion and Literature in Seventeenth-Century England* (London, 1990)

Hilary Hinds, *God's Englishwomen: Seventeenth-Century Radical Sectarian Writing and Feminist Criticism* (Manchester, 1996)

A. MacLachlan, *The Rise and Fall of Revolutionary England: An Essay in the Fabrication of Seventeenth-Century History* (New York, 1996)

R. Terrill, *R. H. Tawney and his Times: Socialism as Fellowship* (London, 1974)

Local and regional

Cynthia Herrup, 'The counties and the country: some thoughts on seventeenth-century historiography', *Soc. Hist.*, viii (1983)

C. Holmes, 'The country community in early Stuart historiography', *JBS*, xix (1980)

R. C. Richardson (ed.), *The English Civil Wars: Local Aspects* (Stroud, 1997)

Politics, political culture, revisionism

G. Burgess, 'On revisionism: an analysis of early Stuart historiography in the 1970s and 1980s', *HJ*, xxxiii (1990)

W. H. Dray, 'J. H. Hexter, neo-Whiggism and early Stuart historiography', *Hist. and Theory*, xxvi (1987)

Mary Fulbrook, 'The English Revolution and the revisionist revolt', *Soc. Hist.*, vii (1982)

J. H. Hexter, 'The early Stuarts and parliament: Old Hat and *Nouvelle Vague*', *Parliamentary Hist.*, i (1981)

T. K. Rabb, 'Parliament and society in early Stuart England: the legacy of Wallace Notestein', *AHR*, lxxvii (1972)

K. Sharpe, *Politics and Ideas in Early Stuart England* (London, 1989)

History from below

J. C. Davis, *Fear, Myth and History: The Ranters and the Historians* (Cambridge, 1986)

C. Hill, 'The lost Ranters? A critique of J. C. Davis', *Hist. Workshop. J.*, 24 (1987)

C. Hill, *The World Turned Upside Down: Radical Ideas during the English Revolution* (London, 1972)

H. J. Kaye, *The British Marxist Historians* (Cambridge, 1984)

B. Manning, *The English People and the English Revolution* (2nd edn, London, 1991)

Reverberations

T. Aston (ed.), *Crisis in Europe 1560–1660* (London, 1965)

C. Brinton, *The Anatomy of Revolution* (New York, 1938, rev. edn, 1965)

J. C. D. Clark, *Revolution and Rebellion: State and Society in England in the Seventeenth and Eighteenth Centuries* (Cambridge, 1986)

J. A. Goldstone, *Revolution and Rebellion in the Early Modern World* (Berkeley and Los Angeles, CA, 1991)

C. Hill, *Some Intellectual Consequences of the English Revolution* (London, 1980)

B. Moore, *The Social Origins of Dictatorship and Democracy* (Harmondsworth, 1973)

J. G. A. Pocock (ed.), *Three British Revolutions: 1641, 1688, 1776* (Princeton, NJ, 1980)

M. Walzer, *The Revolution of the Saints: A Study of the Origins of Radical Politics* (London, 1966)

INDEX

Note: 'n.' after a page number refers to a note on that page.

Dray, W. H. 132
Duffin, Anne 179
Dugdale, William 22–4
Durston, Christopher 153–5
Dutch Wars 29

Eales, Jacqueline 153–4, 176–7
East Anglia 166–7, 173
Eastern Association 173
Eccleshall, Robert 228
Echard, Laurence 40, 44, 45–6, 60
n.9
Edwards, Owen Dudley 81
Eikon Basilike 230
electorate 188–9
Eliot, T. S. 124
Elizabeth I, Queen 14, 30
Elton, G. R. 114, 150, 199, 203,
239–40
English Historical Review 83
Evans, John T. 178–9
Everitt, Alan 122, 170–2, 176
Exeter 179

family unit 154–5
Farrow, W. J. 164
Ferguson, Niall 249
Figgis, J. N. 228
Finch, Mary 167
Fincham, Kenneth 152–3
Firth, C. H. 35, 91, 100–4,
204
Fisher, F. J. 123
Fletcher, Anthony 156–7, 169, 172,
199, 203, 218
Forbes, Duncan 53–4
Foster, Elizabeth R. 204
Franklin, Benjamin 57
French Revolution 63–73 *passim*,
87, 245, 246
French Revolution (1830) 71
French Revolution (1848) 71
Fulbrook, Mary 132
Fuller, Thomas 11

Gangraena 197
Gardiner, S. R. 6, 83, 91–5, 101–2,
110, 131, 137, 204, 218, 220,
232
General Crisis of the seventeenth
century 241–2, 250 n.8
Gentles, Ian 178
gentry 150–1, 155, 166–9, 170–2
gentry controversy 17, 118–21
Geyl, Pieter vii
Gibbon, Edward 42
Gladstone, W. E. 95
Glorious Revolution 42, 58, 109,
193
Godwin, William 5, 66–9, 72 n.13
Goldsmith, M. M. 25
Goldstone, Jack 245–6
Gooch, G. P. 92
Gould, Mark 147–8
Grand Remonstrance 49
Great Reform Act 81
Green, J. R. 90–1
Greenleaf, W. H. 228
Guizot, François 86–9, 240

Hainsworth, Roger 213
Hallam, Henry 76–8, 87
Halley, Robert 163
Hamburger, J. 81
Hammond, John and Barbara 185
Hampden, John 33, 58, 76
Harleys (Brampton Bryan)
176–7
Harrington, James 16–18, 56, 87,
117, 229
Harris, Tim 190–1
Heal, Felicity 150–1
Heath, James 22
Heinemann, Margot 231
Henrietta Maria, Queen 14, 226
Hervey, Lord John 53
Hexter, J. H. 120, 137, 206–7, 208,
234 n.8
Heylyn, Peter 12